ON SECULARIZATION

I have found David Martin's work tremendously useful and illuminating for my own reflections on modernity, secularization and Christian faith. I see Martin as having transformed the discussion about secularization, moving us onto a different track. Some of the latest fruits of his reflections are offered in this new work.
Charles Taylor, Emeritus Professor of Philosophy, McGill University

This is a fascinating and challenging book from a leading sociologist whose reflections make a major contribution towards understanding the cultural dynamics of secularization. Martin's book will be essential reading for undergraduate and postgraduate students in the sociology of religion, religious studies, contemporary Christianity as well as scholars with a serious interest in these fields. This important and rewarding book will stand as a landmark study for years to come.
Jonathan S. Fish, University of Leeds

'Secularization' has been hotly debated since it was first subjected to critical attention in the mid-sixties by David Martin, before he sketched a 'General Theory' in 1969.

On Secularization presents David Martin's reassessment of the key issues: with particular regard to the special situation of religion in Western Europe, and questions in the global context including Pentecostalism in Latin America and Africa. Concluding with examinations of Pluralism, Christian Language, and Christianity and Politics, this book offers students and other readers of social theory and sociology of religion an invaluable reappraisal of Christianity and Secularization. It represents the most comprehensive sociology of contemporary Christianity, set in historical depth.

D1376033

On Secularization

Towards a Revised General Theory

DAVID MARTIN
London School of Economics, UK

ASHGATE

Published by
Ashgate Publishing Limited
Gower House
Croft Road
Aldershot
Hants GU11 3HR
England

Ashgate Publishing Company
Suite 420
101 Cherry Street
Burlington, VT 05401-4405
USA

Ashgate website: http://www.ashgate.com

British Library Cataloguing in Publication Data
Martin, David
    On secularization : towards a revised general theory
    1. Secularization (Theology)
    I. Title
    261

Library of Congress Cataloging-in-Publication Data
Martin, David 1929–
    On secularization : towards a revised general theory / David Martin ;
foreword by Charles Taylor.
        p. cm.
    Includes index.
    ISBN 0–7546–5314–5 (hardcover : alk. paper) – ISBN 0–7546–5322–6
(pbk. : alk. paper) 1. Secularization (Theology) I. Title.

    BT83.7.M38   2005
    306.6 — dc22

                                                                    2004023751

ISBN 0 7546 5314 5 (Hbk); 0 7546 5322 6 (Pbk)

Typeset by Express Typesetters Ltd, Farnham
Printed and bound in Great Britain by TJ International Ltd, Padstow, Cornwall

For Yvonne Brown,
whose expertise over thirty
years provided the medium
of the message,
with love

And for Jonathan and Emma

Contents

Acknowledgements and Sources

Chapter 1: Given in the Magna Aula of the University of Timişoara, Romania in 1994 and published in *Religion*, Vol. 15 (1995), pp. 295–303.

Chapter 2: Given at an Oxford conference (St Catherine's College) in 1999 and published in Donald M. Lewis, *Christianity Reborn: The Global Expansion of Evangelicalism in the Twentieth Century*, Cambridge, UK and Grand Rapids, MI: Eerdmans, 2004.

Chapter 3: Given at a conference arranged by the Templeton Foundation in Paris, 1 and 2 May 2004.

Chapter 4: Given at a conference at the Goethe University, Frankfurt in March 2003 and published in the conference papers, edited by Nicola Köck.

Chapter 5: Given to the Reflection Group, chaired by Romano Prodi, Brussels, May 2003, published in *Transit*, 26, winter 2003–4, pp. 120–44.

Chapter 6: Published as chapter 1 in *Rethinking Church, State and Modernity. Canada between Europe and America*, edited by David Lyon and Marguerite Van Die, University of Toronto Press, 2000, pp. 23–33.

Chapter 7: Given as a keynote address at the Bavarian American Academy, Munich, June 2004.

Chapter 8: Given as a keynote address for a conference on Church and State in Europe in the Houses of Parliament, Budapest, September 2004.

Chapter 9: Given as a keynote address at the University of Otago, Dunedin, New Zealand, December 2002.

Chapter 10: Conference in Amsterdam on Master Narratives, April 2002.

Chapter 11: Cambridge University, late 2001, one of a series for the Cambridge Theological Federation.

Chapter 12: Conference at Dresden Technological University, July 2003.

Chapter 13: Furfey Lecture, Atlanta, August 2003, published in *Sociology of Religion*, 65: 4, pp. 341–56.

Foreword

In writing this foreword, I have an acute sense of trespass. David Martin is an eminent sociologist, who also is deeply grounded in theology; I am a mere amateur in both fields, albeit a very interested one. But just because I am an avid consumer rather than a producer of texts in these disciplines, I can say something of why I have found David Martin's work so tremendously useful and illuminating for my own reflections on modernity, secularization and Christian faith.

I see Martin as having transformed the discussion about secularization in two very important ways. The first is that he has put the debate through what I would call a 'hermeneutical' turn. That is, instead of trying to define how 'modernity', in the singular, has brought about or is bringing about universally certain changes we define as 'secularization' (rationalization, privatization, differentiation etc.), Martin has moved us all onto a different track. He took seriously the (in retrospect, obvious) plurality of national and regional trajectories, and showed how the whole dynamic of what we call secularization was quite different in Anglo-Protestant cultures than it was in organic and uniformly Catholic societies. This initial distinction was refined, developed and added to, and the result is a rich understanding of particular situations, not only in the West, but on the global scene. In other words, he let history, culture, different theologies and ecclesial structures back in to the subject, and made it possible to face some of the awkward facts on the ground that mainstream sociology too effortlessly ignored. Some of the latest fruits of these reflections occur in this collection, notably in Parts II and III.

The second big change is related to the first. I have said that Martin made us recognize different dynamics of 'secularization', where the original theories assumed a single one. The assumption of singularity, which usually applied to 'modernity' itself, as well as to the rise of the secular – the idea, in other words, that a single process was marching through history, making over cultures one after another to a single ultimate model – was nourished by an underlying family of 'master narratives', which for various reasons relegated religion to the pre-modern phase of human development, and saw it as eventually headed for at best marginal status in the society of the future. There were various reasons why this was thought to be inevitable: it could be the march of science, or the advance of technology, or the development of modern, individualist, consumer society; but the direction was held to be fixed.

Underlying this was a kind of secular–liberal triumphalism, uncannily similar to the triumphalism of some Christian missions in the late nineteenth and early twentieth centuries. It is all too easy for these two modes of linear optimism to lock horns, so that each delights in bringing the bad news to the other: the empty churches of Europe on the one hand, and the 'resurgence' of religion in the Third World on the other.

This triumphalism is a travesty of Christian faith (and, I would argue as well, of the best forms of secular humanism) but what we very much needed (I speak here from the Christian side) was an exploration of other models of Christian history. I have found his development of these to be one of the most valuable and exciting aspects of Martin's work.

The 'dialectical' view which he develops in the Introduction to this volume is, I believe, immensely fruitful. Christian 'incursions', the attempted remakings of the world to conform to the Gospel, stand themselves in perpetual danger of being or becoming also remakings of the Gospel to fit the world. They can't simply be registered as definitive gains; but nor should they be simply repudiated as blank betrayals. They contain some element, or perhaps better, hover on the brink, of both.

I believe that one should see the secular modern West as the product of one such large-scale 'incursion', that of Latin Christendom, which in the later Middle Ages embarked on a long series of reforms (including but not confined to the Reformation) that ended up creating the disciplined, productive, pacified, rights-affirming world we live in, within the intellectual framework of a clear natural/supernatural distinction unique in human history hitherto. For many in our civilization, this has become the major implementation of Christian faith; for others it is an early version which has been superseded by the (more rational, consistent) secular variant. (For others again, of course, suffering from partial historical amnesia, it was won only through the overthrow of religion.)

The identification is a travesty (and the superseders and rejecters also travesty the faith in their own way). But that doesn't mean that the whole development is to be deplored. We're not about to dust off Pius IX's Syllabus. It is in fact in the very nature of Christian faith to produce such transformations of the world, such secular expressions, one might say, and then to recover the Christian language in which to live in them and speak to them in a stance of benign-but-critical non-identity. In this regard, David Martin's reflections on Christian language, as in the last two chapters of this collection, are of the greatest contemporary relevance.

Charles Taylor

Introduction

This book documents part of an intellectual journey roughly over the two years 2002–4, with regard to Christianity and secularization, which had begun about four decades earlier with a critique of the concept of secularization. It came to interim fruition with 'Notes Towards a General Theory of Secularization', published in *The European Journal of Sociology* in December 1969, which comprised the first chapter of *A General Theory of Secularization* published by Blackwell in 1978. The chapters here are 'Notes Towards' a revised 'General Theory'; a summary of the four decades work appeared in the article 'Secularization and the Future of Christianity', which was published in *The Journal of Contemporary Religion*, 20 (2), May 2005.

My intellectual journey took a different turn in 1986 when I began to look at Christianity in the developing world, in particular evangelicalism, initially in Latin America, and latterly in Africa and globally. Thus the first two chapters under the heading 'Orientations' are focused respectively on two basic phases, one mainly concerned with Europe and North America, the other with Latin America, Africa and Asia. Both *Tongues of Fire* (1990) and *Pentecostalism – The World Their Parish* (2002), published by Blackwell, attempted to show how the extraordinary changes they charted fitted into the original general theory, and the latter book included an extended survey of the specifically European situation. That survey indicates how I might treat Europe in a revised general theory. Both Europe and Latin America were discussed in my *Forbidden Revolutions* (SPCK, 1996), where I compared the Pentecostal Revolution in Latin America with that in Eastern Europe in 1989–90. The point here is that the dominant grand narrative of the Western intelligentsia disallowed both developments, so it was important to say why. For that matter the Pentecostal Revolution still does not figure on the horizon because it is not political.

The work of 2002–4, ten of the thirteen chapters presented here, began with an invitation from David Ford and Daniel Hardie to contribute in late 2001 to a series of lectures on pluralism for the Cambridge Theological Federation. It ended with the Furfey Lecture in Atlanta, Georgia in August 2003, chaired by Grace Davie, with the lecture for the Templeton Foundation in Paris in May 2004, and addresses to the Bavarian American Academy and a conference in the Hungarian Houses of Parliament in respectively June and September. In between there were two especially significant encounters, one in Amsterdam, the other in Brussels.

The conference in Amsterdam was concerned with alternative master narratives to secularization, which stimulated me to look at the issue of master narratives, but I also had the privilege of encountering Charles Taylor and his work. I realized then, as I should have realized long before, that my often-repeated concern about the gap between accounts of secularization seen from the philosophical viewpoint and standard sociological accounts was less relevant than it had been. Charles Taylor was bridging the gap and the pontoons were, so to speak, meeting in the middle. Progress was actually being made in a field that has sometimes seemed to comprise endless revisiting. (Another scholar building such bridges in modern British history is Simon Green.)

The other encounter arose from an invitation to present a paper in the period before the advent of the draft European Constitution, to a Reflection Group chaired in Brussels by Romano Prodi, President of the EU. That pushed me back to re-examining the European material from a new angle, as did an invitation a little earlier from Professor Übermann of the Goethe University, Frankfurt.

Perhaps I might add that Chapters 3 and 7, given in Paris and Munich respectively, are twinned. Chapter 7 in particular marks a push into new territory, fraught with risk and (I hope) promise, because of its free treatment of myth, theology and sociology. The background of strained German–American relations in the context of the Iraq War will be readily understood, and it picks up the theme of triumphalism raised in Charles Taylor's Foreword.

Of course, invitations come with requests for particular approaches, which may include the suggestion that you rethink previous work, for example, my early critique of secularization in the 1960s, and the general theory of the 1970s. Inevitably that involves some repetition, even the reuse of examples. One cannot, through either modesty or arrogance, avoid these restatements.

Three of the thirteen chapters were written before 2002–4. As already indicated, the first chapter was an orientation given to a lay audience in Timişoara, and the second an orientation to the global situation in the specific context of evangelicalism, which immediately trailed and previewed *Pentecostalism – The World Their Parish* in 2002. Perhaps I may add here that an address given as the keynote in Dallas, Texas, on 20 January 2005 at a conference organized by the Roman Catholic movement 'New Evangelization', provides a succinct account of what a revised General Theory would look like. It is published in the *Journal of Contemporary Religion* 20:2 2005 as 'Secularization and the Future of Christianity', and deals in particular with master narratives, with the contrast between Anglo-American and Catholic trajectories, with contemporary individualization, and with the conclusion of the two centuries of contestation, 1789–1989. Chapter 6 on Canada was given at a conference in the late 1990s in Kingston, Ontario, and enabled me to explore the hybrid pattern of secularization in Canada 'between Europe and America'. Obviously hybrids are of particular theoretical interest.

The three final chapters comprise 'Commentary' and are crucial, at least for me, because they look back, in the context of secularization, to themes of constant personal and intellectual concern. These themes are Christian language and its nature; and Christianity and politics, war and peace. I am particularly grateful to Klaus Tanner of the Martin Luther University of Halle-Wittenberg for giving me the opportunity to present the second of these final chapters at his seminar in Dresden. The last chapter looks back to my *Does Christianity Cause War?* (1997) as well as to a portrait of the politician as moral hero I drew three decades ago in an essay on R.D. Laing by way of contrast with the existential heroism promoted in the 1960s.[1] This final chapter had the Iraq War in the backround and could have been called 'The Prime Minister, the Archbishop and Mr John Humphrys, although its scope is very much more gereral than that. Both these chapters were later given to seminars at Durham University in November 2003.

At one point I intended to include two further chapters, one based on writing up a lecture given to clergy at Christchurch, Oxford, on 'Secularization in England' at the invitation of Henry Mayr-Harting, and the other a piece solicited for a symposium on the New Zealand theologian Lloyd Geering, which was to have dealt with secularization as treated by 'secular theologians'. Both the lecture and the proposed article pushed the argument about secularization further by way of serious speculation, and I have used sketches for them as the basis of the rest of this Introduction, beginning with the concept of Christian dialectic as I deployed it in the address at Christchurch. The specifically English context has been mostly shorn away to leave a structure of argument about the Christian West as such.

A Dialectic of Faith and Nature?

The Christian dialectic, realized for socio-historical reasons in the West rather than the East, depends on the contrast between 'the world' and 'the kingdom', and on the persistent secularization of Christian seeds sown abroad in the world as signs of the kingdom. The result is intermittent ferment within Christian civilization, because God is distinguished from Caesar, and Church from State, and because the inner kingdom of the spirit bursts the bonds of the letter of the law and of the institution. So, a whole civilization is rendered precarious. The Gospel itself lays down the cultural slipways of secularization, making it difficult for the institutional Church to resist a momentum in which it shares. However, there are, as I shall suggest, built-in limits.

Crucially I argue that instead of regarding secularization as a once-for-all unilateral process, one might rather think in terms of successive Christianizations followed or accompanied by recoils. Each Christianization is a salient of faith driven into the secular from a different angle, each pays a characteristic cost which affects the character of the recoil, and each undergoes a partial collapse into some version of 'nature'.

In what follows I am thinking speculatively in terms of four Christianizations, each overlapping the others, and each creating massive wakes which are still with us, either remotely or more immediately. I identify, first, a Catholic Christianization in two versions: the conversion of monarchs (and so of peoples), and the conversion of the urban masses by the friars. I then identify a Protestant Christianization in two versions: one seeking to extend monasticism to all Christian people but effectively corralling them in the nation, and the other realized in the creation of evangelical and Pietist subcultures. This last collapsed quite recently so we are immediately in its wake. If one wanted to illustrate how we are still affected both by the varied successive Christianizations and by the relapses into nature, one might choose attitudes to baptism. Thus baptism may be seen as a right belonging to everyone within Christendom, or to a citizen of the nation, or as a rite of passage into a denominational subculture. In terms of relapses into nature it may be understood magically, or rejected as unnecessary because birth itself is regarded as the one true sacrament.[2]

Turning to the core of the argument, one has to indicate the specific costs attached to each Christianization as well as the various relapses into nature, beginning with the Catholic Christianization in both its versions.

Christianity began as a burgeoning and voluntaristic subculture, but its initial mass conversions mostly came about through the conversion of queens and kings (often in that order), not just the Emperor Constantine but Oswald, Olaf, Vladimir and many more. This incurred the cost of assimilating faith to power, hierarchy, war, compulsion and violence, as well as setting the scene for tensions between Church and State. The second mass conversion was undertaken by the friars among the urban masses of medieval Europe, and the cost incurred here was a division into the athletes of God and the also-rans, into the celibate and the spiritual, as contrasted with the domestic and the reproductive. The Catholic system went into the crisis of the Reformation by way of the Protestant attempt to break down this division, and include everyone equally 'by grace'. Within Catholicism the reversion to nature manifested itself in several ways: in the new visibility of the natural world, for example in St Francis and Petrarch; in an unstable mixture of rationality, protoscience and alchemy; and in the recognition of the naked facts of political nature in Machiavelli.

The Protestant attempt at universalizing the monastic ideal ran into the antimony of grace and nature and, in this case, the cost was paid in terms of election and/or perfectionist striving laid on everyone, with intermittent outbreaks of antinomian moral chaos. There are various options open once you attempt to universalize the Gospel. One involves election according to God's predestinate will, which can lead to the elect imposing a godly government on a whole society as in Calvinist Geneva and Massachusetts. Another is the Anabaptist pursuit of perfection which can only work when it is hived off into a self-selected group or territorially segregated community. Both of these options, especially when they are in mutual interaction, can tighten tensions to the point where the moral structure of society itself totters, and crashes in the kind of chaos that occurred in Münster or in England during the Civil War. In the long run the intellectual structure of Calvinist election evolves into a naturalistic and rationalistic moralism: Richard Price and Joseph Priestley.

The Lutheran option works by covering everyone by grace alone, rather than by works, while holding the perfection of the invisible Church permanently in abeyance. This forces the dynamic of grace and nature into a settled routine before it breaks out again within the inner chamber of the soul and in small intimate groupings by way of infusions of divine love.

Both the Calvinist and Lutheran options rest on the universal priesthood of all believers. They imply the extension of a lay ethos to the point where the international orders of priests, monks and friars are abolished. The Church becomes assimilated to the State, the sacred ministry becomes yet another profession and the monastic brotherhood is converted into the reproductive family. Another way of putting this is to say that Fathers-in-God become fathers of their peoples, or else they are just ordinary fathers marrying and begetting. In other words the special social structures designed to carry and mediate grace revert to the 'natural' formations of ethnicity and the family. However, that was only one of the reversions to nature within Protestantism. Nature also asserted itself in terms of the autonomy of individual reason and of empirical reality: Herbert of Cherbury and Locke.

Finally, the Christianizations attempted through the evangelical and Pietist 'Awakenings', first in the North Atlantic world, and nowadays globally through Pentecostalism, were based on individual heartwork and inward feeling. The cost here was, and still is, paid in terms of some degree of lesion with the sciences of nature, as well as in terms of the creation of denominational subcultures which set up boundaries between the committed and the uncommitted. In practice one cannot convert everybody, which means that the idea of being Christian comes to refer to a subcultural lifestyle not a whole society. At the same time this kind of Pietist, evangelical or Pentecostal subculture runs alongside modernization in a mutually supportive manner, first in relation to the Industrial Revolution, and now throughout the developing world, especially in Africa, Latin America and the Pacific rim. Denominational subcultures are positively related to modernization.

Almost from the start this evangelical Christianization runs alongside, and even overlaps, a Romantic return to nature. Evangelicalism and Romanticism both appeal to the heart, in the one case through conversion and adoration of God, in the other case through sincerity, acting naturally rather than artificially, and through adoration of nature. Today we live in the wake of both, which means we combine a pure inwardness derived residually from evangelical heartwork with a Romantic myth of the sacred environment. That myth is propagated by contemporary education and the media to the exclusion of the creative tensions built into salvation history and all the associated ideas of historical sequence, freedom, choice and moral consequence. Naturalism embraced in this comprehensive way offers very little resistance to ancient ideas of fate and fortune, or to manipulative magic and superstition. It is also vulnerable to a very different reversion to nature, based on the Darwinian struggle for survival, now propagated increasingly through 'cognitive science' or biogenetic determinism. Whereas Romanticism responded to nature as a source of moral and emotional truth, as though it were already the 'peaceable kingdom' envisaged in prophecy, in the version represented by Darwin and Nietzsche, nature is completely amoral. Furthermore, any morality that may be proposed on Darwinian premises lacks any epistemological backing. This is a point made with particular force by Charles Taylor.

The evangelical Christianization, with the subcultures it created, lasted from the early nineteenth to the mid-twentieth century, when boundaries as such were undermined by the flood-waters of the natural, the primitive, the ahistorical and the primordial. However, in some ways evangelicalism retained its boundaries and survived better than movements lacking boundaries or, like the Student Christian Movement, taking them down and disappearing into 'the world'.

In spite of this necessary retention of institutional and conceptual boundaries, evangelicalism incurs a cost on account of the ease with which heartwork can be taken to imply that there is no need for efficacious ritual and institutional mediation. Ritual and mediation are all too easily dismissed as mere mumbojumbo and priestcraft: that is the sentiment or sediment deposited by a receding Protestantism. Christianity comes to be popularly received as no more than neighbourliness or decent personal attitudes and well-meaning sentiment. Decency is the eminently natural virtue and in political terms it has to provide the agreed point of reference for moral consensus. It offers the working version of faith in the political sphere. The reason is that a public institution, like a road roundabout, requires a decent law-abiding citizenry, not Christianity.

If childbirth is the all-sufficient natural sacrament, with no loss on account of sin or necessary benefit of grace, then Church and community are once more at one, the dialectic is over, and we, in our inwardness and sincerity, are reunited with nature. The cost of the return to nature is paid in terms of a loss of freedom, and of moral and historical consequentiality. It is no accident that God, freedom, truth, human uniqueness and responsibility, as well as every kind of qualitative difference, have all been attacked simultaneously.

The various reversions to nature occurring in Christian history are seldom simply reversions to paganism, though these do occur, initially in the Renaissance but more particularly in the nineteenth century when an over-intellectualized and moralistic presentation of Christianity leads to a search for religious contents elsewhere. In practice it is not easy to shake off the sense of forward movement and historical purpose derived from Christianity in order to embrace mere rotation or to accept a meaningless passage of time and change leading nowhere. Certainly the Enlightenment did not attempt to do that and, in any case, there is a positive Jewish and Christian understanding of nature which checks any straightforward adoption of paganism. The creation is, after all, regarded as good, and not just as a vale of tears. Its order derives from the operation of the divine reason or wisdom, and man also is made in the rational image of God. In the great period of change in the seventeenth century, Christian, Jewish and indeed Neoplatonic resources could be resorted to and were able to find highly attractive expression, for example, in Vaughan, Traherne and Henry More. A century and a half later poets such as Coleridge, Wordsworth and Novalis, who were progenitors of a Romantic response to nature, might set Romanticism in a Christian or semi-Christian frame. That kind of

Christian Romanticism is still diffusely present in a great deal of contemporary sentiment about faith, nature, mountains and landscape. Even today the world of feeling promoted by an idealized Celtic paganism mingles with an idealized Celtic Christianity and with 'creation spirituality'. The symbol of the candle is simultaneously a sign of returning natural light and of the advent of the Redeemer. Wagnerian myth in *Parsifal* is not alone in combining the two. Why else the double charge and mutual exchange of meanings between evil and the 'works of darkness' or between the rising sun and the Risen Son – or in 'Wie schön leuchtet der Morgenstern' ('How brightly shines the Morning Star')? Why else are churches aligned to the East apart from 'Ex Oriente Lux'? The Wisdom tradition, in particular, provides Christianity's reserve repertoire, one which is able to unite a Solomonic admiration for nature with desire for the coming embodiment of the incarnate Word. Science and 'measure' can complement redemption, and so the dialectic tension of grace and nature can be eased without being destroyed.

The Relation of Faith and the Secular, and the Variety of Secularization Stories

In the sketch just provided I have attempted to present a speculative history of Christian incursions on secular nature, each of which sets up its own particular tension and then shifts again towards nature and the natural in both Christian and non-Christian forms. In certain respects these tensions have a perennial character, so that the problem of including everybody in the overall religious frame affects Catholicism in relation to the monarchs of Christendom while it affects Protestantism in relation to monarchs and/or nations and nation-states. Inclusion requires dilution. In the same way the problem of bounded subcultures based on self-selection and semi-segregation affects Catholic orders, perfectionist communitarian enclaves and Protestant voluntary denominations alike. However, in the Catholic case the boundary or limit is accepted in principle, whereas in the case of Protestant denominations it is painfully encountered in practice. Eager evangelists discover that the kingdom of God does not come either in the USA or in Britain, and recognize how membership may recede as well as expand. Optimism about expansion may then mutate into pessimism or self-flagellation about failure, or constant search for the right formula. Simon Green brilliantly analyses all this in his *Religion in the Age of Decline* (1996).

This sketch should not be seen as simply a theological account of culture, but also and independently a sociological account of culture analysing the modes whereby faith inserts itself in society when it is a faith simultaneously accepting the goodness of the created order and strenuously seeking its transformation by an appeal to the Gospel. As I shall emphasize again later, the distinctive character of my approach lies in the intimate correlation between the theological and the sociological accounts, so that faith is understood in terms of its social incarnations and in its dialectic relation to nature as observed in action. In a rather similar way a typological approach in theology can be correlated though not merged with a structuralist account in sociology as the basis for a seamless discourse.

A dialectical approach based on an account of successive religious transformations in their varying encounters with social realities (or social nature) as understood by sociology differs considerably from standard narratives of secularization. Characteristically these narratives join together the varied elements of nature, whether physical or social, to create a running narrative of the steady supersession of religion. The recoils are limited and the varied Christianizations scanted. Once there was *a* religious past, and that has bit by bit emerged as *the* secular future. The natural (often equated with science) wins out over religion through uninterrupted increments, however much religion resists and engages in rearguard actions.

The most usual secularization story of this kind starts with (say) Roger Bacon, Machiavelli and Petrarch, moves to the empiricism of Francis Bacon and the rationalism of the French, and to some extent the German, Enlightenments. It then proceeds to Schopenhauer and Nietzsche and sundry prophets of modernity, (say) Darwin, Freud, Marx and Sartre, up to any number of contemporary figures, such as Russell, Ayer and Rorty. Often enough this story of the triumph of the secular combines description of the process with overt or covert prescription of the outcome. Secularization is both noted and promoted. As a result the dialectic of successive Christian incursions becomes occluded, along with the distinctive character of a Christian civilization as compared with any other. As Charles Taylor has pointed out, the Christian sources of contemporary mentalities are overlooked because no longer identified by their 'Christian names'.

Given that the secularization story as just outlined is based on the idea of 'The World we have Lost' – the title of Peter Laslett's book positing an unequivocal religious past – we retroject our own contemporary assumptions onto the nature of the process. *Some* kind of process has certainly occurred, but it may not be quite the one we have retrospectively constructed. As a result retrospective accounts too often treat phenomena of a religious character as interim formations prior to a secular denouement. There are, for example, numerous accounts of Christian socialism which treat it as 'only' an interim anticipation of real secular socialism. There are also accounts of the genuine gains of religion in industrial urban society which treat them as illusory and some kind of survival.

More specifically, standard renderings of crucial episodes, such as the Darwinian controversy, are routinely cast in terms of enlightened science breaking through the darkness of religious resistance, all oblivious to the critique of that approach mounted by recent revisionist historiography. Again, to take a contemporary example, suicide bombing may be traced simply and solely to sources in regressive religion as it reacts to secular pressure, and not to its original sources in the secular nationalism of the Tamil Tigers or the late-nineteenth-century secular propaganda of the deed. This can only happen because the ruling paradigm renders the idea 'obvious'.

The most recent example to come my way can be found in the connection suggested between Ruskin's 'loss of faith' and his emergence as one of the defining prophets of modernity. Michael Wheeler in his *Ruskin's God* shows this was not at all the case, and he traces this type of misrepresentation to our own contemporary cultural presumptions.[3] Of course, such presumptions are in themselves evidence for a *kind* of secularization story, at least among sections of the Western intelligentsia, but it is not necessarily the one that the intelligentsia tells itself – and the world.

What needs to be attempted is a sociological account of certain episodes in the history of the Western intelligentsia in its struggle for ideological power with rival groups, including the clergy. An episode of particular interest in my view occurs between about 1870 and 1910, the effect of which is to lead contemporary intellectuals to envisage secularization as due to the implausibility of *beliefs*, and to divide the world up into a negatively weighted contrast between people described as 'believers' and people who are not. This approach, based on a particular and restricted kind of intellectual attitude relating to credibility, is generalized to the characterization of secularization as such. In fact the world is not like that, even allowing for the undoubted 'trickle-down effects' of intellectual attitudes through the control of media and education, or even the effects of 'rationalized' activities in the Weberian sense. Sociology itself proceeds in terms of 'beliefs' held to this or that extent rather than features of religion or spirituality which 'snag' people positively or negatively, which may have little to do with intellectual credibility and owe much more to social alignments, atmospherics and myths. If one wants to see secularization stories of this kind at work, then they can be read in almost any biography of people of this period from 1870 to 1910.

Secularization stories of this partial kind, while not straightforwardly wrong or merely ideological and prescriptive, tend most of all to stress changes in our understanding of physical and biological nature, treating changes in our understanding of social nature as secondary, and changes in the arts as illustrative afterthoughts. Of course, these weightings may vary, and sociological accounts, such as are given by my colleagues and myself, inevitably lay stress on changes in society and social understanding, with the progress of the natural and biological sciences treated as tangential and contributory. In my own work I have tried to modify the standard sociological approach by taking into account secularization stories of all kinds, including those found in art, literature and music. Indeed, in my *Christian Language and its Mutations* (2002) I concentrate on music to some extent because it is the form of human activity closest to and most intimately associated with religion. A 'Whig' interpretation of the history of music in terms of straightforward secularization just doesn't work.

In emphasizing the ubiquity of secularization stories, and the varied ways they combine prescription and description, it may help to take an example from children's literature, which could easily be assimilated to the discussion of secular theologians almost immediately following. My literary example is Philip Pullman, and what characterizes him, and secular theology alike, is the fusion of prescription and description, which is so much easier to get away with in fantasy rather than discursive prose. Critics do not ordinarily subject an imaginative writer to a reality check based on sociological analysis, as they might do in the case of a secular theologian.

In Pullman's trilogy, as in all stories with an arbitrary closure, the reader is left with little idea of what it would take, beyond work and study, to bring about the republic of heaven on earth, or how the collapse of the 'Authority' (or God) solves the problem of power which Pullman has arbitrarily identified with the evils of the institutional Church rather than as a feature of social structures as such. Unlike John Milton, his source and model, Pullman does not have to face the dilemmas of power and high office in his republic of heaven. What he has come up with is just another version of what Eric Voegelin called the 'immanentization' of the eschaton.

I am saying that in originally attempting to construct and now to revise a theory of secularization, I have throughout faced the problem of skewed intellectual and social histories, as well as imaginatively powerful secularization stories half-hidden in history and literature. The problem can be exacerbated by theologies which take off from these skewed histories, particularly those based on assumptions of unilateral and uniform intellectual advance which, nevertheless, go on to announce the arrival of the secular age as a kind of epiphany. Having utilized a story based (say) on the progress of scientific understanding, one then, as by a non-scientific leap of faith, discerns the signs of the times in order to declare the 'acceptable year' in which the inner meaning of Christianity is finally realized in secular reality. Heaven has been finally earthed and so heavens above are surplus to requirements, or a kind of surplus supplying fuller, deeper resonance to a secular hope. The dialectic lapses because shorn of transcendence.

However, the emptying out of the sea of faith into the secular reality as described and prescribed by (say) a secular theologian such as Don Cupitt is not the only theological response. In John Milbank's work quite the reverse happens, because the autonomy of secular understanding by way of social theory is treated simply as an enclosed discourse without objective criteria of its own. Social theory is accused of policing the sublime *and* declared off limits, while Christianity itself is credited with its own social theory based on harmony and peace.

This very much contrasts with Don Cupitt's approach, which is not to dismiss sociology in principle but totally to ignore it in practice, using 'ordinary-language' philosophy to trace the epiphany of the secular in such fragments of hearsay on the Cambridge omnibus as may selectively illustrate its arrival. There is no notion of answerability to evidence in this, but only evangelical proclamation stood on its head and preached over and over again to create the new Church of the 'non-realist God'.

One might cite many other examples of secular theology, such as Harvey Cox's announcement, in an early phase of his writing, of the arrival of 'The Secular City', or the reconstruction of Jesus by the Jesus seminar as a secular sage to serve the secular age. But Cupitt and Milbank between them serve well enough to exemplify significant extremes whereby the dialectic lapses, either by the final earthing of transcendence or by the swallowing up of secular reality and understanding in transcendence and theology.

My own view, as stated below, argues that once the dialectic between transforming vision and a natural and social reality characterized as good has been introduced into history, it does not and perhaps cannot lapse. Rather it mutates in different variants, sometimes under misleading names, so that we miss its secret presence.

The key to my own work over four decades, for example in Part II of *Christian Language and Its Mutations* (2002), lies most clearly in the dialectic between the transforming vision of peace and harmony in its Christian version, and in its derivative Enlightenment variant, and the social realities of power and violence. But I also touch on parallel tensions relating to artistic beauty and the erotic, and note the tension between Christian notions of mutuality and self-giving and the social science of economics, as that is based on permanent realities of pleasure and profit, expansion and survival. None of these realities of power or wealth are in themselves radically evil, but they do provide the occasions through which radical evil can manifest itself. Of the coiled-up presence of radical evil I have no doubt.

In my view, sociology (like economics) is ideologically inflected, and even infected, especially by enlightened assumptions. Thus far Milbank is right, though the point has been made many times before by sociologists.[4] At the same time, sociology provides, and analyses, the reality checks faced by Christian and enlightened sentimentality alike, using sentimentality in both its strict and popular senses. Sociology, above all in relation to power and violence and to the international order and disorder, explains why and how Christianity in its challenge to 'the world' partly succumbs to it and becomes part of its legitimation and support. That is easy to grasp. The same is true of the aspirations of the Enlightenment and of any 'republic of heaven' you care to envisage. That appears less easy to grasp, though no less obvious. So, not only can a sociology be constructed that takes into account the social dynamic introduced by the transcendent vision, and the pressure it exercises on mundane time, but a theology may likewise be constructed which takes into account the interpenetration of the ways of earth and the ways of heaven. A realist theology is precisely that. Christianity works in that way because that is the way it is.

A Personal View of the Dialectic

In my own view, then, the dialectic continues.[5] My argument would rest on Troeltsch, Weber, Richard and Reinhold Niebuhr, and it relates to the Christian repertoire and the adaptation of its images to new worldly contexts, above all power.

The key elements in that repertoire concern the radical reversals of the kingdom, the identification of the divine with powerlessness in the Incarnation, and the reversal of Babel in the universal speech of Pentecost. All of these encounter the inherent character of human society, necessarily based on authority and power, as well as based on a solidarity against 'the other'. So the *logic* of Christianity, exemplified in its repertoire of images, encounters the *logic* of social organization. It simultaneously adapts to it and infiltrates it with contrary imaginations. And, of course, no society could be constructed on the sole basis of such imaginations: such a society only becomes really present in the enactments and sequences of liturgy.[6]

Other elements also exhibit the same dialectic, for example, the tension between the transforming transcendence of liturgical poetry and drama, and the everyday as realized in the communal aspects of a simple meal, or the tension between visions of redemption based on the free gift of grace and ordinary moral common sense about balanced and symmetrical exchange. What Donald Davie called the Christian oxymoron, its fruitful, creative contradiction, occurs and recurs in every sphere, while also constantly mutating. I believe in that oxymoron: accepting but transforming, incarnate yet transcendent. It is the kingdom of heaven seeking to enlarge its colonies on earth. Those colonies are located in the sacraments, in experiments in fraternity, in the universal speech of Pentecost, and in seeds of hope cast far outside the boundaries of the Church. I also believe, as against John Milbank, that sociology can provide a context for a theology which, while played in a different key, remains faithfully rooted in the core repertoire of Christianity. That is because it is not inevitably an alien discourse but engages with the way things are, and the way things happen. The key to the Christian dialectic is the concept of 'the world', and sociology tells us how that world works. What sociology and economics alike testify to is the continuity through all modalities, religious or enlightened, of the secular principles of power seeking, pleasure, survival and profit. They can and should be challenged, but they had better not be ignored or dismissed, not least because they are the stuff of a serious theological engagement and of Christianity's own proper activity.

Notes

1 David Martin, *Does Christianity Cause War?*, Oxford: Clarendon Press, 1997; and David Martin, 'R.D. Laing: Psychiatry and Apocalypse', *Dissent*, June 1971, pp. 250–51.

2 For an indication of the *terminus ad quem* of pagan naturalism see Michael York, *Pagan Theology: Paganism as a World Religion,* New York: New York University Press, 2003; and for similar tendencies held in check by Christianity see Richard Thomas, *Counting People In. Changing the way we think about Christianity and the Church*, London: SPCK, 2003. For reactions to moralism see Hans Kippenberg, *Discovering Religious History in the Modern Age*, Princeton: Princeton University Press, 2002.

3 Michael Wheeler *Ruskin's God*, Cambridge: Cambridge University Press, 1999. For a modern reversion to the Wisdom tradition see Jacques Dupuis, *Christianity and the Religions. From Confrontation to Dialogue,* London: DLT, 2003.

4   See Kieran Flanagan, *The Enchantment of Sociology*, London: Macmillan, 1996.

5   I have drawn this from my own (solicited) response to comments on my theological position by Ian Markham in the journal *Conversations in Religion and Theology*, March 2004, published by Blackwell, pp. 33–41.

6   See Kieran Flanagan, *Sociology and Liturgy*, New York: St Martin's Press, 1991 and Catherine Pickstock, *After Writing. On the Liturgical Consummation of Philosophy*, Oxford: Blackwell, 1998. For an ethnographic approach there is Martin Stringer *On the Perception of Worship*, Birmingham: Birmingham University Press, 1991.

PART I
ORIENTATIONS

CHAPTER 1

Sociology, Religion and Secularization

What follows is an account of an issue that bears centrally on the relationship of sociology to religion and of sociology to theology. It is a retrospective account of a personal encounter with this particular issue. That issue is secularization. Sociology itself emerged as part of the process of secularization because it represented the autonomous study of Man in Society. But the circumstances of its emergence meant that it gave an absolutely central place to the problem of secularization and encased that problem in an ideological frame, in part derived from the philosophy of history. Sociology itself, as John Milbank has argued, has a deep structure of ideology embedded in its very foundations.[1] However, unlike Milbank I do not believe that its whole discourse is self-contained beyond correction. Ideology, once observed, can be countered. The guiding paradigms of sociology, such as secularization, can be made analytically coherent and descriptively accurate. However, that means reducing 'grand theory' to tendencies which are to be observed in certain definable circumstances and not in others and, moreover, those circumstances need to be seen as varying greatly according to historical context. In what follows, I present the viable core of secularization as the sub-theory of social differentiation. Serious doubts can be raised about the sub-theory of rationalization, and an important work of José Casanova[2] criticizes the sub-theory of privatization (which happens also to have implications for theological reflections on society).

This is why I can be counted both as a theorist of secularization, for example by Frank Lechner,[3] as well as a critic. There is a viable core and a doubtful periphery. I need only add that what follows is a personal account of my own encounter with the problem as perhaps the first person to raise the critical issue in the mid-1960s and, moreover, to do so at a time when some theologians, such as Harvey Cox, were actually celebrating a version of the secularization thesis and glossing it theologically.[4] This is *not* an overview of the debate offering an assessment of such key contributors as Peter Berger, Bryan Wilson, Karel Dobbelaere, Rodney Stark, Thomas Luckmann, Richard Fenn and Steve Bruce. It is a simple personal account offered to a lay audience interested in the relation of sociology to religion, of sociology to theology and of religion to society.

One needs to recall two standard points about sociology in general before coming to the sociology of religion – and secularization – in particular. The first point is that we need to recognize how our knowledge embodies a particular historical, cultural and even personal location. We are able to see precisely because we have a standpoint. That means that the sociologist does not present a package of certified knowledge, but begins a conversation.

The second point is that we see through a grid which *organizes* what we see. This is not just a matter of having a focus, though it is certainly true that you need a focus. Nor is it just a matter of being personally involved, although we are. The notion of a grid refers to the way we automatically structure the whole field of vision. Certain assumptions taken together constitute a paradigm, and as Thomas Kuhn argued, we are extremely reluctant to alter that paradigm. Evidence may pile up against it, but we prefer to keep explaining *away* the evidence to altering the paradigm. Even science tries to achieve some stability of understanding.

What, then, of what used to be the undisputed paradigm of secularization? Sociology and modernity were born together and so the focus of sociology was on what happened to religion under conditions of modernity and accelerating change. Basically it characterized modernity as a scenario in which mankind shifted from the religious mode to the secular. Secularization was made part of a powerful social and historical narrative of what had once been and now was ceasing to be. Emile Durkheim and Max Weber founded their reflections on what they saw as the crisis of religious consciousness. So strong was this presumption that few bothered to articulate the theory in terms of concrete historical analyses and careful examination of statistical data.

Since secularization was the undisputed paradigm, relatively few sociologists took a special interest in religion apart from a debate about Max Weber's thesis that Calvinistic Protestantism was one of the midwives of capitalism and so a sort of prelude to modernity. After all, sociologists had to consider future employment and nobody wants to spend their lives explaining why something is going to be less and less important. At one point I described the sociologist of religion ironically as 'an academic deviant living by a non-existent subject'.[5] But, of course, that situation varied according to the cultural situation of the sociological community in different countries. In North America, after all, church practice had *risen* steadily through the whole period of modernization from 1800 to 1950. Indeed, Jon Butler has described this extraordinary increase in a book entitled *Awash in a Sea of Faith*.[6] Thus, in the USA, there was genuine interest among sociologists represented by such distinguished scholars as Charles Glock, Robert Bellah and Peter Berger. More than that, the political scientist Martin Lipset argued that sociologists laid too much stress on class in understanding political behaviour and should try properly to take into account the role of religion. There was also some interest in European sociology in the condition of the Catholic Church. After all, the Catholic Church was one of the pillars of the European Community after the war. Many of these studies focused on indices of religious practice, on the status groups most likely to be attached to religious institutions, on the milieux most supportive towards religion. Nevertheless, in European sociology the paradigm of secularization remained dominant. Scholars argued that people in the great cities and the administrative and industrial centres were least likely to be religiously involved. Religiosity was concentrated among women and the older groups and in more remote areas.

As for Britain, it was still in a phase of post-war reconstruction and sociologists were more interested in questions of class, living conditions, education and social mobility. There was, for example, a Marxist approach which regarded religion at best as a naïve anticipation of social change, a projection of fantastic hopes that could only be properly realized under scientific socialism. And there was also a strong emphasis on the sifting of facts and statistics. It was only in the 1960s that sociology shifted its focus towards meaning, narrative, symbol and culture, and started to show a greater interest in religion. The result of all this was that religion was treated as a remainder, something left over from the past. That showed itself in two ways. The first was in social anthropology, where the interest in non-European societies required some understanding of religion. In this area there was a very different atmosphere associated with figures such as Mary Douglas, E. Evans-Pritchard and Victor Turner. Victor Turner, for example, focused attention on rites of transition, on the richness of symbols and pilgrimages. Few people realized how important pilgrimage remained in Western society. The second focus of interest was in the emergence of small minority groups, such as Pentecostals and Adventists. Bryan Wilson's school of sociology at Oxford concentrated on sects: categorizing them in types, describing the conditions which favoured their growth, analysing their social constituency and their dynamics. But in this area, explanation was initially dominated by the idea that this kind of religion arose from frustration and deprivation.[7] Eventually the interest shifted to groups associated with the New Age or New Religious Movements offering different kinds of spiritual therapy. In any case, the paradigm of secularization remained undisturbed, at least in the early stages, though there were those who thought the emergence of the New Age groups offered some contrary evidence.[8]

So, where was a critique to come from which might disturb the paradigm? Perhaps in the long run from anthropology, but an important clue was offered by the work of Karl Popper. In his *The Poverty of Historicism*, Popper had criticized the notion of long-term inevitable trends of history from the viewpoint of a philosopher of science.[9] It seemed to me that secularization was just such a trend. Perhaps it could be criticized as an ideological and philosophical imposition *on* history rather than an inference *from* history. So, in 1965, I offered a critique of the concept of secularization.[10] First, I suggested that it was conceptually a hotch-potch of ideas, some of them contradictory. And then I suggested it was *in part* an ideological projection on history based on an apotheosis of reason, on an existentialist anticipation of autonomous man, and on a Marxist leap into freedom and into reality with the conclusion of the historical dialectic in class society. Not so long after, a parallel critique was launched by the American sociologist Andrew Greeley. We were both anxious to underline the extensive influence of religion even in Western European society and the sharp difference between Western Europe and North America. There was, in our view, more than one model of modernity and of the future.[11]

At the same time, there were various important extensions of secularization theory. For example, Peter Berger analysed the growth of pluralism, that is of competing religious (and secular) alternatives, and suggested that it would be difficult to maintain secure religious commitment when faced with so many contradictory beliefs and competing social environnments. However, Berger no longer believes that pluralism leads to a decline in religious commitment. Thomas Luckmann analysed the long-term consequences of the turn to inwardness and subjectivity and argued that this would bring about privatization, which would render religion socially invisible and irrelevant. This thesis concerning the shift to privatization was a major component in revised secularization, holding that society would be run by a rational bureaucracy and by impersonal regulation. It would not require any consensus over values or a religious instruction of personal conscience.[12]

These, then, were some of the reconstructions, mostly based on Western European experience. However, there was one other analysis of the role of Christianity in modern industrial society which has to be mentioned. It was provided in the 1950s and the 1960s by Talcott Parsons. He refined a key component in the theory of secularization, which was the process of social differentiation. A key text for this is his article on Christianity in *The International Encyclopedia of the Social Sciences*.[13] Parsons saw differentiation as the separating out of each social sphere from ecclesiastical control: the state, science and the market, but also law, welfare and education etc. They would gain their own proper autonomy and specific expertise. But being an American reflecting on American experience, Parsons did *not* see this as a decline, but as change enabling religion better to fulfil its proper role. No longer, for example, was it tied into the *realpolitik* of the state but liberated to be itself. Social differentiation also predicted the extension of religious competition and pluralism.

Arguably, social differentiation offered the most useful element in the paradigm of secularization. It was the analytic core to which the statistical data, for example, the inverse relationship between religious practice and the size of the city, should be related. It also seemed crystal clear that secularization varied enormously. Not only was it very different in North America and Western Europe, both of them modern societies, but it varied also within these cultural areas. Social differentiation and the general statistical tendencies had to be passed through historical filters in a major effort of cross-cultural comparison. I projected this in the *European Journal of Sociology* in 1969 and completed it in *A General Theory of Secularization*, published in 1978.[14] The aim was to *ground* the theory and turn it from an inevitable trend into something that happened in *this* way, or alternatively, in *that* according to historical circumstances.

The prime historical circumstance was the difference between those countries, mainly Protestant, where Enlightenment and religion overlapped and even fused, and those countries, mainly Catholic, where Enlightenment and religion clashed. Another crucial historical circumstance was the presence of a religious monopoly or some degree of pluralism. Thus in England and Holland there was some degree of pluralism, and in the USA an even greater pluralism that led to the separation of Church and State. The conclusion that followed from these historical comparisons was that religion flourished most luxuriantly under modern conditions where church and state were separated and where there was religious pluralism and competition. It is true that the original expansion of religion in England with the arrival of religious variety and industrial society was followed in the twentieth century by a decline. This is probably due in the main to the retention of a link between State and Church and of a link between the social élite and the Church. The question is much disputed.

However, there were other major variations on the pattern of secularization. These occurred where the Church and nation fused in a common cause against alien government. The same pattern of cultural resistance aided and infused by religion was observable in micro-nationalisms – Brittany, the Basques and so on. This raised the question whether Eastern Europe, with its pattern of government by Soviet-style dictators ought also to have a rather distinctive pattern. After all, it contained so many countries where religion was the carrier of national culture. Poland offered the pre-eminent example, but the same was true of Romania, as well as Slovakia, Croatia, Serbia, western Ukraine, Greece and other countries. Also, the experience of some of those countries under communism had given religion a role as the only possible focus of an independent personal or social existence. On the other hand, there were complicated differences in secularization, for example, between highly secularized Estonia and militantly Catholic Poland, as well as between Romania and Bulgaria.[15] Nothing is simple. Maybe Bulgaria, as a Slavic nation, had imitated the Russian pattern, whereas Romania with its strong Latin traditions had emphasized the union of religion with the defence of its historic culture.

However, a question had to be asked about the impact of social differentiation. That theory implied a break-up of all kinds of monopoly, whether it was of a political ideology or a religion. In the field of religion one would expect a continuing identification between historic churches and national and ethnic identity, but one would also expect the onset of pluralism and the emergence of several denominations. Initially, that would be a shock but it would also help vitalize the religious field by competition. This, indeed, is now happening. The Ukraine, for example, is already a religiously pluralistic society. After all, that development was already massively present in Latin America.

This leads on to the other major variation in Latin America. Initially, Latin America seemed to recapitulate the intense conflict in European Catholic societies, particularly in countries which were virtually European, such as Uruguay. But it became clear that something rather different was happening. First, the secularized radical élites had not succeeded in destroying the spiritual premiss in the lives of ordinary people. But beyond that the Catholic Church had, to some extent, eased itself out of its old alliances and state connections. It had emerged as a popular church, opposed to the National Security State, attacking corruption and identifying itself with the poor. Even more important perhaps was the emergence of massive pluralism, parallel to the pluralism of the USA but generated in the main from *within* Latin American culture. I tried to cope with this extraordinary development in a

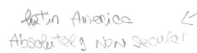

book called *Tongues of Fire* (1990). I also tried to relate this to a vast extension of Pentecostal and evangelical Christianity in the Third World, especially parts of Asia, for example Korea, and sub-Saharan Africa.[16] In this development, a Christianity based on the Holy Spirit set off a process of personal social reform, trying to restore the dignity of women, to support the integrity of the family and attack violence and corruption in the state.

To this comparative-historical analysis, where the broad trends to social differentiation had very different social consequences according to the cultural matrix in which they occurred, I added an analysis in terms of centre and periphery derived from the work of Edward Shils, who (incidentally) offered a sympathetic account of religion quite outside the secularization model in his work on *Tradition* (1981). Given that the great urban centres of Western Europe, such as Amsterdam, Paris, London etc., were core areas of secularization, they nevertheless, encountered various kinds of cultural resistance in the peripheries. In Britain, for example, the peripheries would be Wales, Scotland and Ireland, and in France, Alsace and Brittany. Of course, not all peripheries were 'behind'. Some, such as Alsace, the Basques and the Banat, were highly developed.[17]

From the mid-1960s to the mid-1980s the paradigm of secularization shifted under a critique mounted by various scholars, until what had previously been accepted without demur was now dismissed by many as a sociological 'myth'. This was an extraordinary reversal: just as in human history, the unexpected happens. Rodney Stark and William Bainbridge were particularly incisive in providing an account of the persistent renewal of religion in response to the need for compensation. A powerful resistance in favour of the old paradigm was, however, maintained by Bryan Wilson and Steve Bruce, and also by Karel Dobbelaere, who analysed both the decline of religious practice in Belgium as a core culture of the European Community and the freeing of social sectors from ecclesiastical control. This debate can best be viewed from an eirenic standpoint in the volume edited by Steve Bruce, *Religion and Modernisation*.[18]

During this whole period the grip of empiricism had been loosened by a new emphasis on meaning and narrative, on culture and symbol and on phenomenology. The range of matters which came within the purview of sociology, and could be treated as real and important, dramatically increased, and that increase included religion. These shifts are too complex for analysis here, except to say that the 1960s, which led to a decrease in religious participation, also encouraged this increase in the range of things which might be sympathetically studied.

However, we now need a final brief summary bringing the analytic history down to the present. There were three developments of the utmost importance. The first was the extension of the Western European pattern out from its core areas, deepening their secularity, and to some extent corroding the resistance of the peripheries. Church attendances fell, particularly after the cultural crisis of 1968. And the decline was most marked in France and Holland. So were the secularization theorists right after all?

Recently Peter Berger has raised the question: 'Is Europe exceptional?' That implies the further question as to whether it can be regarded as a model of what one day will happen universally from Atlanta to Timbuktu. If it is exceptional, we have to locate a specific factor, and the most likely candidate is the long-term after-effects of sometime monopolistic systems, and of strongly placed secularist élites, especially in education and the media. Maybe secularization was so vigorous and penetrating in Western Europe precisely because Christianity had been so long intertwined with the structures of power and because the Enlightenment needed so strong a thrust to undermine the status quo.

Alternatively, it might indeed be the case that cultural individualism was being continually extended to the point where it affected *all* the old markers of identity and authority. After all, what were the principal characteristics of the crisis of the late 1960s? They were the growth of new attitudes towards moral discipline and authority. So far as morality was concerned people grew less inclined to accept rules, and began to dissolve the sense of obligation into a utilitarian calculus of happiness. So far as authority was concerned, the figures of authority lost their capacity and will to impose and be imposing. *All* the main institutions were subjected to criticism and irony: politics, religion, the monarchy. It appeared that there were no examples of endeavour which might be held up for imitation and emulation. Each person sought a radical individual essence and self-fulfilment. That meant that all the ties of belonging loosened, including national identity and political identity. The great narratives of Western culture, including progress itself, ceased to motivate and command dedication. Individuals put their own packages together out of whatever cultural materials seemed to serve their own personal preference. Religion itself became a preference, and one which included all kinds of experimentation, with New Age cults or ancient pagan superstitions. The only consensus appeared to be concern for health and worry over the purity of foods and pollution of the environment. Whether all these shifts amounted to a new stage labelled 'post-modernity' hardly matters. They certainly travelled in the wake of 1968 and affected religion adversely. They combined with the remaining thrust of Enlightenment antagonism to bring about the unique degree of secularity currently observable in Western Europe.

This is not to say there were no kinds of religiosity able to make headway in such an atmosphere. The most notable survivor was evangelical Christianity, which took some elements of the expressive individualism of post-modernity but controlled them with a strong sense of moral obligation and loyalty to the community. Individual feelings were released but balanced and checked by moral disciplines and priorities.

That was one major shift: the expansion of individualism and the privatization of life and religion, partly expressed and partly controlled by evangelicalism. But there was another major shift: the churches themselves emerged as players on the social stage. Privatization ought to mean the disappearance of the churches from debate, but precisely the opposite happened. As churches gave up their links with the old structures of power, they emerged as social actors, taking up various causes and even being listened to. This reversal of privatization has been most persuasively ‣charted in José Casanova's, *Public Religions in the Modern World*.[19]

I conclude by summing up the effects of social differentiation and the paradoxical response where churches have acquired a public voice. In his important book, José Casanova argues that in the 1980s religion reversed one of the presuppositions of secularization theory by refusing to be privatized and marginalized. It emerged as a major actor in the public sphere and seemed able to articulate many of the concerns of civil society: pollution, abortion, problems of migration, racial prejudice, state repression and economic exploitation, depending on the context. In the USA, for example, the Roman Catholic Church initiated major debates on the economy and defence. In Casanova's view the Roman Catholic Church has accepted the liberal concept of the secular state, but rejects the privatization of religion. Other examples one might give from Britain are the debates on defence and the inner city, and the way in which the Labour Party leadership has increasingly jettisoned any element of Marxism and has revived roots in Christian Social Democracy.

The churches' most dramatic contributions were to the changes in Eastern Europe during 1989–90: the role of the Catholic Church in relation to Solidarity, of the Lutheran Church in Germany as a channel of popular discontent. The example of the Lutheran Church in Germany indicates that even a quite weak Church can provide a social space in which to raise the problems of civil society. In Romania there were the remarkable events sparked off in the Banat by the defiance of a Hungarian Reformed pastor. All in all, it seems that in various contexts religion acts as a repository of human values and transcendental reference which can be activated in the realm of civil society. One does not have to agree with all its manifestations to regard it as an important contribution and one running counter to the thesis of privatization. Indeed, more than one sociologist has argued along these lines. Peter Beyer, for example, in his *Religion and Globalization*,[20] has suggested that in a functionally differentiated society it is an advantage to be the guardian of broad non-specific values which nevertheless call forth total commitment. Believers need not mobilize to restrict and hinder *other* voices, but they can constitute a community of faith and of values which makes a central contribution both to the core values which made society possible and to the debate over public priorities.

Conclusion

What, then, in conclusion? First, as concerns the approach of the human sciences there has been a signal advance from the idea that we dispense authoritative packages of knowledge, either concerning brute empirical fact or the supposed dynamics of history, to the idea that we enter a conversation with others on the basis of certain criteria of logic, evidence, coherence and comparison. We have become fully conscious that we are putting forward tentative hypotheses which are ordered by controlling paradigms and assumptions. The material of our scientific scrutiny comprises worlds of meaning and symbol and these are part of a narrative of personal motives and social projects that takes unexpected turns.[21] These shifts have made it more possible to pursue the sociology of religion in a spirit of sympathetic understanding rather than see faith as an alienated delusion destined to disappear in the process of rationalization and the dialectics of history.

Notes

1   John Milbank, *Theology and Social Theory,* Oxford: Blackwell, 1990.

2   José Casanova, *Public Religions in the Modern World*, Chicago: University of Chicago Press, 1994.

3   Frank Lechner, 'The case against secularisation: a rebuttal', *Social Forces*, Vol. 69, 1991.

4   Harvey Cox, *Fire from Heaven*, Reading, MA: Addison-Wesley, 1994.

5   David Martin, 'The sociology of religion: a case of status deprivation?', *British Journal of Sociology*, Vol. XVII, No.4 (17 December, 1966), pp. 353–9.

6   Jon Butler, *Awash in a Sea of Faith*, London and Cambridge, MA: Harvard University Press, 1990.

7   First challenged by James Beckford in *The Trumpet of Prophecy*, Oxford: Blackwell, 1975.

8   See the sections on New Religions in Stewart Sutherland and Peter Clarke (eds), *The Study of Religion, Traditional Religion and New Religion*, London: Routledge, 1988.

9   Karl Popper, *The Poverty of Historicism*, London: Routledge, 1957.

10   David Martin, 'Towards eliminating the concept of secularisation', in Julius Gould (ed.), *Penguin Survey of the Social Sciences*, London: Penguin, 1965; reprinted in David Martin, *The Religious and the Secular*, London: Routledge, 1969.

11   Andrew Greeley, *Unsecular Man: the Persistence of Religion*, New York: Schocken, 1972.

12   Bryan Wilson, *Religion in Sociological Perspective*, Oxford: Oxford University Press, 1982.

13   Talcott Parsons, 'Christianity', in David Sills (ed.), *The International Encyclopedia of Social Sciences*, New York: Macmillan and Free Press, 1968.

14   David Martin, 'Notes towards a general theory of secularisation', *European Journal of Sociology*, December 1969, pp. 192–201; and David Martin, *A General Theory of Secularization*, Oxford: Blackwell, 1978.

15   David Martin, 'Religion in contemporary Europe', in John Fulton and Peter Gee (eds), *Religion in Contemporary Europe*, Lampeter: Edward Mellen Press, 1994, pp. 1–15.

16   David Martin, *Tongues of Fire*, Oxford: Blackwell, 1990.

17   David Martin, 'The Religious Politics of Two Rival Peripheries: Preliminary Excursus on Center and Periphery', in Liah Greenfield and Michel Martin (eds), *Center: Ideas and Institutions*, Chicago: University of Chicago Press, 1988, pp. 29–41.

18   Steve Bruce (ed.), *Religion and Modernisation*, Oxford: Clarendon Press, 1992; and Philip Hammond (ed.), *The Sacred in a Secular Age*, Berkeley: The University of California Press, 1982.

19   José Casanova, *Public Religions in the Modern World*.

20   Peter Beyer, *Religion and Globalization*, London: Sage, 1994.

21   David Martin, *The Breaking of the Image*, Oxford: Blackwell, 1980.

CHAPTER 2

Evangelical Expansion in Global Society

The expansion of evangelical Christianity, and more especially of its potent Pentecostal mutation, is closely related to the emergence of a global society. The essence of globalization is the increasing speed of movement as people, ideas, images and capital take advantage of modern means of communication. As we all know, what began with road, canal and railway is now communication by jet and internet. The advertisement pages of newspapers are just one indication that the major social catalyst of mass tourism can take us to remotest Amazonia or Borneo. However, the consequences for religion on our planet are less obvious. In the early part of the twentieth century the extension of Methodist chapels in the surrounding area of Mexico City followed the line of the British-built railways. More recently new roads out of Mérida in the Yucatán and out of La Paz in Bolivia mark out the route of evangelical dissemination. Like any other kind of message, evangelical messages travel to the jungles of Irian on the Papuan border and to the remotest valleys of Nepal.

Whatever the complicated mesh of factors contributing to this process, a major agent of change over the last half-millennium has been the ability of capital to create an international economy. Wealth could not be constrained within the borders of the bureaucratic empires of France and Spain; it went with the flow of the commercial empires of Holland, England and the USA. All three of these Protestant North Atlantic powers abandoned the holism of their Catholic rivals, not only as a principle of social organization but also as a mode of social and philosophical understanding. At the same time, though to different degrees, all three countries were incubators of the voluntary principle in religion. That principle detaches religion from the polity, from state power and from an anchorage in the territorial community. It also detached the work of the missionary from the work of soldier and trader. Of course, the detachment was bound to be partial, and in fact in the Anglo-American empires the Bible travelled in partial partnership with the sword. Nevertheless, the break was of world-historical significance. The British Empire did not become Anglican in the way Spain's Latin American Empire became assimilated to Latin Christendom. Indeed in some areas imperial administrators actively inhibited missionary activity.

A further consequence of the breakdown of holism and the establishment of the voluntary principle was the way religion was able partially to absorb the Enlightenment and avoid the outright clash which tore apart Latin cultures, above all France. The proximity of the established clergy to the secular intelligentsia also meant that the Enlightenment could filter selectively into religion, creating versions of Christianity such as Unitarianism, which acted as a buffer zone. Clerical conservatives did not struggle with secularist liberals for control of the state, as happened all over Latin Europe and Latin America. The closest approximation was the mid-nineteenth-century tension between Protestant-dominated states and Catholic minorities in Germany, Switzerland and Holland.

The period of modernization also saw a shift from hierarchy and ascribed status towards an increasing emphasis on merit and achievement and towards semi-autonomous class cultures. Within these cultures people were able to associate in terms of felt affinity rather than economic subordination. However, that had rather distinct consequences in the Protestant North of Europe, and in the societies of the North Atlantic. In such societies, and above all in the English-speaking world, the all-encompassing unity based on social and ecclesiastical hierarchy crumbled. It did so in three successive stages, beginning in the 1590s, accelerating from 1790 to 1850, and renewing the impulse again in the early 1900s. Very loosely these stages correspond to a movement towards a lay, popular and enthusiastic Christianity, culminating in Pentecostal awakenings with a particularly powerful and influential eruption in Los Angeles in 1906. These awakenings were themselves harbingers of global society and their spread corresponded to the movement of lay people around the globe, to South Africa, Norway, Sicily, Korea or the Southern Cone of Latin America. No sooner converted than *en route*.

The people travelling around the globe with evangelical and Pentecostal messages were energetic and intelligent, of little education, and authorized only by the Spirit. The missionaries who preceded them as earlier messengers of a global faith had been only modestly educated, but they were at least authorized and prepared. In Pentecostalism Christianity had generated an autonomous lay culture, once again composed, as in the New Testament, of 'ignorant and unlearned men', and empowered by the Spirit with all that implies for good and ill in the exercise of personal authority. This was not a diaspora of liberal resource persons.

They represented the furthest extension of the voluntary principle not merely by being free of the state but free to feed off the Bible raw, and create whatever organization that seemed to imply. Not being weighed down by sponsorship of a social or ecclesiastical hierarchy or the relation of faith to territorial identity, they could treat the world as their parish.[1] Frontiers meant little, whether they were the catchment areas established by missionary societies or the implicit catchment areas of long-established Christian civilization, such as Latin America.

Coming as they mostly did from the North Atlantic, they exploited the intimations of global society created by the spread of English in association with the British and American empires, and by extension Spanish, as a second metropolitan language. At the same time, they rapidly became indigenous or inspired indigenous associates, in part because of the remarkable resonance between their Spirit-filled religion and the spiritist layer of worldwide shamanism. So what began with minor hints of global religion, such as Moravians on the Atlantic coast of Nicaragua, Mennonites in Mexico, or Methodists in Sierra Leone, expanded until the world capital of Pentecostalism was not the City of Angels but São Paulo or Seoul.

Evangelicals are not, of course, the only beneficiaries of modern communications. The neo-Buddhist Soka Gakkai is now established in Hawaii, in the area of Los Angeles, as well as in São Paulo. Furthermore, the empire can strike back as the spiritual conquistadores of La Luz del Mundo carry their messages to the USA and the Brazilian Universal Church of the Kingdom of God makes converts in Portugal. Catholic and evangelical messengers from Brazil are now active in Mozambique and Zimbabwean Pentecostals in London.

Nor is this global mobility confined to transnational denominations, but is exemplified in para-church organizations, such as Caritas, Adveniat or the evangelical development agency 'World Vision'. One might add here that although transnational denominations are competing on an open market and are prone to multiple schisms, nevertheless they also foster a kind of ecumenism in spirit, and often come together for mass meetings. Here they realize that they count.

None of this means that the primordial relation of religion to local community and to territory is abolished, or that people no longer acquire their lifelong religion at birth. Moreover, since the rise of nationalism over the past half-millennium religion has been closely bound in with ethnic identity, and the Church has been subordinate to the State. That subordination was as true of Hispanic Christianity as of Anglican Christianity. For Louis XIV 'L'Eglise c'est moi', and eventually monarchical prerogatives passed to the nation, the people and the national culture. Today Islam makes a point of being a complete system coextensive with society, and with ambitions to become the global faith. In Latin America the ecclesiastical élites still address the nation and the Church educates the national élite. For that matter the base communities are predicated on the hegemonic idea. In each locality the ties of faith are the links of the fiesta and godparenthood. All that implies that conversion to another faith involves opting out of the national identity and its historic culture. In Thailand and Burma the prestige of state, élite and the majority culture of the core areas of the nation are linked to Buddhism. Nor does globalization lead unambiguously to a relativization of such ties. The effect of missions is often to stimulate the receiving culture to renew its own boundaries and also to emulate the attractions of the new faith from within its own resources. The sense that a local religion was normal and inevitable, which existed before global contact, mutates into militancy and explicit exclusion of alternatives, as can be observed all over the Middle East, in the Indian sub-continent, and the Balkans. What had been coexistence in Albania or Lebanon becomes religio-ethnic cleansing.

However, this militant reaction to the onset of pluralism and competition on the part of the majority culture has interesting implications for transnational faiths. Just as majorities accentuate their cultural self-definition, so also do minorities. Under pressure from the majority and conscious of the global options open to them they may adopt evangelical Christianity, with the result that the global becomes once again embodied in a particular territorial identity. Sectors of the Aymará in the Andes are a case in point. Hindus in Java, for example, coming under Muslim pressure, opted for Christianity. Some of the minority ethnic groups of the Russian Federation have reacted to Orthodox Christianity through self-conscious paganism, just as some Afro-Americans have opted for Islam. All over the world a new self-consciousness is engendered by global contact. Minority peoples affirm difference, equality and identity, in Thailand or Malaysia or Myanmar or wherever.

We have identified two obvious processes. One has to do with the emergence of voluntary religious associations, initially in the North Atlantic world and spreading in partial alignment with the English language and Anglo-American influence. The other has to do with the emergence of minority self-consciousness which evades the pressure exercised by local majorities, by linking itself to evangelicalism as an expression of transnational modernity. Self-conscious identities breed their mirror images bolstered by difference, and evangelicalism is able to express that difference. Given that the USA is both the remaining superpower and an attractive expression of cultural modernity, evangelicalism enjoys an aura of association. Obviously the adoption of evangelicalism (or Mormonism or Jehovah's Witnesses) by minorities will run along the lines of fissure within that particular society, one sector developing in contradistinction to another.

One further tendency present in global society and relevant to evangelical expansion is a heightened sense of individuality as the self is released from the constraints of extended kin and the continuities of local community. The idea of conversion by a personal transaction is part of that individualization, because of its inwardness and its dependence on choice. It is a drama in the person through an incubation of experience generated by the Church, and then stabilized and moulded by its collective disciplines. Plainly an established Church, built into the community and sacralizing its mores, is always suspicious of the emotional transactions which give second birth to individual selves, whereas a transnational denomination may embrace them. However, what remains highly problematic is the different course of individualization in the developing world compared with that in the developed world. In the developing world evangelicalism (and other sources of inward personal transaction) manages to inhibit the fragmentations which so evidently follow from individualization in the developed world. In the USA, however, religious voluntary associations may inhibit individual fragmentation to some extent, but the rate of divorce is the highest anywhere. The problem has to be flagged as needing more research.

Kinds of Faith Community

Before proceeding further one ought perhaps to indicate the core members of the evangelical family under consideration and also their extensions. Clearly the historical core is the Pietism of Northern Europe as active in the evangelical awakenings of Anglo-America and their revivalist variants. Then a further closely related awakening occurs in classical Pentecostalism through the mediation of

Methodist holiness movements. That in turn generates or runs in parallel with the gospel of health and wealth and various free-floating charismatic movements both outside and crossing the borders of the historic churches in a kind of ecumenism in the Spirit. In Latin America, for example, one encounters historic churches 'in renewal'. All kinds of combinations occur whereby Pentecostalism overlaps Afro-South American *cura divina* or global shamanism or religious contents semi-suppressed by colonial Christianity or varieties of Christian Zionism or Ethiopianism. Beyond that, and more or less distinct from evangelicalism, are semi-Judaic versions of Christianity such as Adventism, the New Israelites, the Mormons and the Witnesses. Though these constitute separate genealogies their trajectories of conversion intertwine with evangelical expansion while their American associations and the consequences of their ethos are somewhat similar. Indeed, the American associations are often more obvious with Mormons and Witnesses than with Pentecostals.

Contrast: Developed and Developing World

Two further preliminary questions have to be explored which have links with the earlier point about the differing effects of individualization in the developing and the developed world. First, why is it that in the developed world evangelicals are the dominant partner whereas in the rest of the world Pentecostals have increasingly become dominant, though not everywhere to the same extent? Second, why is it that within the developed world the degree of evangelical influence corresponds to a spectrum running from Northern Europe through England to its peripheries, and thence through such English-speaking democracies as Canada and Australia to its apogee in the USA? That second question is relatively easy to answer since it corresponds to the space allowed for the institutional reproduction of subculture through the erosion of established, hierarchical and centralized religious forms by disestablished, populist and federal ones. In Canada, for example, there remain shadow establishments in French and in Anglo-Scottish Canada which have inhibited an evangelical expansion on the American scale, as well as switching the pattern of secularization since the 1960s in a European rather than an American direction.[2] Within the British Isles each of the territorial peripheries has generated larger evangelical constituencies than England itself, and it is arguable that lines of connection run between these and the largest evangelical peripheries in the USA. In England it is not too difficult to see how the command posts of establishment in education and communications have switched from a vaguely religious ethos to a vaguely secularist one. Nevertheless, whether or not there is a cultural command economy, evangelicals constitute the liveliest sector across the North Atlantic spectrum.

Even if that analysis remains speculative, the question of Pentecostal dominance beyond the North Atlantic sphere is more puzzling, even if one takes into account the historical priority of evangelicalism in the North Atlantic area. After all, evangelicalism has been established for a long time in parts of the Anglo-Caribbean, and yet in contemporary Jamaica it has been eroded until Pentecostalism is arguably the established faith.[3] There are also those who believe that a parallel erosion of Pentecostalism itself by neo-Pentecostalism is occurring in Brazil, Argentina and parts of Asia and Africa. However, leaving that aside as disputable, it remains clear that in some countries, such as Zimbabwe, Pentecostalism runs at 10 per cent of the population, and even in Korea mounts a very strong challenge to an established evangelical tradition.

Perhaps the most promising line of explanation rests on the universal layer of spiritism outside the North Atlantic and continental European cultural sphere which resonates with the potent combination of black and white motifs in Pentecostalism. To that one might add a form of development outside the developed 'West' which leaps through the global expansion of capitalism from the pre-modern to the post-modern. Of course, there are Western-influenced élites in many parts of the developing world, for example Singapore, but the mass of the population has not passed through a modern developmental phase. That is as true of Latin America as elsewhere. The liberal élites absorbed a mixture of Anglo-American pragmatism and Latin European anti-clerical radicalism, especially the latter since they were after all Latins, but they did not follow up European success in spreading that metropolitan ideology downward to large sectors of the population. Those sectors still embraced an unstable mixture of Catholicism and pre-Columbian faiths. So far as Africa was concerned, the evangelical thrust, in partial cooperation with colonialism, achieved a very partial modernization, again largely confined to emerging élites. The Protestant penetration in Africa was as unstable as the Catholic penetration in Latin America. Thus the masses both in Latin America and Africa were vulnerable to Pentecostalism. Asia was a different matter, perhaps best understood in terms of the vulnerability of areas or groups marginal to the dominant traditions. In this context the whole of Korea was vulnerable in relation to the dominance of Japan; the Chinese minorities in different parts of Asia were also vulnerable, for example in Malaysia and Singapore, as well as the peripheral peoples of Thailand, Burma, the Philippines, India, Malaysia and Indonesia, and even Nepal. Much depends on how far a folk tradition has been partially absorbed by a developed high tradition in association with the state and national solidarity. Where that has occurred, as in Buddhist Thailand and Burma, conversion is not very likely. On the other hand, where there is a folk tradition unabsorbed by a high tradition and without reinforcement from national solidarity, for example Taoism in Singapore, then conversion can be quite rapid.

Western Europe

Western Europe represents the most secular group of cultures in the modern world, with the vines of faith twined round crumbling and centralized establishments and with exposure both to classical modernity and to an élite tradition of militant secularity capable of reproducing itself among the masses. Given the secular tilt in the Western European heartlands, its extension beyond the French epicentre under the auspices of the EU has led to rapid secularization in Belgium and Spain. A further belt of post-Protestant secularity extends from Birmingham and Amsterdam to Berlin and Tallinn. Few footholds are available to Pentecostalism and evangelicalism except for the interstitial culture of the gypsies and the margins in Portugal and southern Italy. In Portugal the Brazilian 'Universal Church' is now the second largest religious body; and in Italy south of Ancona Pentecostalism, as well as the Witnesses, has made significant inroads, perhaps 1–2 per cent of the population of the area. Within the UK, Pentecostal and holiness movements have had their successes among the Caribbean population, reinforcing their original culture and offering protective solidarity, especially for women. Within Scandinavia there is a Pentecostal constituency of quite long standing, taking over where the 'inner mission' left off. However, the Social Democratic ethos is not conducive to expansion, though a notably successful 'Faith Mission' operates in Uppsala.

Eastern Europe

Things are rather different in Eastern Europe, where Turkish overlordship followed by Russian communist domination has reinforced ethno-religion. In Poland ethno-religion has been combined with high practice, though not obedience to Catholic norms, whereas in Serbia it is more a matter of identification, but in either case to adopt another faith is to desert the national tradition. Similar situations are found in Croatia, Slovakia and Lithuania. However, in some cases religion was historically out of alignment with ethnic tradition and national solidarity, and so failed to reproduce itself under communist pressure, as for example in the Czech Republic, East Germany and Estonia. So, in Poland, evangelicalism does not extend beyond about 0.1 per cent and also makes few inroads into the areas of successful secularist indoctrination. That means that (gypsies apart) the main areas of vulnerability are at the junction of traditions, notably the multicultural marchlands of Transylvania and the western Ukraine. In Transylvania, for example, German Baptists made some impact among Hungarians in the late nineteenth century, and there has been a rapid expansion among both Romanians and Hungarians since the 1970s, accompanied by an even more rapid expansion of Pentecostalism and even some charismatic Calvinism. Perhaps the evangelical constituency in Romania as a whole is 1–2 per cent. The minority Protestant culture of Hungary and the uncertain Catholicism of Budapest also display a certain vulnerability to a Faith Mission, which appeals to some in the new middle classes, including new entrepreneurs.

Latin America

In Western and Eastern Europe evangelical incursions have been minor. In Latin America by contrast, they have been major, varying between 4 per cent and 30 per cent, with an average for the whole continent of about 10 per cent. The classical evangelicalism arrived in the nineteenth century, making a minor impact in the lower middle classes, and Pentecostalism arrived in the early twentieth, though the main expansion has been since the 1960s. The classic incursion of Pentecostalism has been among the poor, but not the poorest, so that in some suburbs of Santiago the active evangelical population is about the same size as the active Catholic population. Two varieties are most in evidence here: the major denominations of the Methodist Pentecostal Church (or the Assemblies of God), and small groupings with exotic names often around a husband and wife, and honeycombing whole areas.

The situation in Latin America is one where the Catholic Church has been institutionally weakened either by state control as in Brazil or state hostility as in Guatemala, but this hostility or indifference has not been transmitted to the masses outside Cuba and Uruguay. This has assisted the intertwining of folk motifs with Catholicism, and it was this unstable combination that began to collapse in the 1960s with the arrival of global communications and a global economy. Since that time competitive pluralism has become a norm, and has linked together the fluidity of the pre-modern situation with the post-modern. Pentecostalism and evangelical renewal have offered a new voice, a fresh space for the adoption of transforming disciplines which fast-forward the aspirations of millions as they move from countryside to mega-city. Also offered is a protective capsule for women and opportunity for the reformation of the family.

However, there are other manifestations, appealing to somewhat different constituencies and directed towards a variety of spiritual needs. In the case of the Universal Church of the Kingdom of God one has a very rapidly expanding movement promoting 'liberation', both of mind and body, and having a large black constituency.[4] It takes over cinemas or else erects large buildings which open on to the street, into which people wander at any time, and its services have a format strongly resembling a television show. Its pastors are spiritual and material hustlers and offer miracles and 'liberation' as the first inducement to faith. The 'Universal Church' is highly controversial, not least because it is heavily involved in radio and television to the point of being in rivalry with the vast conglomerate 'Globo'. Another source of controversy is its dramatic warfare against the gods of the spiritists: a case of fighting fire with fire, but also of the incorporation of Afro-Brazilian cultural resources.

In other cases one has free-floating charismatic groups, some of them breaking away from the restrictive moral practices of the classical Pentecostals, and often appealing to quite youthful middle-class and professional groups who have been involved in the drug culture. One of the largest of these is 'Renascer' or 'Born Again in Christ', which nightly fills an ex-cinema with the equivalent of spiritual 'shows' and claims extensive success in the reclamation of young people from personal deterioration. This kind of charismatic Christianity, deploying all the appurtenances of modern technology in the style of the contemporary media, operates in contexts remote from the conventional church, whether it is a huge arena or else in the basements of middle-class homes. In such homes one may have a couple of dozen charismatic-minded families meeting together to sing their songs, to meditate on scripture under each other's guidance, and to share their everyday concerns.

These charismatic manifestations among the better off, dealing as much with stress, psychic and professional problems as bodily ills, are all over the Southern Cone, not only Brazil, but in Uruguay and – quite dramatically – in Argentina.[5] What we see here is the adaptability of mutations of the evangelical impulse to different social niches in a rapidly developing world. The global reach is indicated by the international connections and criss-crossing trails: from Nigeria to Atlanta to Manila to Bucharest to Seoul and to Buenos Aires. Nowhere in the world is there a clearer manifestation of the rapid take-off of middle-class charismatic and neo-Pentecostal Christianity and its ability to affect other denominations than in Argentina.

Though evangelical churches arrived in Argentina well over a century ago, and Pentecostalism as early as 1906, the initial impact was slight, apart from modest gains in lower-middle-class sectors by Baptists and Brethren. As everywhere else, this began to change in the 1950s, as Pentecostalism showed its capacity to 'key in' to popular culture. But not until the 1980s, with the crisis in political legitimacy, was there any dramatic movement. Pentecostals, who had comprised 2 per cent in the 1970s, comprised 5 per cent by the mid-1990s, and the members of the Assemblies of God numbered nearly half a million. In the 1980s there were ten extra churches per year in Buenos Aires, and seventeen per year in the next decade. Evangelical churches in the capital exceeded Catholic churches in number, and if the participation of Catholics was some 5 per cent of nominal adherents, then at least a quarter of the active Christian constituency was evangelical.

The character of this expansion contrasts with the classical Pentecostalism hitherto dominant elsewhere in South America. Centred in Bible Institutes and with many mega-churches the emphasis is on spiritual warfare, exorcism, divine healing, charismatic gifts and empowerment in everyday life and professional activity. Modern technology and contemporary popular culture are everywhere in evidence: Christian rock, musical events, videos, periodicals, new hymns and a general atmosphere of perpetual motion and theatricality. Though there is some evangelical concern over accusations of financial and sexual misconduct, and thinly veiled eroticism, as well as about irrationality and a cheapening of the experience of salvation, nevertheless the same charismatic styles have penetrated the historic churches (as I discovered on attending an Anglican church in a comfortable suburb of Santiago) and there is a considerable amount of mutual cooperation. The smudging of boundaries and leakage of members aroused considerable concern at the 1998 Lambeth Conference.

Also in Latin America one may find creative reformations of suppressed or despised cultural contents, as well as supportive spiritual depots for groups on the move. La Luz del Mundo is an extraordinary case, since it also revives Judaic elements appropriate to peoplehood. In that respect it resembles the Mormons and the New Israelites of Peru. Members of La Luz del Mundo often travel backward and forward between Mexico and the USA, finding in their churches supply dumps and resting places for renewal among people of their own kind. At their main base in Guadalajara they effectively run part of the city, creating a complex of schools and hospitals in an area which replicates the geography of Palestine around their vast temple. This holds many thousands. The group is run by an almost messianic figure, descended from the founder, and assembles emblems of its power, in such Ethiopian manifestations as the lions in its zoo and the flags of the nations missionized by the new 'conquistadores' of the spirit. The light of the world not only flashes out to the rest of the city by laser beam, but descends annually through an aperture on to the head of the leader. This pre-Columbian reminiscence resonates with the way the temple architecture reflects Aztec models. Indeed, the group seems to have a considerable appeal for non-Hispanic peoples rather as the Universal Church has for blacks.

In Latin America there are many instances of reactions by ethnic minority groups to the increasing pressure of a Hispanic nationalism in terms of a new evangelical identity, sometimes reinforced by a symbolic association with the prestige of the USA. This means, other things being equal, that countries with large ethnic minorities could undergo extensive evangelical inundation. The Maya, the Mapuche, the Quechua and numerous others are, so to speak, at risk, and all offer evidence of the effects. A paradigmatic example occurs among the Aymará of Bolivia, as recently studied by Andrew Canessa.[6] The evidence of the tentacles of modernity is the relationship between good roads from the capital, La Paz, and the incidence of evangelical conversion, as well as the trail from the countryside to La Paz, marked by a migration of souls as well as bodies. The most interesting aspect of Canessa's study is the way the converted Aymará succeeded in reversing the stereotype of their ethnic character. In the Hispanic stereotype they were identified as lazy, undisciplined, backward, given to intoxicants, whereas in their own revised estimate they were exemplary models of modernity in dress and habits. It also appears that once in La Paz, the Aymaré found in their churches a space for their language, as well as opportunity for family discipline and mutual support among the women.

Asia

Similar manifestations can be found all over the Pacific rim from Seoul to Manila and Hong Kong. Drawing on the work of Michael Hill and his associates in Singapore, we can say that Christianity in a mixed Malay, Chinese and Indian society is mainly Chinese with a significant Indian minority, though in its charismatic form it shows a characteristic capacity to break down ethnic barriers.[7] Singapore after independence concentrated initially on economic advance but later turned to the moral dimension of nation building. In education that stimulated some interest in Confucian ethics, believed to be conducive to order and an economic ethos. Malays as Muslims were suspected of disloyalty and Christians suspected of social activism.

Then in the late 1980s there emerged a dramatic shift among young, high-status, English-educated Chinese to charismatic Christianity, with some further interest in Buddhism or else secular irreligiosity. Young Chinese gravitate from the amorphous Taoism of the majority, so that about one in four of those in tertiary or university education are Christians. Protestant Christianity is viewed as modern and international and offers an orderly rational world, in which there is opportunity for personal expression, musical catharsis and close contact in a democratic atmosphere. Everything changes and yet the charismatic churches establish a continuity with the ancient spiritist tradition and its proffered mundane benefits. In the mainly Muslim context of (western) Malaysia, Michael Northcott argues that charismatic and Pentecostal churches offer the most significant challenge to the former mission churches.[8] Indifferent to liberal theology and the comparative analysis of religions, they combine Asian and Western cultural forms with a celebration of the spirit in everyday life and oral tradition in the mode of the New Testament. Charismatic Christianity is at home in the middle class of a modernizing society which is for the first time in reach of material goods, and yet it has a strong sense of the supernatural realized in renewed personal identities and moral reformation. In one direction a sense of crisis not unconnected with ethnic tensions is symbolized in millennial anticipation, while in another direction continuity with the past is assured by drawing on indigenous shamanism (while suspecting it elsewhere as demonic). This capacity to draw on shamanistic spiritism parallels the Korean experience. As in Singapore, there is some relation between social mobility and speaking English, and this fits in well with a gospel of health and prosperity. It also makes the movement open to an evident North American influence.

As has been noticed in urban South Africa and Latin America, the energies of charismatic Christianity cross ethnic lines, though some churches are distinctively Indian, such as the Pentecostal Church of Malaysia, while others have a majority Chinese membership. The Full Gospel Assemblies have a strong lay leadership, with a cell structure and frequent meetings in homes. Its members dress in smart modern styles and deploy elements of television culture and popular music. However, the largest impact of charismatic Christianity is in fact within the Roman Catholic Church through parish-based renewal groups. The historic Protestant Churches find themselves in more of a dilemma, uneasy about the theological trends but anxious not to be overtaken in numbers and influence.

Of course, it would be easy to multiply instances of this evangelical mutation in other parts of the aspiring sectors of the rapidly developing world, above all Korea, which is by now a society very extensively Christianized, but the objective is not to provide an exhaustive survey.

The next kind of expansion to be considered involves an appeal to groups at the ethnic margin of societies hitherto without distinct religious self-consciousness. It is, of course, modern global communication which helps arouse this consciousness. Interesting instances of this are in Nepal, Burma and Thailand, and these run parallel to modest expansions in the major cities of the kind just discussed. In Nepal, Burma and Thailand there is a strong religious identity espoused by the state and by a majority population infused by ethnic nationalism which inhibits conversion as involving loss of status and community membership. For the tribes at the geographical margin therefore, the attraction of conversion includes an assertion of identity, equality and difference.

Looking a little more closely at Nepal,[9] there are now a couple of hundred churches in Katmandu, run by Nepalese, and a perceived relation between Christianity, modernity and global scope. Yet the areas of greatest success occur among the Tibeto-Burmese in semi-autonomous valleys north-west of the capital. Lines of conversion run along the differences of lineage and may involve whole villages under local leadership, though where habitation is dispersed adhesion is individual or familial. Pastors tend to be hostile to the lamas and there is dispute about the legitimacy of traditional sacred powers. The groups operating in this area are the Nepalese Christian Fellowship, Gospel for Asia, and Baptists of the New Life Mission Church, who have health and educational facilities.

In Thailand conversion has for a long time been largely confined to the hill tribes and border groups.[10] Traditionally Christians in Bangkok have tended to be Chinese or Vietnamese Catholics. And yet with the establishment of a Pentecostal Church in the capital in 1981, a Thai leadership emerged for the first time and within five years the congregation had grown to five thousand, utilizing the cell structure pioneered in Korea. As in Korea (and elsewhere) elements of local culture have re-emerged in Christian guise in spite of official repudiation, notably the Thai hierarchy of merit. Pentecostals are now 5 per cent of all Protestant Christians: to what extent the characteristic Pentecostal dynamic has been reinforced by the crisis in political legitimacy is difficult to say. So we see here the coexistence of different patterns, at the centre of the society and at the margin.

If we turn to India as discussed by Susan Bayley, we find that a large proportion of (south) Indian Christians now belong to activist churches which emphasize the gifts of the Spirit, including prayer, healing, exorcism and prophecy.[11] They have charismatic leaders and promote corporate and individual discipline. At their heart are assemblies of lay people under lay leadership with little regard for established hierarchies. Women find the assemblies particularly attractive and enjoy the special opportunities they offer them. The professional and commercial middle classes are also attracted, both by the new churches and by parallel changes in the older Christian bodies, including Catholicism. The problem for the older bodies is their seeming relativistic and anodyne liberalism challenged by a very Indian reclamation of living presences and concrete powers, even though some idioms and organizational models come from elsewhere. As in Malaysia communal tension plays a role and the new movements mark out a terrain and defend a genuine if fragile Christian stake in the social order against a Hindu vocabulary of exclusion.

The imponderable element here is China, with about one-sixth of the world's population. It is clear that evangelical Christianity has some appeal for the Chinese diaspora, and that there is a fairly easy transition to it from Chinese folk religiosity. Leaving aside the bodies granted official acceptance in the more repressive period of communist rule up to the 1980s, an extensive underground Christianity developed in the form of conservative evangelical house churches. The main areas of expansion were in the south-eastern coastal provinces and overlapped areas of long-established Christian activity. There was also rapid growth in the 1980s in some inland rural provinces. This rapid growth has been termed 'Christianity fever' and appears to involve some subsumption of folk practices. The main traditions are conservative in an Anglo-American mode, in keeping with the original missionary presence. As for the house church movement, it was lay in inspiration, with many female workers, and at least a sector of it offered healing, spiritual gifts and exorcism. The influence of this sector is very evident in recent revivals along the Korean border. The view of 'the world' without was apolitical, though the government displayed some unease after the Tiananmen Square crisis of June 1989. A middle-range estimate suggests that evangelical Christians are about 3 per cent of the total Chinese population.[12]

Africa

In Africa we find variations on these themes. Nigeria is the largest nation in Africa, divided roughly half and half between Christians and Muslims, but ruled until 1998 by a largely Muslim military establishment. Ruth Marshall regards Pentecostalism as creating an autonomous space over against corruption, monopolies of power, state violence and economic exploitation. Within this space is room for new practices assisting survival. She identifies two main niches which are clearly parallel to those observable in Latin America. One consists of denominational mission churches like the Assemblies of God and their indigenous counterparts. Within these enclaves narratives of conversion contrast helplessness with empowerment and invite believers into a world of equality and self-worth negating the hierarchies of wealth or age. Strong boundaries against 'the world' and communal solidarity provide rudimentary social security and mutual assistance; and counselling is available on financial and marital matters.

The other main niche is a transdenominational charismatic movement, appealing to the young and mobile, with a strong base in the universities. Prosperity is treated as a mark of divine favour and yet, at the same time, mere appetite is controlled by the rules and by norms of economic reliability and trust. There is a network of patrons and clients in the community, as well as private hospitals, kindergartens and maternity wards. In such groups young women achieve by merit what might otherwise only be obtained by sexual favours, and they also have a chance to meet reliable, considerate spouses. Infidelity is treated according to a common standard for men and women, and marital disputes are adjudicated by the pastor. It also seems that choice of partner crosses ethnic lines more frequently than elsewhere. There is in such groups a global consciousness and a capacity to exercise pressure, sometimes in the context of communal tensions. As so often, the danger lies in concentrations of power and displays of success cancelling the atmosphere of participation, as well as alliances between leaderships and politicians with doubtful records.[13]

The other African examples chosen are the Peki Ewe in Ghana studied by Birgit Meyer, and the Pentecostals in Zimbabwe studied by David Maxwell. Birgit Meyer's work illustrates the relation between the oldest evangelistic layer of German Pietism and contemporary Pentecostalism, as well as the way older cultural resources are reassembled inside a new format.[14] The original missionaries were – as so often – rather poorly educated men sent from their native Germany by upper-class sponsors. Though their Pietism was not that far from African religion, they diabolized it. Conversion was initially infrequent but by 1915 about one-third of the Peki were Christians of various kinds. Motivations were related to a desire to achieve goods through faith as well as health and educational advancement, though this was not what the missionaries actually preached. Many evaded missionary control and slid back into the old ways, until the 1960s a serious expansion of Pentecostalism began, with healings and vibrant services setting aside written orders and taken by untrained pastors. This was part of an undertone of protest against a religion based on rules which neglected the spirit.

One major difference was that whereas the mission church envisaged a permanent shift to Christianity, Pentecostals maintained continuous warfare with the real powers of the old order. By projecting this contest in stories and media presentation they not only revived the healing practices and exorcisms of primitive Christianity, but allowed believers to revisit the past safely armed by Christian prophylaxis. The older practice was incorporated in the new, including bodily movements and gestures. Once again this parallels the operation of Pentecostals in other contexts: the transplantation of the old within the new, without the kind of radical disenchantment which expels the whole world of the spirit. It is clear that Meyer rejects the idea of Pentecostalism as an alien import. Rather, she views it as providing a space for believers to negotiate modernity, especially as women strive for multiple adjustments within the family. Spiritual resource and communal support enable people to stand independently on their own two feet. It also allows hope for material betterment in a capitalist economy to burgeon without selling out to worldly seductions. As to the association of religion with betterment and 'goods', it clearly resonated with traditional African motifs and needed little stimulus from elsewhere.

A somewhat different negotiation of modernity is analysed by David Maxwell in the context of Zimbabwe, and his analyses show just how evangelical and Pentecostal Christianity enter into different niches in the social economy, in this case, for example, the search for independence on the part of young men and women.[15] As in Ghana, in Zimbabwe the Pentecostal churches make up a sizeable proportion of the population, maybe 10 per cent. In other words the proportions reached in (non-Islamic) Africa match those in Latin America. Moreover, so far as timing goes, processes in the two continents mirror each other, with Africa about a decade behind. The two processes also have in common the multiplicity of sources, a two-way traffic with North America, and a history which begins earlier than is generally realized, as well as a great deal of creative indigenous invention bringing about a post-modern 'bricolage'. Maxwell also identifies an initial and rapid indigenization, followed by expansive transnational ambitions.

Though a fractious family, the Pentecostals coming to southern Africa saw themselves as harbingers of a worldwide movement, both transnational and moving across the boundaries of denomination. The initial awakenings were in 1908, about the same time as in Chile and Brazil. They reached Southern Rhodesia within the next decade and by the 1920s Pentecostal movements had penetrated deep into the burgeoning urban centres, countering the personal social disintegrations of violence, promiscuity, alcoholism, gambling and crime. They created, as they do now in Latin America, a counter-society based on work, self-discipline, the integrity of the family and the mutuality of the Church.

An interesting characteristic of Pentecostals was their indifference to the packaging of discrete territories by missionaries and to the 'civilizing mission' the missionaries shared with the colonial administration. This offensiveness was compounded by their indifference to the invented tradition of the rulers who were a pillar of that administration. Maxwell comments that in southern as in central Africa, Pentecostals (like Witnesses) delegitimated chiefs by demonizing ancestor religion, provided young labour migrants anxious to retain their wages with legitimate reasons to break free from traditional commensality, and gave young women legitimate reasons to challenge patriarchal authority.[16] In short, these were poorly educated men and women behaving and speaking in modes outside colonial control and so defined as on the margin of subversion. Here one observes the extent of the sociocultural changes that have been initated by the interaction of the local and global, black and white, in the first half of the century, and continuing at an accelerated pace in the second half.

David Maxwell stresses the versatility of Pentecostalism, sometimes poised against the partial cooption of historic denominations by the state in the form of NGOs (non-governmental organizations), sometimes filling in gaps in the legitimation of doubtful regimes criticized by these denominations. It secures personal and collective buoyancy along the networks of labour migrating to the towns by undermining the moral ties and local gerontocracy and creating a new time and space within the church. It deploys modern media and music, creates self-reliance and 'testifies' an economic culture into existence as it 'sings away' poverty. Maxwell points also to the emergence of a tension as an older and more populist Pentecostalism acknowledging suffering and the danger of riches, and valuing humility, meets a smoother Christianity susceptible to personality cults, display, greed and opportunistic political alliances. At the leadership level it succumbs to bureaucracy and 'authoritarianism'.

An interesting example of the replication of Latin American (especially Brazilian) developments is provided in the tiny country of Cape Verde. Early incursions of Adventists and Nazarenes are now stalled as the field is disputed by 'American' groups (Mormons, Witnesses) classical Pentecostals and the Brazilian 'Universal Church'. The practices of the Universal Church chime well with Afro-Portuguese spirituality.[17]

The object of the foregoing is not to provide an overall assessment of the global expansion of evangelical and especially Pentecostal Christianity, but to outline some of the kinds of religious bodies and the kinds of social niches they occupy. I could have taken very different examples comparing, for example, the successful alignment of evangelical and Pentecostal Christianity with Korean cultural identity with the resistance encountered in Japan. But whatever examples I took, they would illustrate an 'awakening' to messages circulating around a world increasingly unified by modern communication, an engagement with capitalist transformations, the creation of voluntary transnational bodies operating across boundaries, and a mingling of motifs from the original North Atlantic heartlands of evangelical Christianity with indigenous motifs and initiatives. In Latin America and Africa, as elsewhere, this mode of religiosity helps prise people out of old frameworks and reassembles old elements within a new format.

In summary form, evangelical Christianity, and by extension Pentecostalism, is a manifestation of modernity in so far as it is a voluntary association occupying a space within the cultural sphere and established across national borders. Within that space people who are on the move, geographically and socially, revise their moral selves and their domestic roles so as to reintegrate the family, and they also are accorded opportunity to participate and lead. The disciplines of the group generate solidarity and assist every kind of betterment, including material betterment, and that incidental link becomes explicit in the gospel of health and prosperity. This kind of Christianity manifests an ecumenism of the spirit while being organizationally fissiparous, and cuts loose from Western professional theology as it enables lay people to feed at will on the biblical text. It is indifferent to the ideological maps of the Western secular intelligentsia and allows an eruption from below which unites the despised peripheries of the North Atlantic to the poor and the ethnically marginal groups of the South Atlantic and elsewhere. In doing so it shows some capacity to cross ethnic boundaries.

As a self-generated vehicle of the aspiring poor it picks up contents within the universal shamanistic layer of spiritism overlaid by colonialism and integrates them into the frame of Holy Spirit Christianity. It is also well adapted to newly emerging middle classes, protecting them from psychic disintegrations and erecting zones of moral and professional integrity. In all its forms it has a special appeal to women, offering them opportunity for expression as well as havens of security and respect. It stands for the domestic table over against the street and the bar and the machismo culture of violence and indulgence. It is, arguably – with Catholicism, Islam and Western secularity – one of the half-dozen or so basic responses to the modern world. That, at least, is Peter Berger's view. Its global character is indicated by the symbol of the gift of a universal voice beyond the Babel of competing languages.

To put it another way, a particular kind of global transition is occurring, engendered in the West by a fusion of black and white popular and populist religion which rejects the sponsorship and agenda of the post-Protestant and post-Catholic intelligentsias of sometime Christendom, along with their theological allies. It coincides with emergent self-consciousness in many different niches; it fuses ancient and post-modern; it operates across national and ethnic boundaries; and it keys in to local resources while framing them in a Christian format, mainly through indigenous carriers. It resonates least in areas of apathy left by collapsing establishments, especially where élite carriers of anti-clerical tradition have used centralized state power to erase the spiritual premise, as in France, (East) Germany or Uruguay. It also makes little headway where there is a unity of state, society and local community which drastically inhibits individual choice, for example, in Buddhist, Hindu and above all Islamic contexts. Where it operates politically its stance depends on context, but in terms of a space for autonomous social learning and revision of social roles, and for institution building between state and individual, it is implicitly democratic as well as economically entrepreneurial.[18]

Notes

1   David Martin, *The World Their Parish. Pentecostalism as Cultural Revolution and Global Option*, Oxford: Blackwell, 2001; Bernice Martin, 'New Mutations of the Protestant Ethic Among Latin American Pentecostals', *Religion*, Vol. 25 (1995), pp. 101–17.

2   David Martin, 'Canada in Comparative Perspective', in David Lyon and Marguerite Van Die (eds), *Rethinking Church, State and Modernity: Canada Between Europe and America*, Toronto: University of Toronto Press, 2000, pp. 23–33 and 'From pre- to post-modernity in Latin America', in Paul Heelas (ed.), *Religion, Modernity and Post-Modernity*, Oxford: Blackwell, 1998, pp. 102–46.

3   Diane Austin-Broos, *Jamaican Genesis. Religion and the Politics of Moral Order*, Chicago: Chicago University Press, 1997.

4   David Lehmann, *Struggle for the Spirit*, Cambridge: Polity Press, 1996.

5   Daniel Míguez, *Spiritual Bonfire in Argentina*, Amsterdam: CEDLA, 1998.

6   Andrew Canessa, 'The Politics of the Pacha: the conflict of values in a Bolivian Aymará community', University of London Ph.D. thesis, 1993.

7   Michael Hill and Liam Kwen Fee, *The Politics of Nation Building and Citizenship in Singapore*, London: 1995 and Tong Chee Kiong, 'The Rationalization of Religion in Singapore', in Tong Chee Kiong et al., *Imagining Singapore*, Singapore: Times Academic Press, pp. 276–98.

8   Michael Northcott, 'A Survey of the Rise of Charismatic Christianity in Malaysia', *Asian Journal of Theology*, Vol. 4, No. 1 (1990), pp. 266–78.

9   Blandine Ripert, 'Christianisme et Pouvoirs Locaux dans une vallée Tamang du Népal Central', *Archives de Sciences Sociales des Religions,* Vol. 99 (July–Sept. 1997), pp. 69–86.

10   Charles Keyes, 'Why the Thai are not Christians: Buddhist and Christian Conversion in Thailand', in Robert Hefner (ed.), *Conversion to Christianity*, Berkeley: University of California Press, 1993, pp. 259–84; Philip Hughes, 'The Assimilation of Christianity in Thai Culture', *Religion*, Vol. 14, (1984), pp. 313–36, and Edwin Zehner, 'Merit, Man and Ministry', *Social Compass*, Vol. 38, No. 2 (1996), pp. 155–75.

11   Susan Bayley, 'Christians and Competing Fundamentalisms in South Indian Society', in Martin Marty and J. Scott Appleby (eds), *Accounting for Fundamentalisms*, Chicago: Chicago University Press, 1994.

12   I have drawn inter alia on a paper circulated in 1991 by Alan Hunter and Chan Kim-Kwong.

13   Ruth Marshall-Fratani, 'Power in the Name of Jesus', *Review of African Political Economy*, No. 52 (Nov. 1991), pp. 21–37.

14   Birgit Meyer, *Translating the Devil*, Edinburgh: Edinburgh University Press, 2000.

15   David Maxwell, 'The Church and the Democratisation of Africa: The Case of Zimbabwe', in Paul Gifford (ed.), *The Christian Churches and Africa's Democratization*, Leiden: E.J. Brill, 1990.

16   David Maxwell, 'Witches, Prophets and Avenging Spirits', *The Journal of Religion in Africa*, Vol. 25, No. 3 (1995), pp. 309–39 and *Christians and Chiefs in Zimbabwe*, Edinburgh: Edinburgh University Press, 1999.

17   Anne Stensfold, 'A Wave of Conversion: Protestantism in Cape Verde', *Religion,* Vol. 29, No. 4 (1999), pp. 337–46.

18   See Paul Freston, *Evangelicals and Politics in Asia, Africa and Latin America*, Cambridge: Cambridge University Press, 2000.

PART II
EUROPE

CHAPTER 3

Rival Patterns of Secularization and their 'Triumphal Ways'

In this chapter I want to show above all else how religion is deeply implicated in all kinds of things that are not included in a purist definition of religion.[1] The patterns of connection that interest sociologists of religion are patterns of culture profoundly stained in this way or that by religious colouring. Politics and religion may be joined or separated in different ways in varying national contexts, but in any given case politics and religion are isomorphic. You read from the one to the other.

I am going to offer some sketches which rework a framework I devised in 1969 in the early stages of *A General Theory of Secularization*.[2] In that work I focused on Europe and the North Atlantic, and I argued that the master narratives we use to organize the data of seculariazation, such as privatization, individualization, rationalization and social differentiation, mislead us because they suggest a single track to a common terminus. We are beguiled by all those dangerous nouns of process ending in 'ization'. Yet it is obvious that Anglo-Protestant trends follow different paths to Latin Catholic ones. Different kinds of theology and church organization are bound up in different histories and cultures. The liberal enlightened narrative that generated secularization grows out of its political pursuit as well as out of its *observation*, and even that narrative patently diverges into rival versions. The conflict of Church and State in the Third French Republic ending in separation in 1905 was one version, but in the later history of Eastern Europe post-1945 a much more militant historicized Enlightenment tried to deliver secularization by Caesarean section and political fiat. Apart from the Czech Republic, Estonia, Latvia and the former GDR, that failed, and it produced a pattern of religious revival very different from what occurred in Western Europe over the same period. I went to Bulgaria in 1967 to observe what was hailed as the paradigm of successful secularization, only to find later, in 2000, that Bulgarian levels of religion had revived and risen to meet declining levels in Britain.[3] As I have extended my studies to Latin America and Africa it has become increasingly clear that Western Europe might be the odd one out.

Over the last decade I have reworked my 'General Theory' in various ways, beginning with visualizations designed to help my American students understand the differences between North Atlantic Anglo-Protestant patterns in their American and English variants, and Catholic patterns, beginning with France.[4] I started with visualizing the organization of sacred space in Washington as the centre of American society, then moved to London and Paris, before shifting to Central and Eastern Europe – Vienna, Budapest, Bucharest, St Petersburg and so on. In the end it all became very complicated because I also looked at the varying organizations of sacred space in the regional peripheries, contrasting Madrid and Barcelona, Paris and Strasbourg, London and Edinburgh, and running into the numerous awkward problems of the kind that are the creative grit of a theory. Just where, for example, is the periphery of Italy? Is it the whole peninsula south of Ancona? Could it be that Italy is the wrong kind of shape for peripheries as compared to 'square' countries like Spain and France? Happily the problems of those peripheries and their distinctive religious cultures are not necessary to the sketches and visualizations I offer now.

Some Initial Visualizations

Permit me to simplify. Washington is a sacred field, surrounded by Greek and Roman temples, with an Egyptian (or Masonic) obelisk in the centre. The national cathedrals lie at a discreet distance symbolizing separation of Church and State. But inside the Lincoln Memorial is an American résumée of the biblical narrative. So this is New Rome and New Israel combined. In Washington we have the classical *novus ordo seclorum*, the new order of the world, and the biblical exodus. It unites the advent and the eschaton.

In Paris you have a classical temple, the Panthéon, which was originally the church of St Geneviève, patroness of Paris, and is now the mausoleum of the Republic, militant and triumphant. To quote Auguste Comte, this is Catholicism without God. The Arc de Triomphe, higher and bigger than any Roman arch, proclaims that Paris is yet another New Rome. This New Rome is in conflict with *Roman* Catholicism, represented in the old centre of the Île de La Cité by Notre Dame, and on Montmartre by the Sacré Coeur, built expressly to rebuke the faithless city below. Looking at this ensemble of rival locations of the sacred you see how an older France, once the powerhouse of Christendom in the early days of the University of Paris, became the powerhouse of global secularity. Moreover, the ties of memory and recollection that still bound the old France to the new have been partly broken. Amnesia has replaced partial recollection. The Parisian basin remains punctuated by bastions of Christian civilization like Chartres, Soissons, Beauvais and Senlis, but these are temples whose meaning is half-forgotten, stranded in a secular wasteland.

London is different again: it lacks the straight lines of Paris and Washington and rejects what Pascal called the spirit of geometry. St Paul's dominates the City like another Capitol, but one reflecting an enlightened religion not an enlightened secular polity. The Houses of Parliament are classical in shape, but Christian and Gothic in execution and ornamental style. Westminster Abbey, nestling nearby to symbolize the historic closeness of Church and State, has a medieval body and an enlightened frontage. London has no 'grands boulevards' like Paris (or Vienna), and the triumphal ways projected from St Paul's to the Palace and from Regent's Park to the Mall never materialized. Grandeur of that sort was frustrated. People who do not need constitutions do not need triumphal ways driven through the city in the spirit of geometry. As Peter Akroyd and Nikolaus Pevsner have suggested, the spirit of the English sacred as embodied in space, time and architecture is horizontal, eclectic, additive, hybrid. Façades stay in place, even as the substance of the spirit has moved. It is not necessary to renovate all the sacred scenery.

I need to pause here to draw out just where these spatial visualizations and implied reworkings of my general theory are going. I accept that there are certain master trends, or *grands récits*, like individualization, and like social differentiation – meaning by that the freeing of sectors of social life such as education and welfare from ecclesiastical oversight. But my visual models show how they mutate and how they are inflected and deflected by what Max Weber called 'the switchmen' of history. The USA and France are fraternal versions of the Enlightenment, symbolized by the gift of the Statue of Liberty by France to America in 1876, and by the fact that Washington was designed by a Frenchman. But they are also rival universalisms, whereas Britain and the USA are not in that kind of rivalry. The English Revolution of 1642-60 was completed by the American Revolution of 1776, just as the British Empire was succeeded by the American empire: 'La république impériale' as Raymond Aron called it. No wonder Britain sided with the USA over Iraq (if for very complex, unarticulated reasons), or that the francophile intelligentsia in Britain violently disagreed.

Some Extended Visualizations

I want now to extend my argument and my visualizations from the old democracies of the West to the old enlightened autocracies of Central and Eastern Europe. That means going first of all to the Austro-Hungarian Empire, and to Vienna and Budapest. These are the two cities that in the 1680s repelled the Turkish thrust into the European heartland. That is something you will see dramatically illustrated at Leopoldsberg, outside Vienna, where the crucial battle was fought. Enlightened autocracy in Europe tells a story of the subordination of Church to State at least as complete as the subordination achieved by Henry VIII in England. In Vienna the Stephansdom Quarter adjoins the Hofburg Quarter, and the medieval architecture of St Stephen's cathedral is a supporting buttress of the Classical and Baroque architecture of the imperial Habsburgs.

Sacred space in Budapest tells a similar tale. In Budapest a clear axis runs from the imperial palace on the hill of Buda to the nineteenth-century cathedral in the centre of Pest. If you want to visualize the collusions of political and ecclesiastical power, you go up river from Budapest to Eztergom, the Hungarian Rheims, where you will find a cathedral modelled on St Peter's, Rome. This vast edifice proclaims another New Rome, this time appealing to a Catholic triumphalism. Of course, in Central Europe you also need to point to monuments of Romantic nationalism or of rising democratic aspirations, such as St Paul's Church, Frankfurt, where the German Parliament assembled for the historic gathering of 1848, or the magnificent Parliament building in Budapest raised by the Danube to echo and rival the Westminster Parliament by the Thames.

You can extend these sacred emplacements of enlightened empire to St Petersburg or to Berlin and Potsdam. All these empires collapsed between 1917 and 1919, and left a deposit capable of mutating into secular tyrannies: the Nazi atavism that proposed new triumphal ways in Berlin, and the communist enlightenment that planned new triumphal ways for St Petersburg.

The new communist enlightenment in Russia only released its colonies in 1989–91, after subjecting them to enforced secularization, and the 'secular religion' of communism. I use the paradoxical 'secular religion' term because just as national politics reproduces the morphology of a nation's religion, so communism reproduces the morphology of Christianity. In theory and in practice it consigns an earlier religion to the past with no right to leak into the future, it divides the world into polar rivalries of good and evil, and cherishes an eschatological anticipation of a new world to come after a time of troubles. The logic of communist triumphalism meant that the triumphalism of the Catholic Church had to be put down, just as established Christianity found it difficult to countenance the obduracy of God's original Chosen People. Communist triumphalism also ran headlong into the enlightened Protestant triumphalism of the USA. It proclaimed (in Nikita Khrushchev's words) 'We will bury you first.'

I mentioned earlier the special pattern of forcible secularization and religious revival to be found in Eastern Europe. You might call this ethno-religious resistance because it was rooted in the way Romantic versions of national identity were prefigured by religious identity. Not all the relations between religion and nationhood were positive, of course. Castle Hill, Prague may still speak of a union of political power with the Catholic Church, but because Catholicism was reimposed on the Czech people by the Austrian Habsburgs, the national myth ran counter to Catholicism. The myth looked back to Jan Hus, but following defeat in the early seventeenth century Czech Protestantism had been reduced to a shadow. Of course, there are also complicated and more recent factors to do with the tension between the Czech and German languages: the point remains that the Catholic Church was vulnerable to the secularization imposed from 1948 on. Today the Czech Republic and the former East Germany are secular heartlands rivalling Paris.[5]

Romania lies at the other end of the spectrum of possibilities: it manifests ethno-religion *par excellence*. It has remained religiously vital, sustained by the sense of being a Latin island in a Slav sea, and by a national communism opposed to Russian domination. The union of faith and peoplehood, forged against the Turks, survived the forcible indoctrination of the clergy and the brutal megalomania of President Ceauşescu. Many of the churches of Bucharest were destroyed with much of the rest of the city when Ceauşescu created a triumphal way ending in a palace which rivals Versailles in size. Romania is still ruled by cadres which have survived from the communist regime, in spite of the revolution of December 1989. Yet there is a palpable religious revival, mainly Orthodox and centred in the monasteries in the East, but including evangelicals and Pentecostals in the west of the country. Figures for belief in God are among the highest in Europe.

Contrasts: Vilnius, Helsinki, Amsterdam

Where shall I look for my final examples? I take one from Western Europe: Amsterdam. This is the cultural capital of a country with a dramatic profile of secularization since the 1960s which some see as a portent of future developments. The other two examples are Vilnius in Lithuania, and Helsinki in Finland, because they both illustrate the mobilization of ethno-religious identity against tsarist and then communist tyranny. They also both enable me to expand my reflections, Helsinki being the capital of an advanced Protestant and Social Democratic country, while Vilnius is the capital of a relatively poor country with roots in rural Catholic devotion.

Taking Vilnius first, it is the furthest node of Catholic Baroque civilization going north-east.[6] In a way it is an extension of Polish Catholicism in spite of a love–hate relationship between little Lithuania and its larger neighbour. Vilnius lies at a border with the Protestant Baltic, White Russian Orthodoxy and Polish Catholicism, and until recently it was a multicultural city. However, like Poland, the appalling events of World War II, above all the extermination of the Jews, but also a major exodus of the Poles, have made it much more homogeneous, ethnically and, therefore, religiously. It also has links, like Poland, with a large diaspora in the USA, and like Poland it has seen the USA as its protecting power against Russia. The second language is now English, and now that it has entered the EU it may well look with other such countries to Britain for leadership.

Because of Russian violence and attempts to expropriate symbols of Lithuanian identity, especially Catholic ones, the old Romantic nationalism has become much more explicitly religious. The same is true of Romania: the symbols of national revolution in 1989 were much more religious than those of the national revolution of 1848. The great symbol of Lithuania is the three crosses on the hill above the city. The Russians blew them up; so, with independence they were raised again, larger and higher. The churches of Lithuania are now regularly full of people, though levels of belief and practice are not as high as in Poland.

But what kind of Catholicism are we talking about in Lithuania, especially in Vilnius? After all, there are different layers and kinds of Catholicism in Europe, all the way from the folk Catholicism of the Mediterranean littoral to the socially critical and intellectual Catholicism of the Netherlands.

Built into the remaining old walls of Vilnius, above what are known as the Gates of Dawn, is a shrine to Our Lady of Vilnius, who is a source of healing and protectress of the country. Crowds of pilgrims converge daily on this shrine displaying every sign of devotion to the holy icon of the Virgin. The young priests who celebrate Mass there seem to be trying to control this intense folk devotion, and you also wonder about its meaning for some of the young people (especially the young males), whose body language and dress contrasts so sharply with the comportment of the older men and women.

The large congregations for Mass are not marked by this kind of intensity or even by much sense of participation. You sense a strong attachment to Catholic identity but, as elsewhere, a lack of strong affection for the reforms of Vatican 2 or of respect for the norms of familial behaviour promulgated by the Church as an institution. After all, even in Poland, where the Catholic Church, led by a Polish pope, contributed so much to the demise of communism, the post-1990 Church was unable to assert any control over sexual mores, or to influence the secular law. Attachment, respect and identity do not imply obedience to what the Church decrees.

Opposite the old city across the river are the communist housing blocks of the old regime and the new skyscrapers of a recently arrived finance capitalism, while around the peripheries are new industries which will draw on cheap labour with EU membership, and in time feed a consumerist ethos. Catholicism and Orthodoxy alike look askance at this aspect of Americanization and global capitalism, but what threat it signifies for the future of religion is uncertain. After all, in Western Europe it may signify relatively empty churches, but in the USA it signifies some of the highest levels of practice and belief in the developed world.

Helsinki, as the capital of Finland, exemplifies an astonishingly homogeneous Scandinavian culture, Social Democratic politically, and religiously Lutheran. Identification, as manifested in the rates of confirmation, is high. Moreover, the Lutheran Pietist inheritance leaves a deposit of inward personal faith considerably more marked in Finland and Norway, the colonized countries, than in Denmark and Sweden, the colonizers. Religion in Finland has also been reinforced by the wars with Russia and by being at a border with Russian Orthodoxy.

At the centre of Helsinki is the Senate Square, flanked by cathedral and university, and by the administration. It is a miniature version of the absolutist enlightened style of St Petersburg, and was created as such by the Russians, who ruled Finland for a century up to 1918. Yet there are later and very different concentrations of symbolic power elsewhere in the city, for example the Romantic national vernacular of the station, of the National Museum and National Gallery, or the institutional emplacements of Social Democracy, or Stockmann's vast *galleria* for the religion of shopping, as well as the early modernist innovations of Alvar Aalto, for example, the Finlandia Hall. Perhaps the most characteristic architectural expression of Helsinki lies in the handsome suburbs built in Jugendstil, a style that has been characterized as distinctively secular, Gaudí excepted. Most interesting religiously is the semi-underground Temppeliaukio church, visited daily by thousands of tourists and pilgrims. As usual, the difference between tourist and pilgrim is not all that clear, but the visitors nearly all light candles, and many pray.

The remarkable reservoirs of religious and national feeling – again the difference between them is not all that clear – are dramatically revealed in the special 'city' weekend in Helsinki. At the heart of this weekend is the St Thomas Mass in the cathedral for those who wish to stand uncertainly in the vestibule of faith. At the climax of the weekend the central square overflows with tens of thousands of people, as searchlights circle the cathedral dome, *Finlandia* is played, and the cathedral fills over and over again with communicants. Perhaps another manifestation of religious emotion, in Finland as in Estonia, is to be found in massed choral singing. Choirs are expressions of social capital, and they also have historic links with churches. It is certainly worth noticing that some of the best contemporary religious music has emerged from just those Scandinavian countries which we rightly regard as among the most secular anywhere. Arvo Pärt is an Estonian who, like others known as the 'holy minimalists', writes in a sacred and hieratic idiom that clearly resonates with contemporary spirituality.

Contemporary spirituality in Finland and other advanced countries is both pre-modern and post-modern, as the popularity of minimalists like Górecki, Adams and Tavener suggests. On the one hand there is the extensive revival of early music, mostly religious, and the remarkable attraction of religious texts for recent and contemporary composers, in conspicuously secular countries like Holland, Britain and in Scandinavia. The dual potential of the pre- and post-modern is evident in the appeal of pilgrimage and Orthodox spirituality on the one hand, and of charismatic, Pentecostal and 'Faith' movements on the other.

Orthodoxy and Pentecostalism may appear to be opposites, but they both focus on worship, in contrast to the more rationalistic churches. They appeal to the spirit, the one as *dunamis*, that is, dynamically, the other as *stasis*, that is, meditatively, and in the context of liturgy. This appeal, which can be picked up even in Finland, for example in the crowds that flock to major Orthodox festivals in Åbo, has its counterpart in a theological concern, rejecting the fragmentation of the Enlightenment approach to religion in favour of the integrated approach of Orthodoxy, based in worship. Moreover, you need to ask serious questions about why the modernizing trends in liturgy, based on clarity and explanation, have a relatively modest appeal to so-called modern people. Orthodoxy pursues none of the causes central to the liberal theological agenda such as social activism and internationalism. Yet even in countries like Russia and Bulgaria, where Orthodoxy was severely repressed and was at quite a low ebb some decades ago, it has recovered. It reaches the parts of the soul the others don't reach and it reaches back into the past and the national patrimony. In St Petersburg, built expressly as the Russian city of the Western Enlightenment, the churches are now restored and in constant use by devoutly preoccupied people of all ages.

The parallels in the West are to be found in the popularity of the most ancient forms of religion, pilgrimages and festivals, for example, in Spain, and in the lighting of candles in joy or in mourning. What does not appeal is sitting in a pew for a religious lecture. The verbalism and moralism of Protestantism have been its downfall, as the state of Calvinist churches from Switzerland to Holland and Scotland indicates. Their genuine virtues are now discounted in favour of the kinds of faith that are more tangible, and more immediately promising.

Pentecostalism is pre-eminently tangible, and full of promises, but one needs to make a distinction between the classical Pentecostalism that appeals in parts of southern Italy, like Sicily, or to gypsies in Eastern Europe, or to migrants from the Caribbean and Africa, and the charismatic movements active in the middle classes of Britain, and even France. So-called 'Faith' movements often make an appeal to mobile people in the most secular environments, for example, in Budapest and Uppsala, and there is a highly successful Lutheran ministry of this type in Helsinki, run by a pastor with 'golden hands'.

In what I have just suggested I am pointing to aspects of modern spirituality that reach back into the recesses of the religious impulse, for healing, or therapy, for ecstasy or prosperity, or the need for prayer and the response to mystery. These aspects are observable in the most secular contexts, for example, in Scandinavia. There is a sense in which we live in an Age of the Spirit, rather as Joachim of Fiore expected many centuries ago.

What, then, of the Age of the Spirit in Amsterdam? Amsterdam is the cultural capital of Holland, and one of the capitals of secularity along a fault line moving from Birmingham to Hamburg and Berlin. It was one of the first cities to embrace a tolerant pluralism, and it also exemplifies a major sequence in the secular process (to be observed equally in Boston, Edinburgh and Cambridge, England) which is the erosion of Calvinism into a Unitarian Enlightenment.

Up to the 1960s, which were everywhere a watershed, Dutch practice was very high, securely banked up in segregated religious cultures, Catholic, Reformed, Re-Reformed and so on. When the protective dykes collapsed, the religious pressure dropped sharply. Today the explicitly non-affiliated are in the way of being a majority, even though explicit religious practice remains higher than in England. The decline has been as dramatic as in Québec, and the two would repay sustained comparison.

In Amsterdam the spatial clues lie in the absence of a clear focal point. The federal and dispersed nature of Dutch society and politics is manifest in a dispersion of the sacred. But there is another point worth considering. It is that there *was* once a Catholic centre to Amsterdam before it was forcibly converted to Protestantism, and that centre is now the university. The university can be seen as a mutation of the Universal Church, so the sacred can be relocated in the University of Amsterdam. Alternatively it can be found in the Rijksmuseum or the Concertgebouw Hall. Likewise in Boston the sacred can be relocated in Symphony Hall and the Art Museum. These are some of the centres of contemporary contemplation, ecstasy and spiritual renewal. But in Boston this happens *alongside* the churches, whereas in Holland it happens instead of them.

In recapitulation, my argument runs something like this: there are some broad trends, such as detachment from ecclesiastical loyalties and habits, coupled with some disillusion with institutions as such, and a search for manifestations of the spirit. This search can find satisfaction in highly personal therapeutic engagements and small intimate cells or in the most ancient forms of the religious impulse, the festival, the pilgrimage, or the prayer in the numinous or sacred location. These rival trends are inflected or deflected by the varieties of historical experience.

Implications For Research

I conclude by drawing out some of the implications for future research and exploration. One implication is very clear: you cannot separate the nature of the religious culture from that of the political culture or that of the intellectual culture. National character and religious character are woven closely together, and there is no proper sociology of religion that is not also a sociology of morals and mores. Research needs to pursue trails across conventional boundaries.

So much of the relevant material is soft: it can be sifted but not quantified. We are looking at daisy chains of meaning. The repetition of the same act, such as rites of baptism or confirmation, are not replications of the same meaning, and you have to trace how meanings change over time. Semantics matter.

Religious practice is sustained by networks over space and time, and you have to ascertain how governing attitudes to religion in those networks are either hostile or supportive. In these networks shifting vocabularies are significant and you have to probe just what is meant, for example, by the increasing use of the word 'spirituality' instead of religion or faith. Shifting attitudes to *all* kinds of institutional commitment, whether religious, political or communal, are also significant. It may be that people are less willing to sink long-term psychic capital in institutions of any sort where the return is not immediately obvious.

In England I think the study by Linda Woodhead, Paul Heelas and others of networks of belonging in the small town of Kendal offers an exemplar of careful research which takes proper account of changes in a locality over time.[7] It shows spiritual networks almost as influential as churches. Moreover, religion is so much a matter of family dynamics, habits and personal autobiography that you really need to uncover life stories and spiritual biographies, especially in the fluid period of adolescence. What are the peer-group pressures adolescents encounter on the use of time and the expression of taste?

These kinds of study are at the micro-level, but there are wider-ranging enquiries that might look into the focus of seriousness in the arts and music, and what kinds of messages these communicate. There are also seeming spiritual wastelands, for example, East Germany, where it seems there is hardly a breath stirring. This, after all, was a region where the government was overthrown in 1989 by processions emerging from churches with much of the appearance of religious revival, and yet it all petered out into nothingness. Has this anything to do with lack of vitality in the whole culture: hopelessness, depression, meaninglessness? In East Germany you have an example of de-Christianization carried out over more than half a century since 1933, with no special resources of resistance such as existed in Russia. The 'Youth Ceremony' successfully displaced Confirmation and remains popular. East Germany is close to a *tabula rasa*, so that the guides in Erfurt Cathedral have to explain meanings to people with no access to them at all. Yet for Bach the cathedral had standing room only.[8]

I would add two kinds of enquiry which seem to me worth pursuing. The first relates to the place of religion in mutually supportive activities, by which I mean the way it is interfused or *not* with other ways of spending time. I have never forgotten a paper by the late Basil Bernstein in which he described how ritual placement around the Jewish family table reinforced the solidarity of faith and its continuity over generations. There are Christian and certainly Muslim analogues of this, though in modern Christianity there is a significant absence of supportive familial rituals. Is Protestantism too inward, too dependent on explicit, sincere commitment, compared with the performance of the rite?

The other enquiry relates to ownership in the Church. An Anglican priest who is a friend of mine commented that in his Bristol parish people owned the parish church to the point of being upset when unfamiliar things happened. In that respect it was the remaining nationalized industry, but as with nationalized industries in general, people had explicitly to be encouraged to take up their rights and invited to enter the building. Immediately you want to compare that with the situation in the USA where the building is not only 'owned' but entered easily with no real anxiety about class or style or speech – or gender – as well as standing at the centre of an extensive network of different activities. In England, if there is such a network it is a musical one. Social capital as church membership overlaps social capital in choirs and choral societies. Moreover, I would add that the Church in England has a large penumbra of occasional attachment rooted in this equivocal ownership, which appears absent in Holland. As already indicated, there is in Holland a higher level of practice and a higher level of explicit non-attachment. It is these variations that are most worth pursuing, particularly if those who see the Dutch situation as a portent of the future are right.

Notes

1   This chapter was originally a lecture given under the aegis of the Templeton Foundation in a Cistercian Abbey close to Paris on 1 May 2004. I am most grateful to the Foundation for the honour, hospitality and opportunity offered on that occasion.

2   David Martin, *A General Theory of Secularization*, Oxford: Blackwell, 1978. Chapter 1 reproduces the original 1969 article outlining the theory.

3   Andrew Greeley, *Religion in Europe at the End of the Second Millennium*, New Brunswick: Transaction, 2003.

4   See David Martin, *Christian Language and its Mutations*, Aldershot: Ashgate, 2002, Part IV.

5   Thomas DaCosta Kaufman, *Court, Cloister and City*, London: Weidenfeld and Nicolson, 1995; and Peter Demetz, *Prague in Black and Gold*, London: Penguin, 1997.

6   Tomas Venclova, *Vilnius*, Vilnius: R. Paknio Leidykla, 2001.

7   See Paul Heelas and Benjamin Seel, 'An Ageing New Age?', in Linda Woodhead, Grace Davie and Paul Heelas (eds), *Predicting Religion: Christian Secular and Alternative Futures*, Aldershot: Ashgate, 2003, pp. 229–47.

8   Thomas Schmidt and Monika Wohlrab-Sahr, 'Still the Most Areligious Part of the World', *International Journal of Practical Theology*, Vol. 7 (2003), pp. 86–100.

CHAPTER 4

Comparative Secularization
North and South

Introduction

I have been asked to restate my understanding of secularization based on my enquiries over nearly forty years, since I raised the issue in 1965. Minimally that means I have to provide a brief account of my *General Theory of Secularization* (1978) and its subsequent extension in two books about Latin America, and some marginal extensions into Africa.[1] After that I need to devise a fresh approach. That will be based first of all on a tour through the peripheries of Europe around the compass, north-west, north-east, south-west and south-east. This will illustrate some of the analytic principles I believe important. A linking section on Turkey discusses a semi-Westernized Islamic country mainly to raise the question of how far secularization applies outside a Christian context. I come then to the main section of the essay, which turns on comparisons between two versions of the Protestant North, North America and Northern Europe, and two versions of the Catholic South, Latin America and Latin Europe. From time to time I try to indicate my most recent approach, which is to translate the process of secularization, notably the key component of social differentiation but also centre–periphery dynamics, in three dimensions. This I do by reference to the changing dispositions of sacred and secular space in cities and their architecture, including architectural style.

A General Theory in Summary

Like most important concepts, such as God and religion, secularization is semantically rich, contradictory and paradoxical, as well as saturated in resonances, many of them to do with the immanent direction of history. A theory of secularization therefore has to delimit its meaning and reduce the resonances. In my own *General Theory* I dealt mainly with Christianity as institution, belief and practice, in its positive and negative relationships with modernity. Rather than rely on the broad abstract processes believed to bear on secularization, such as rationalization or privatization, I concentrated on the theory of social differentiation in relation to a number of key historical filters. These historical filters were crucial since they served to direct, deflect or inflect secularization in this way and that. The most important and decisive filters were in fact Protestant Northern Europe, Protestant North America, Latin Europe and (as later developed) Latin America, and

I was especially exercised by the effect of varying degrees of religious monopoly and competitive pluralism.

Glossing the argument a little, pluralism was initiated in North-west Europe, in particular in Holland, extended in Britain and realized in North America. So it is possible to have an analytic key based on Anglo-American pluralism which regards Britain as an interim experiment half-way between the full-scale entrepreneurial religion of the USA and the religious state monopolies or duopolies of the continent, such as the monopolies of Scandinavia and the duopoly of Germany.

I also used the concept of centre and periphery both to contrast metropolitan secularity with provincial religiosity (for example the contrast between Paris and Strasbourg or Oslo and Bergen) and to suggest wider relationships such as that between the Roman centre in the northern Mediterranean and peripheries north-west and north-east in Ireland and Poland–Lithuania. These two examples were the most obvious cases of peripheries where religion doubled for an absent state in nations under alien rule, but there were further cases in Croatia and Slovakia, and related cases in distinctive regions like Catholic southern Germany, southern Holland and the Swiss Catholic cantons, or Protestant Wales and Protestant eastern Hungary.

The many empirical generalizations about the relation of religion to class, status, urbanization, changes in local community, and industrialization had to be run through the historical filters to see in what ways they might be deflected and inflected, given that simple correlations are not enough. For example, two countries may share a common characteristic such as pluralism, but if the postulated consequences of pluralism do not appear in one case, that is not quite the end of the matter because specific combinations and ensembles affect all the other elements in the combination.

Further Elements

The first of these elements can be stated baldly. It is the close relation between religious morphology and political morphology, such as common patterns of centralization and monopoly. Hence the importance of linking the sociology of religion to political sociology, and thinking in terms of religio-political complexes. The second element is the disjunction between the secularization stories arising from intelligentsias and the history of ideas, and the stories derived from studies of popular beliefs and practices. One wants to know whether the notion of the avant-garde is just a conceit, more particularly a French intellectual conceit, and whether there are key strata promoting secularization, such as teachers or scientists or engineers.

The third element has already been mentioned and it involves an attempt to relate the secularization stories told in the arts, initially in music, but then in the architecture of sacred and secular urban space, to more standard secularization stories. The temporal trajectories are conspicuously not unilinear in the arts, but one can contrast the minimal sacred–secular differentiation of the Peter–Paul fortress in St Petersburg with the clear difference between Signoria and Duomo in Florence and (say) the wide dispersal of the sacred in Boston, a 'heavenly city' in both the Christian and enlightened sense. One can also contrast the different kinds of historical filter by looking at the subordinate role of churches in the classical profile of Schinkel's Berlin, the embattled rival bastions of Notre Dame and the Sacré Coeur and the Place de la Bastille and the Panthéon in Paris, and the partial pluralism of the triangular arrangements, Catholic, Anglican and Free Church, in Westminster, London. The three dispositions of sacred space all differ from Washington with its two national cathedrals separated from the sacred field of the Capitol, with its Athenian classical temples, and an Egyptian obelisk. In Washington, Enlightenment and Christianity are distinct but positively related, as they are in England, Scotland, Holland and Germany. That positive relation is of major importance.

Meanings are lodged in iconography or architectural style: the distinctive oriental styles of many synagogues, for example in Budapest, drawing attention to the distinctive character of minority ghettos, the Byzantine character of the Catholic cathedral in Victoria St, Westminster indicating separation and distance, the iconography of the Sagrada Familia in Barcelona coding a 'fortress Catholicism', and the geopolitical statements embodied in (say) the German church erected in Strasbourg post-1870 and the Alexander Nevsky Cathedral in Sofia built about the same time. If I have spent disproportionate time on this three-dimensional unfolding of sacred–secular dynamics it is to emphasize the major political and geopolitical dimensions, as well as recapitulating some of the historical filters.

Peripheries: a Grand Tour of the Compass

My chosen peripheries are Ireland in the context of the British Isles, Finland in the context of Scandinavia, Catalonia in the context of Spain, and Greece in the context of the Balkans. Each case illustrates something of the range of analytic principles without attempting more than a hint of what a full analysis might involve. In the (Catholic) Irish case there is the role of nationalism in relation to alien governance and proximity to a rival Protestant nationalism, as well as geopolitical position. The same elements are present in Finland, that is, a close proximity to a dominating atheist or Orthodox Russian nationalism. Catalonia introduces an ambiguity based on bourgeois links to Paris as the secularist global capital, as well as a regional nationalism based on language and religion. Greece also presents ambiguous elements based on its dual role as heir to Byzantium at a major border with Islam, and as progenitor of Western rationality and democracy. Its religious nationalism has been reinforced by the history of Ottoman domination, and by the way in which it has both received a diaspora and created one, especially in the USA. In Ireland, Catalonia, Greece and even in Finland it is worth commenting on the increasing contemporary role of pilgrimage and communal festival in fostering religious vitality.

So, then, in all these instances we observe how religion is reinforced by the heightened self-consciousness of a threatened or dominated nation, and in three of them there is the further reinforcement of proximity to a major religio-political border. That reinforcement in turn relates to geopolitical position, so that historically Ireland has been an embattled periphery of England seeking alliances with Catholic France and Spain (and now pursuing close ties with the EU) while Greece retains irredentist ambitions connected with being a broken-off fragment of imperial Byzantium, and allies itself to Orthodox Serbia and Russia, for example in the war over Kosovo. Greece has felt doubly threatened by the historic intrusion of the Western powers, like France and Venice, and by Turkey, though in the nineteenth century Greece enjoyed the 'love affair' pursued by Britain, France and Germany. Catalonia also has a special view of itself based on an expansive past and the constant threat of assimilation or conquest, as the monuments of Barcelona amply testify, such as the Christopher Columbus statue and the Philip IV arch. Finnish self-consciousness is high not only on account of Russian domination so clearly demonstrated in Helsinki's Alexanderplatz, echoing St Petersburg, but also on account of Swedish domination. Like Greece it has felt endangered from all sides, and so in recent times has sought a mediating role. Finland is of special interest as it belongs to a northern Lutheran periphery of five countries, where Sweden and Denmark as the ex-imperial powers are more secular than Norway, Finland and (maybe) Iceland as the ex-colonies. All the Scandinavian countries illustrate how uniform is the modern mirror-image of an established religious monopoly in the more recent political monopoly of Social Democracy: the city hall in Stockholm poised against the Gamla Strana, or 'Old Town'.

These examples of subordinated peoples at borders raise further questions. One is how far language cooperates with religion or alternatively can take over from it as a carrier of national consciousness. Another is the degree to which the national consciousness of the dominating nations at the apogee of their imperial power is also aligned with religiosity, if in a way different from what one observes in dominated nations. The imperial past of Sweden and Denmark is distant, and so perhaps irrelevant, but that aspect is clearly observable in nineteenth-century Britain and twentieth-century America. Russia is interesting, since the collapse of the Soviet Union in 1989–90 saw the re-emergence of the Orthodox Church as a historic symbol, for example the rebuilding of the Christ the Saviour Cathedral razed by Stalin, and the recent rise in observance of the Lenten fast among young people.

That kind of symbolic identification, not necessarily connected with frequent church attendance, is a potent presence in the rise of pilgrimages and festivals connected with sacred sites: in Serbia Kosovo, in Greece Tinos, in Catalonia Montserrat, in Aragon El Pilar, in Galicia Santiago, in Finland the Tempeliaukio Church and the St Thomas Mass at the City Festival in Helsinki, in Ireland Knock, and also at Medjugorje, Lourdes and Fatima. All these pilgrimage sites stimulated religious identities at the margins and peripheries, and have their political and geopolitical resonances, as Milošević's use of Kosovo illustrates.

The final issue relates to the role of diaspora, especially in relation to Greece, Ireland – and also Turkey. Greece and Turkey have both been engaged in more than a century of exchange of populations and dispersion, and it seems that whereas language may sometimes take over from religion in the home country, in the diaspora religion takes over from language, apart that is from liturgical language. Jews and Armenians are obvious further examples of nations in diaspora. The reinforcement of religion in diaspora is illustrated by the increased religiosity of people forced by ethnic cleansing to 'return' to their home country, as for example the Greeks in western Turkey forced after two-and-a-half millennia to leave for mainland Greece.

Turkey: a Hermeneutic Problem

The example of Greece at a turbulent border marked by constant ethnic cleansing, especially since nationalism gave deeper meaning to the territorial borders of ethnicity, allows one to move to Turkey. Since 1922 Turkey has progressively become increasingly religiously homogeneous, and indeed the whole Middle East follows suit, as secular nationalism and religious nationalism alike expel or pressurize the enclaves of difference. Similar moves are even proposed in India, where the religion is supposed to be tolerant and peaceful, and the horrors of partition are merely one example of what the idea of a nation entails.

Turkey is also the most Westernized of Islamic nations, even more so than Egypt, and aspires to join the European Union. That Westernization can itself be read as secularization in so far as it has meant a separation of religious and secular powers and attempts by élites to damp down the fires of religion similar to those adopted by secular élites in the Catholic West. Thus far there are important cross-cultural similarities, yet when I attempted to include Turkey in my *General Theory* I gave up in the face of an ensemble or set of relations so different to any of the many variants of sometime Christendom. Turkey was the best case for the application of secularization theory and it proved resistant, and that in turn makes one query the idea that contemporary Islamic revival is just a phase prior to real secularization, rather like fortress Catholicism from 1850 to 1960. Just as the wave of militant religio-nationalism emerging in fifteenth-century Spain anticipated today's wave of militant religious nationalism in Islamia, so the phase of interim resistance to modernity represented by 'fortress Catholicism' is being replicated in Islamia, except that in Christendom there was a sequence, whereas in Islamia it is following rather than initiating a path, which means that the two processes are to some extent superimposed.

One obvious similarity between Christendom and Islamia is the way in which religion and nationalism become fused, under the pressure of colonial or quasi-colonial status, even when political decolonization has been in principle achieved. The cultural colonization remains, in part because it is fused with modernization and what is still the preponderant influence of the dominant nation. There is also a continuing reflex of humiliation and reassertion which appeals to God or Allah as the great restorer of lost political and cultural fortunes. Those who propose compromises with modernity and with liberalism are no longer able to make their voices heard, and so compromising élites have to resort to illiberal force, as in Turkey and Egypt.

However, the colonial mentality and the 'integral' impulses that accompany it, in Poland and in Ireland (especially after the new republican constitution in 1937), and indeed in parts of South-eastern Europe such as Serbia, Romania, Greece and Bulgaria, is a majority phenomenon in Islamia rather than a minority one as in Christendom. Moreover, there are consequences which have few precedents in Christian societies. The kind of *integrista* reaction such as existed in much of Latin America, militantly opposed to Protestant and capitalist modernity, is present in both civilizations. But in Islamia the current of religio-political protest against the compromising and sometimes semi-secular élites can simultaneously combine reformist impulses based on the democratic will with the *integrista* impulse to impose Sharia law on everybody, to reject totally democratic pluralism and extrude non-Islamic groups. Hence the pressure resulting in the prudential migration of Middle Eastern Christians, and the tensions along the sub-Saharan Islamic–Christian borders. At any rate in Turkey we have a secular élite relying intermittently on military force to face down an Islamic revivalism which combines reforming impulses with potential moves in an Islamicist direction.

The Turkish example, then, exhibits some similarities with some of the processes undergone in the West, particularly (as will be discussed later) the inability of the radical secular élites to resocialize the masses in their values. Here Turkey and much of Latin America (Uruguay conspicuously excepted), as well as parts of Eastern Europe, appear very similar. One also might be able to construct a spectrum of response to modernity rather along the lines explored in Steve Bruce's *Religion and Politics* (2003), where Protestantism and Judaism are aligned with modernity, Catholicism resistant and Islamia very resistant, and this would correspond to types of social integration and degrees of individualization in the three cases.[2] One might bring to bear hypotheses about the contrast between an externally manifest and ritual religion based on pressures toward public performance and a collective mode of strong integration, and personally appropriated faith which has lost or repudiated the support of external rite and duty. From this perspective Protestantism has become dangerously attenuated and reduced to free-floating cultural motifs on account of its stress on spontaneity and inwardness at the expense of ritual performance and memorization. Catholicism has recently followed the same dangerous path, while retaining communitarian resources. Islam, helped by its location in societies at a developmental level prior to individualization and privatization, as well as by the absence of Reformation and Enlightenment, continues successfully to mobilize resistance through young counter-élites and the 'peasantry' *en route* from country to city. One might rephrase that by suggesting that Islam has always held to a religious programme based on success, particularly in integrating a society around the law, and allowing comparatively little neutral secular space. Of course, in so far as one uses classical secularization theory to characterize Islam as undeveloped with respect to internalization, privatization, pluralism and democracy, one is using precisely the criteria which derive from Western developments and the Gestalt initiated by the Reformation and the Enlightenment. One is also ignoring the huge variety of possibilities within contemporary Islam.

North America: Northern Europe

Inevitably one begins this central part of the argument with an extended analysis of the USA, which presents the quintessential combination of semi-partnership between Enlightenment and Reformation, in particular the way enlightened élites have rested on cultural bases in provincial religiosity. It also offers the maximum contrast to Islamia. The USA is increasingly in conflict with the Islamic world, after having successfully struggled to convert American Catholicism to its own cultural emphases. The first 'clash of civilizations' was with Catholicism, and the second is now in progress with Islam.

However, the discussion that follows concentrates on the contrast, and maybe the conflict, of the American model with an 'old' Europe of declining state churches characterized by the regulatory activity of the state in major spheres of social life. Though the focus of the contrast is Northern Europe, and indeed on the particular role of Britain and Canada as culturally half-way across the Atlantic, some of the contrasts apply to Europe as such. That Britain should have sided with the USA over the issue of Iraq, and France not, is just one geopolitical example of how religio-political complexes and alignments persist. In line with the earlier sections of this essay, I am extending the range of analytic principles and hermeneutic perplexities as I proceed, particularly as they arise in the USA, and then asking how they might be applied in Europe.

Unlike the rest of 'the West', the USA is religious and uniquely pluralistic. I am aware that this characterization has been challenged, and the whole issue of pluralism is a matter of debate. That Americans exaggerate their church attendance seems highly likely, but practice is certainly higher than in Europe and levels of belief (of all kinds, one may say) astonishing. Nowhere else does the devil on his own trump Charles Darwin. American political leaders deploy religious rhetoric in a way unimaginable in Britain or Europe, and they mostly mean it.

The USA has to be the fulcrum of this discussion not only because it is simultaneously at the forefront of 'development' and yet religious, but because it disseminates its culture and religion elsewhere. To be a hegemon (or hyperpower in current terminology) involves the exercise of superior power, but where that power is based on ideas and a loosely associated religiosity as it was in nineteenth-century Britain and is now in the USA, the consequences greatly exceed those following from the mere exercise of power. The Ottoman Empire has 'left not a wrack behind'. The consequences of Anglo-American empire include, for example, what has been called 'the Anglosphere' and the English language, as a creole of French and German. This is where the comparison between the USA, Britain and Canada (and Australia) becomes useful, particularly if comparison with the five Scandinavian countries is included. Britain incubated American pluralism yet more resembles Scandinavia in its degree of secularization, while Canada has simultaneously moved closer to the USA, economically at least, while in the sphere of religious culture it has begun to follow the British and even the European pattern.

When considering the USA, the issue of the specific ensemble, even the Gestalt, emerges with particular relevance. The combination of elements, fused together, affects the whole tone and direction of the religio-political culture. For example, the postulated trend towards rationalization, which is advanced in the USA in the highest degree, seems not to have the effects attributed to it in Europe. Perhaps the effects are blunted or even negated by the other elements present, or maybe the effects attributed to it in Europe are imposed on the data rather than derived from it. Alternatively, perhaps American evangelicalism is a religious mode especially capable of combining disenchantment in the public sphere and separation of powers with private religiosity.

The same query arises with respect to the observed tendency towards individualization and subjectivity, which in Europe fragments the local and communal religiosity of 'established' churches, while in the USA it may lead to some fragmentation but also throws up new denominational forms combining services to cater for subjectivity along with community enthusiasm, as in churches of 'The New Reformation'. The American aspiration to self-fulfilment is somehow harmonized with Christianity, just as it was in the Renaissance, though the same question arises as in the Renaissance: is this real Christianity?

Here lies a major hermeneutic question. Is there a Christian core persisting through all mutations, contemporary consumerism, including the idolization of the American Way of Life? The question of the continuity of the Christian core is perennial (for example, with respect to the changing meaning of baptism) but it enters into discussion of religion in the USA with special force because the churches there are so aligned with the American ethos. It is what conspicuously distinguishes them from British and continental churches, which are not so closely aligned, particularly when it comes to economic culture, and even (since 1945) when it comes to nationalism. Could this be the crucial difference: being transfixed by the past as in Europe and constantly adjusting to the present and the future as in the USA?

The most frequently cited reasons for American religiosity turn on the pluralism of 'The First New Nation', the severance of any particular church or religion from the power of the state finalized in the First Amendment, the role of religion in holding migrant communities together, and the federal rather than centralized mode of American governance. After all, the thirteen colonies on the way to becoming the USA never had to throw off an aristocratic stratum linked to established Church and land, except marginally in its break with Britain, which was as much a civil war within the North Atlantic communities as a revolution. England had developed a commercial bourgeois culture from the early eighteenth century on, indeed back to the times of the first civil war and revolution of 1642–60 and the second revolution of 1688–9 with the arrival of Dutch William. That was shared with the North American colonies; and Amsterdam, London and Boston were way-stations toward a tolerant, lay Protestant enlightened mode of life. It is hardly surprising then that the classicism of St Martin-in-the-Fields Church in London provided the template for the churches of New England, and indeed the USA, even today. Perhaps one might recollect that Amsterdam lost its sacred ecclesiastical centre at the Reformation, and the university now stands on that sacred ground. That expropriation of the sacred at the centre of Amsterdam is paradigmatic.

Moreover, the thirteen colonies, already the freest societies in the world, not only drew on the more egalitarian and religiously dissident sectors of English society, but more especially on the egalitarian and religiously dissident peripheries of Ulster, Scotland and Wales. Just as Amsterdam, London and Boston are linked culturally, religiously and architecturally, so the peripheries of Britain are linked to massive 'peripheries' in the American South and English Canada. The trail of the Scottish Presbyterian diaspora can be followed in Calgary, Alberta, in Ballarat, Australia, in Dunedin (Edinburgh), New Zealand, not to mention the Protestant Baltic. Knox Church dominates Dunedin as St Giles dominates Edinburgh, and nothing could be more eloquent than the way eighteenth-century London, Edinburgh, Dublin, Boston and Philadelphia are culturally and architecturally the same civilization, in the precise sense of that word. The Dutch churches of upstate New York exhibit the same affinity.

The key point is that the clash of early modernity with monarchy and established Church had already occurred in England with the Commonwealth of 1649–60, and the revolutionary war of 1776–83 had elements of the same clash, with the ground already conceded in principle in 1649 and in 1689. In this shared development, incubated in a sheltered offshore island and massively realized in a sheltered continent, there emerges the distinctive Anglo-American political style with its further religious roots in Amsterdam, and in German Pietism (and associated Huguenot and Jewish diasporas, such as existed, for example, in Francke's Halle). That is the genealogy of one version of contemporary modernity. Gradually, of course, the key line of that genealogy switched from Britain to the USA, especially after 1914 and 1945. The style of empire also switched from territories held for (initially) commercial reasons, with religion an incidental export, to a capitalist economic empire exporting religion as part of its expansion, and linking together faith and democracy, commercial and religious competition.

As suggested already, the Anglo-American religio-political style is exemplified by the way in which élite or counter-élite strata carry forward a liberal banner not by appeal to 'the people' viewed as 'masses' but allied to provincial bases informed by provincial religiosity. The leaders of liberal advance in eighteenth-century America or nineteenth-century Britain might be agnostic, Deist, Masonic, Episcopalian or Unitarian, but they gained support from a denser provincial religiosity with which they shared commercial practicality, empiricism and pragmatism.

In such a social context intellectual classes given to radical theory did not appear, and in any case could not have the power and influence they exercised in France and Germany. It is true that intellectuals (or more properly, in Anglo-American terms, academics) might be somewhat inclined to the left, but religion *as such* never had to face the kind of concentrated hostility found on the European continent, particularly in France, fount and origin of the war against religion. At most, and especially after the 1960s, they gained influence in key sectors of socialization, education and the media, and in welfare services once associated with the churches.

That influence in such key sectors has been important. It meant that as the state extended its role at the expense of voluntary organizations and churches, demanding secular certificates of competence divorced from any kind of confessional or religious background, the sphere of religion contracted. Even where welfare and educational organizations remained officially under religious aegis their personnel launched pre-emptive strikes in favour of universal secular criteria. Indeed, state-bearing élites and liberalized ecclesiastical élites formed alliances to soften up, undermine and delegitimate resistance at lower social levels among devout and committed people. The question now is whether these liberal and humanist élites, secular and Christian, will retain their influence or their bases in the universities with the advance of a consumer ethos mainly interested in measurable utility. Are the universities ceasing to be bases for diffuse humanism?

In the USA the diffuse federalism of the polity has always limited 'intellectual' influence. But in Britain the secular left now controls centralized institutions like the BBC, shifting them from a diffuse religiosity to a diffuse secularity. In that respect the centralized institutions of Britain resemble those of Scandinavia. Though in most Western countries the influence of the secular and humanist intelligentsias is declining, it remains true that in Britain they have presided over a spiral of religious decline not easily reversed. That is another way of saying that the centralization which in England was once associated with the partial retention of an established church and a generalized Protestantism, along with a Protestant national identity, finds an analogous contemporary realization in the way the secular élite is able to exert influence over centralized institutions on the Scandinavian rather than the North American model.

This argument can be extended to Northern Protestant (and post-Protestant) Europe as a whole. One would enquire, for example, about the degree of centralization available for deployment by the secular élites, let us say in the Third

Republic after 1870, and up to the separation of Church and State in 1905, compared with the relative decentralization of the Länder in Germany. That might be supplemented by examining the consequences of a monopolar religious system in France with a bipolar religious system in Germany; and by comparison between the weakness of the voluntary religious sector in all of Protestant Northern Europe and its strength in Britain and even greater strength in the USA. The power of establishment on the continent and even to some extent in Britain has meant that a welfare view of religion is pervasive, supplemented by a service-station approach to the Church, whereas in the USA religion remains entrepreneurial and activist.

Here we encounter those aspects which link Britain more to the continent than the USA. In Britain and the USA the voluntary religion of the successive evangelical revivals accompanied the entry into modernity post-1790, and in Northern Europe the analogous strain of German Pietism from which it derived worked mainly within the established churches. But in the USA the revivals continued, even though they experienced a liberalization of the mainstream in the twentieth century, while in Britain and the continent they tended to peter out. Again, in the USA, it was the socialism of the late nineteenth century that petered out, whereas in Britain a democratic socialism emerged infused with and even draining off religious impulses. On the continent socialism was more secular, anti-clerical, intellectual and left-wing, though the clash was much less great in Protestant countries than in Catholic ones. It is also arguable that the shock of World War I greatly diminished religious confidence in Britain and Northern Europe, whereas in the USA after 1918 and after 1945 religious and political confidence and power increased.

What then is the significance of Canada as a source of comparison? It is that in the mid-twentieth century Canada seemed to conform to a North American norm of high practice, and yet from the 1960s onward, in spite of increased American influence, it has tended to follow British and European trends. One has to enquire what elements distinguish Canada from the USA and what elements link it to Britain. Clearly Canada is not riding a wave of imperial confidence and lacks a religio-political sense of manifest destiny, preferring mediating roles. The proportion of evangelicals is lower than in the USA though higher than the proportion in Britain. It is to some extent a mosaic of peoples, Greek, Ukrainian or whatever, rather than a melting pot; the state is closer to the British model of welfare provision, and the cultural ethos is more law-abiding than in the USA. Of these perhaps the welfare state model is the most relevant because it may be linked to a smaller role for the voluntary sector which is in turn linked to the existence of religious quasi-establishments in particular regions rather than full-scale pluralism. These are not novelties dating from the 1960s but taken together they suggest a weaker religious dynamic and weaker resistance to the ethos of the 1960s.

The distinction between centre and periphery in Canada seems on the surface not very helpful, because Québec includes about 40 per cent of the Canadian population, and one is left with the east and west coasts, the former more practising and the latter conforming to the lower practice of the whole western littoral of North America. However, Québec is important because it represents a clear version of Europe in North America as compared with relatively faint European echoes in the 'peripheries' of the USA, such as Louisiana and the Hispanic margins in the southwest. If one wants that difference mirrored architecturally one must compare Montréal with the cathedral squares of New Orleans and Santa Fe. Quebec is 'old France' without the revolution, and a place where territory, religion and language together nourished the sense of identity in the absence of independence. Now, however, Québec has total equality, if not more, and self-government. What emerges quite clearly is the sudden decline of Catholic practice in the 1960s as language partly replaced religion at the heart of Quebecois self-consciousness. This is the reverse of what occurs in diasporas, where religion more often displaces language. One also notes the scope this offers for European comparisons, such as Brittany, Bavaria, the Catholic cantons in Switzerland, and southern Catholic Holland, even though language is a relevant factor only in Brittany. The obvious question is why conspicuously practising regions like Brittany, southern Holland and Québec (and Bavaria to some extent) experienced a dramatic change in the 1960s. How much was that due to the 1960s ethos or to the way the Vatican Council undermined the old basis of the Rock of Peter? Was even the Council itself affected by 'the 1960s'? At any rate, one has to set Québec in an analytic frame that includes peripheries in Europe both large and small.

Recapitulation

Thus far the range of analytic principles set out has steadily expanded, so it may help briefly to recapitulate some of them. I am suggesting that there is a complicated symbiosis between religious and political forms, such as one observes with some clarity in the decentralized religio-political voluntary and entrepreneurial culture of the USA, and in the centralized ethos of Scandinavia where a monopoly church found itself mirrored in a dominant Social Democracy. I have suggested also that one pay special attention to the role of élites and counter-élites in relation to the 'masses' they represent and manipulate as, for example, the enlightened élite in the revolutionary early America and the liberal counter-élite in Britain from 1860 to 1914, both of them relating to bases in provincial piety. The issue is how such critical alliances are articulated elsewhere. This is where the role and status of classic intelligentsias comes into play, especially in Catholic countries where they adopt an enlightened and radical anti-clericalism. Britain and North America historically lack this type of intelligentsia, though where such intellectuals emerge they are often francophile.

In the analysis above I pointed to a succession of enlightened élites from Amsterdam to London (and Edinburgh) and thence to Boston, all of them cities with relatively secular rather than sacred profiles and nourishing a pluralist, commercial, non-ecclesiastical culture. All of these decentred centres are rooted in a liberalized Calvinism or Anglicanism which achieves its apogee in the Anglo-Dutch–German culture of the nascent USA. One fresh point is worth making in passing: the way in which the pious lower middle classes of Germany, Scandinavia, Britain and the USA exported themselves and their faith to the whole globe through the missionary movement.

Latin Europe: Latin America

We turn now from the Halle-Amsterdam–London–Boston axis to an axis based on enlightened absolutism (monarchical or Stalinoid) and enlightened liberal imperialism. The key centre is Paris and its satellite or peripheral cities in Brussels, Bucharest, Barcelona, Madrid, Rio de Janeiro, Buenos Aires and Santiago de Chile, as well to some extent Schinkel's Berlin and St Petersburg. Recapitulating, Paris embodies a fundamental historical pattern, first by its emulation of imperial Rome on the part of the absolute monarchs, the first Republic and Napoleon, and then by war between religion and secularism, coded by the Panthéon and the Place de la Bastille, Notre Dame and the Sacré Coeur.

France and French warred with England and English, as they still do to some extent, and French became the lingua franca of radical anti-clericalism, laicity and liberal imperialism. There are other important centres, such as the Vienna of Joseph II and the Lisbon of Pombal. But Paris was the intellectual and artistic lodestone until overtaken by New York after 1940. Guatemala City even has a miniature Eiffel Tower commemorating the anti-clerical revolution of 1870 which in time weakened the Church disastrously, even depriving it of legal personality. One forgets how completely enlightened emperors or radicals all over Latin America, but notably Brazil, subordinated and gutted the Catholic Church, and how that bears on the flourishing of both spiritism and Pentecostalism.

What is presented here is not a model based on diffusion from Paris; the focus is on conditions tuned to the acceptance of such an influence, given that the Church was allied to land in a war with radical liberals. As Rio de Janeiro illustrates through its avenues and their names, Brazil was as hospitable to Comte as Turkey was to Durkheim.

But in Latin America as in Turkey the secularism of the élites could not be transmitted to the mass of the people. They remained in an enchanted, animated universe made up of a mixture of Catholicism and spiritism, which with the onset of Anglo-American influences could be the seed-bed of Pentecostalism and increasing pluralism. There are other factors, of course, such as a different and later phasing of development and one which leapt from the pre-modern to a post-modern service economy. Nevertheless, a major key to what is now a hybrid Latin American pattern and to the quite minor extent of popular secularism lies in the poor communications and disarticulated structures restricting the influence of the radical liberal élites, as it did the influence of Catholic élites at an earlier period. That was *not* the case in the French Third Republic.

In considering just how and why Latin America differs from Latin Europe one has to take into account the British and German influence alongside the French, and the shift from French-speaking among élites to English-speaking, as the USA took over from the British Empire. Protestant Britain, Germany and the USA were models of progress for Latin American radicals, politically, and the Protestant religion was felt to be aligned with progress. From the radical viewpoint, one might not need the specifically Protestant component in Latin America, but one could at least encourage migration, particularly from Germany, from the American South after 1865, and from Britain. Just as people from the peripheries of Britain moved disproportionately to North America, so, too, in Latin America: Scots in Argentina and Chile, the Welsh in Mexico and Patagonia. So a pattern of pluralism was initiated at the margin, along with minor enclaves of converts to evangelicalism in various forms, as well as to Adventism and Mormonism, and later to the Witnesses.

Here one can only pause to notice the religious implications of the migratory backflow of empire, and of migration *around* the periphery of empire. In the former case there is the massive migration of Hispanics to the USA, so reinforcing the southern religious peripheries of America from Florida to California, and also easing adjustment to American society by conversion to Pentecostalism either before or after arrival. In the latter case one has migration around the British Empire, creating major Indian populations in the Caribbean (Trinidad) and Guiana, on the model of Fiji and Natal. There are, of course, always enclaves of diaspora population in major cities, Latin Americans in Boston or Chicago, or partly Catholicized Japanese or Italians in Latin America, and these are either held together by their natal religion or else convert, as many Italians in Brazil have done, to a version of Pentecostalism. Latin Europe and Northern Europe exemplify the same pattern: for example, North African Muslims in France and partly Pentecostalized Caribbeans in Britain. In such secular countries as Britain and France that means that religious practice is quite disproportionately concentrated among migrants. The pattern in the Balkans is rather different: all the enclaves have been pressurized or expelled, from Athens, Belgrade, Sofia – and from Smyrna and Istanbul.

Reference has already been made to the way the Catholicism brought to Latin America from the Iberian peninsula, which was already syncretic, negotiated trade-offs with indigenous religions and spiritist cults, such as Umbanda and Voodoo. In recent times that could foster two developments – either the spread of Pentecostalism among the 'peripheral' native peoples, such as the Maya, Quechua and Mapuche, or neo-paganism. The intellectual and nationalist strata tend to look kindly on neo-paganism, and pre-Christian deities generally, for example in Mexico and Brazil, whereas the people themselves, more interested in modernity than nostalgia and cultural archaeology, tend to prefer Pentecostalism. The same pattern of popular choice is present in those parts of Southern Europe resembling South

America, such as Portugal, the south of Italy – and the gypsies. Neo-paganism in Europe takes many forms: middle-class 'Druidism' in Britain (or Celticism, Catholic and pagan) or the northern gods revived in Germany, above all in Wagnerian mythology.

Perhaps more obvious cases of neo-paganism, or at any rate the political use of pagan myth, lie in the pre-Orthodox cults promoted by the intelligentsia in the Mari Republic in Russia and the appeal to Tamerlane rather than Lenin in some countries of Central Asia. This whole tendency may appear quite minor but it is very much part of the way nationalist intelligentsias legitimate themselves by appealing to some construct of authentic and original religion. In sub-Saharan Africa as well as Latin America there is a major clash between these legitimating nostalgias and the search by mass populations, including native peoples, for entry into the global modern world through Pentecostalism.

The principles invoked so far with respect to the difference between a relatively secular Latin Europe and an inspirited Latin America (or sub-Saharan Africa for that matter) have leaned quite heavily on just how much power of resocialization is available to secular anti-clerical élites, though it may be assumed that degree and kind of economic development also play a role. It has been suggested that the appeal of the Parisian model, combining diffusion of ideas with a replication of similar conditions among Catholic cultures, only affected the élites. Contrariwise the American model, which for brevity I identify with the New York of the eastern heartland and the Dallas of the pious evangelical periphery of 'the South', works by appeal to the masses anxious to enter the global modernity of which the USA is a symbol and lodestone. As a result in Latin America there is a shift from a Catholic monopoly generating a secular, and maybe Marxist, monopoly, in the direction of a pluralistic religio-political hybrid. Some indication of the lowering of the religious–secular tension, especially with the collapse of the Marxist model after 1989, is the fact that the evangelical contender in the Brazilian elections of 2002, the Presbyterian Garotinho, gained 18 per cent of the vote, which then passed to Lula as the candidate for the Workers' Party. No French Protestant has ever gained 18 per cent of the vote on a 'religious' ticket. And, of course, Guatemala has had two evangelical presidents, however dubious their record. The Philippines, which follows the Latin American pattern, has also had a Protestant president, Fidel Ramos.

However, the analytic principle of centre and periphery has not been applied in Latin America except glancingly, with reference to the differential openness of native peoples to evangelical/Pentecostal conversion, from the Mapuche in Chile to the Maya in Central America. That is very important since such partly unassimilated cultures do not exist in the same way in Europe: the Maya and the Mapuche resisted their overlords for centuries. However, the situation is even more complex, since there are also strongly Catholic enclaves in north-central Argentina, the specifically Hispanic region of Colombia (Antioquia) and the Indians of south-west Mexico. These in a way would correspond to the European Catholic enclaves in the Massif

Central or the rural Veneto and the whole lake and mountain region of the Alps, excluding the secular cities of the plain in Switzerland. Analogous Protestant examples might be found in Friesland, Jutland, Västerbottenland, the Scottish Western Isles and eastern Hungary around the 'second Geneva' of Debrecen.

The Yucatán in Mexico is an interesting periphery. It is partly Mayan and has links with other Mayan areas over the border in the periphery of Guatemala. Both areas are vulnerable to evangelical or Pentecostal conversion. Like Wales in the UK, they resisted conquest longest and embraced a dissident faith first. In the Yucatán and Quintana Roo Protestants are about 15 per cent, twice as many as in Mexico overall. When one meets religiously conservative Americans there with Scottish names and small chapels looking as though transplanted from the British peripheries, one wonders whether periphery speaks to periphery, beginning in Britain and passing through the American South to Latin America.

Peripheries and borderlands apart, Pentecostalism in Latin America as in Africa has tended to spread along the lines of migration and communication from countryside to mega-city, whether it be São Paulo or La Paz. That trek to the mega-city, with its attendant Pentecostal caravanserai, has been accelerated greatly since the mid-twentieth century with globalization, and improved communication and ability to move. Over the past half-century Latin America and Africa alike have opened up very rapidly and the openings have included global, transnational religious movements breaking across traditional cultural frontiers, so that Port-au-Prince in Haiti is now 40 per cent Pentecostal, and Brazzaville also has large Pentecostal communities.

For that matter, Liberation Theology, considered as a kind of pluralism *inside* the Catholic Church, also illustrates precisely this transnational migration of ideas and personnel, though at a much higher social level than Pentecostalism, with more centralization and support from international intellectual and financial networks. Whereas Pentecostalism works among the aspiring poor, Liberation Theology derives in part from Catholic intellectuals in Latin America, but also from sources in France and Belgium in what looks like a reprise of the classic French influence, as well as from Germany, and also crucially from New York and Princeton, New Jersey. Liberation Theology represents 'sponsored mobility', Pentecostalism self-help.

Clearly the changes in Latin America, whereby large segments of the population have detached themselves from the linked élites of the Catholic hierarchy and the political class to run their own religious organizations, is subject to several possible interpretations from the viewpoint of secularization. One is that pluralism itself is a harbinger of secularization by breaking down the sacred canopy, and another is that Pentecostalism in the developing world parallels Methodism in industrializing Britain and will soon enter a downward spiral in the same way. Alternatively, it may follow a North American rather than a European trajectory. One does not know. Whatever else is the case it seems that the genealogy following from 1789 has given way to the genealogy of 1649, 1689 and 1776.

Notes

1   David Martin, *A General Theory of Secularization*, Oxford: Blackwell, 1978; David Martin, *Tongues of Fire*, Oxford: Blackwell, 1990; David Martin, *Pentecostalism – The World Their Parish*, Oxford: Blackwell, 2002.

2   Steve Bruce, *Religion and Politics*, Oxford: Blackwell, 2003.

CHAPTER 5

Religion, Secularity, Secularism and European Integration

Prologue

In this essay I shall be making certain assumptions unconnected with any personal views about further European integration. I assume that a question about how religion does or does not contribute to European integration is an empirical question, and if the answer is rather discouraging then that is what I have to report. No doubt the question itself is embedded in normative concerns, such as those now focused on the European Constitution, and it might be possible to respond drawing on carefully selected religious norms relevant to those concerns, but that is not my main task.

I am concerned, then, with the varying states of religion between Galway and Salonika, not with that particular subset of religious norms, of which subsidiarity is a characteristic example, which are capable of being subsumed within the conceptual abstractions dominating the humanist agenda. That is a game worth playing but its rules are already set by that agenda.

Were I to pause briefly and play that game, I would suggest that – classical sources apart – ideas like liberty, equality and fraternity are secular translations of biblical texts, such as our oneness (irrespective of all adventitious characteristics) in Christ, the unity of humanity 'under God', and the way in which every human being is a king and a priest 'unto God'. To this I would add 'Glory to God', 'The Peace of God' and 'Christian liberty' by God's grace. Remove the references to Christ and to God and you arrive at comprehensive mottoes of republican principle and virtue. Since Christian language can in this way be emptied out into ordinary secular currency, the question is whether the specifically religious gold standard, held (literally) in vaults and crypts, is still required as reserve backing, or whether it has been finally converted into the secular. Repudiate that standard and a relativistic nihilism easily follows of the kind brilliantly delineated in John Gray's *Straw Dogs* (2002).

I hold that the hidden gold standard provides permanent backing for secular enlightened usage, while resisting all attempts at a final conversion. Religious language is *sui generis*. In any case, its fundamental grammar of incarnation and redemption, transformation and deformation, acceptance and alienation, sacrifice and resurrection, cannot be incorporated into the public realm without damage and compromise on all sides. A Risorgimento in the secular realm echoes the Resurrection, but cannot be confused with it, any more than a secular Renaissance can be confused with a Second Birth.

Religious language is embedded in specific angles of vision, specific modes of human association, and in sacred places specifically shaped and informed by the gestures, images and exclamations of worship. Such sacred places are scattered all over Europe and are part of its unity, and even if you dismiss Christianity as a lingering or malingering tenant, this deposit of faith remains a social presence and stays a social fact. The normative question can therefore be rephrased to ask how this presence and this fact may or may not be acknowledged in the public realm.

I referred above to the enlightened agenda as a kind of taken-for-granted, and one which, like a media interview, reserves the right to question without itself being questioned. From the protected vantage point of that agenda, enlightened élites presuppose an established universalism which has somehow to cope with, and perhaps override, an awkward, fissiparous and archaic religious particularity. However, in a supposedly post-modern age one is permitted to think outside this protected vantage point. What we have in practice are rivalrous secular universalisms, such as are represented by France, Anglo-America and (until recently) Russia, each in complex encounter with rivalrous religious universalisms. In this encounter there are, for sure, shared wisdoms, complementary vocabularies and perennial common understandings, to be explored and exploited, such as peace with justice and human responsibility. But unless the protocols of human dignity are threatened or violated either by different religions or by different enlightenments, there needs to be respect for difference, and a sense of an unoccupied neutral space. Neither God nor truth can be pre-empted by the secular city. In any case, abstract rights are notoriously capable of being deployed in contrary directions: 'gays' should not be discriminated against when it comes to employment, and religious organizations should be able to employ those who share their ethos.

Enlightenments, then, are in conflict, and the French Enlightenment in particular, as allied to the omnicompetent and secularist state, is challenged by other less statist Enlightenments (English, Scottish, Dutch, German and American). These have had or, in the German case, have lately arrived at, a limited and federal view of the state, and they all present piety and reason in partial alliance. The main historical conflict was between the British and French versions, and that has now become a conflict between the American and French versions, with the British usually leaning westward once push comes to shove. The Anglo-Dutch genealogy of 1689 and the American genealogy of 1776 have long faced the genealogies of 1789 and 1917.

Not only are there characteristic and powerful alliances of Christianity and Enlightenments running east and west all across the northern tier from Harvard to Halle, but there are powerful and parallel lines of theological communication, mostly moving westward from German sources. Religiously, linguistically and historically, Britain looks west to North America as well as to Australasia and the global Anglosphere. This is where the sometime Protestant character of Britain retains some relevance in spite of the passionate love affairs pursued by the educated British middle classes with France, Italy and Greece, in search of places where sensuous relaxation can be briefly indulged under a southern sun. That apart, the post-Protestant North still preens itself on its capacity to internalize rules and laws, rather than to accept them in principle while venally evading them in practice. Whatever may be true of the old border of the magisterial Reformation, mutations of Protestant and Catholic attitudes still remain in force to cause cultural and political misunderstanding.

If there are such palpable if modest differences between north and south, there are more basic differences between west and east, especially north-west and south-east. In the north there is a socially critical religious leadership, including high-calibre lay opinion on such matters as bioethics, whereas in the south the weight of a more traditional Catholicism supports the idea of the Church speaking as a collective voice. Media convenience and political convenience collude with this Catholic view. In the east, and especially the south-east, the accepted role of religious leaderships has been and remains to speak on behalf of nations, even though the concrete norms governing people's lives are not at all subject to ecclesiastical control or guidance. Indeed, in the east, churches damage their moral credibility by seeking power and status.

These comments outline certain basic contrasts in contemporary European religiosity. Perhaps I may summarize. There is a socially concerned 'reformed' Catholicism, particularly where Catholics are effectively a minority. There is an embedded folk Catholicism with its redoubts in the south, but with northern outliers. There is the ethno-religion of Eastern Europe, sometimes with recently renewed links to the state but energized by several different kinds of alien rule. Western Europe has also nurtured ethno-religions, in particular in such niches as the Brittany peninsula and the island of Ireland.

Then there are the two Protestant types of religiosity found right across the northern tier. One is Anglo-Dutch and Anglo-American, based on religion as generating voluntary social capital, either as a passive service station under the shadow of establishment, in the English style, or active, entrepreneurial and competitive, in the American style. The other is Scandinavian and German, with a strong Social Democratic mirror of Lutheran monopoly in Scandinavia, and in Germany a federal state working in partnership with churches to maintain a massive web of social assistance: Gotteshilfe, Selbshilfe, Staatshilfe, Brüderhilfe to use the formulation deployed by Klaus Tanner.

The remaining kinds of religion are the cases of successful secularist indoctrination by the state, in France, the Czech Republic, the former East Germany and Estonia. This is the obverse of religious nationalism, because the success of counter-indoctrination by an ideologically secularist state, whether radical liberal or Marxist, depends to a great extent on whether the Church has been aligned with or opposed to the mobilization of national feeling and the nation-state. Religion and ethnicity either divide the sacred between them, or the sanctity of faith and nation are partially merged. So one needs to understand both how the sacred may occupy rival poles, and how it may partially migrate to occupy a new national sacred space. One also needs to be cautious about projections concerning the demise of sacred nationalism or the sacred nation-state. Its death could well be exaggerated. Sacred nationalism is palpably alive in Croatia, and the sacred nation-state in France.

Since parts of Northern Europe are post-Protestant (in spite of the fact that even in secular Britain 72 per cent identify themselves as Christian), one has also to notice the growth of largely unorganized subjective spiritualities, stressing human potential, sacralizing the individual, and creating a kind of Puritanism based, not on self-control, but on passionate judgements about pure air, racism and green issues. If there is a unifying dimension connecting changes in the Church, charismatic movements and the subjective 'self-religions', it is the world of the spirit, holy or otherwise. Joachim of Fiore would not have been surprised at the arrival of his Third Age of the Holy Spirit.

Some Patterns of Religion in Europe

In what follows I sketch some patterns of religion in Europe which can be mentally superimposed like a set of transparencies. My aim is to suggest what these patterns mean with regard to the integration and fragmentation of Europe, and I should say that they rest upon two premises. The first is that Christianity embodies a dialectic of the religious and the secular which more easily generates secular mutations of faith than straightforward replacements and displacements. The second is that religion should not be regarded as a separate channel of culture but as a distinctive current mingling in the mainstream, sometimes with the flow, sometimes against. These two premises taken in tandem mean that religious forms and moulds are often reflected in secular analogues. The Scandinavian symbiosis of Lutheranism and Social Democracy is a pre-eminent case.

Part of the aim of this essay is to give additional depth to those standard accounts of religiosity which rely on comparative statistics about belief and practice. Counting matters, but one needs some broader account of religion as a mode of social consciousness and identity rooted in history and geography, time and place. Christianity can be viewed as a flexible repertoire of images and gestures, and as a code simultaneously replicating itself and adjusting to social cues and circumstances.

It is better to proceed with concrete illustrations of the different patterns than continue setting out programmatic abstractions. One pattern of changing relations between the religious and the secular can be read at the centre of every European city, though most dramatically so in regional and national capitals. In the Byzantine tradition divine and human sovereignty are placed in intimate juxtaposition at the sacred heart of the city, whereas in a Western Renaissance city like Florence we see the incipient separation of powers in the two distinct spaces of Cathedral and Signoria.

Rome and Paris are ancient cities where a relatively recent history of conflict between religious and secular has been realized in rival architectural emplacements.

In Rome St Peter's is faced off by the vast Victor Emmanuel Monument, though eventually the Via della Conciliazione had to be constructed to bring Vatican City and the national capital back into contact again. In Paris, Notre Dame and the Sacré Coeur represent one kind of sacred centre, where France is the eldest daughter of the Church, while the Panthéon and the Place de la Bastille represent sacred centres where France is the eldest daughter of the revolution.

This paradigmatic urban ecology, with its rival versions of the sacred, signals two centuries of warfare between religion and progress, Church and State, faith and liberal nationalism, clericalism and anti-clericalism, Catholic universality and Enlightenment universality. It provided a model of conflict, and of the attempted supersession of one form of the sacred by another, which was disseminated from Paris to the intelligentsias of Europe and Latin America. The governing concept, enshrined in Paris, and taken for granted in France, was and remains laicity.

However, quite different notions are enshrined (and just as much taken for granted) elsewhere. In Germany, Scandinavia, England and Scotland, piety and Enlightenment lived to some extent in partnership, partly because the Church was subordinate to the State, and overlapped the middle and ruling classes. So, in Berlin and Helsinki, the churches were integrated into a profile which included university, arts and administration within a classical format conveying the power of enlightened absolutism. In Helsinki, Oslo and Stockholm the old centres were later complemented by monuments to Social Democracy and civic consciousness. The modest Enlightenment in England and Scotland integrated modest classical churches into civic squares and bequeathed a model of coexistence to North America which has become the main alternative to the model of warfare and supersession emanating from France.

Clearly, some of the different models of the religious and the secular can be read in the city, literally at a glance. On the one hand Europe is a unity by virtue of the universality of the basic distinction between religious and secular, and the deposit of sacred buildings from Syracuse to Trondheim, and Dublin to Sofia, while on the other it is a diversity by virtue of the different ways the distinction is realized.

This mapping in terms of urban sacred ecology can be supplemented by thinking in terms of architectural styles in a way already hinted at in the references to the classicism of enlightened absolutism in parts of Europe (Charles III, Joseph II, Catherine the Great), and the more modest bourgeois classicism of the Anglo-American tradition. Europe could be looked at, again quite literally, in terms of zones of Counter-Reformation Baroque, the classicism of enlightened absolutism, and the more modest, domestic and bourgeois tradition located in Amsterdam, London, and Boston, New England. These three civic cultures, each rooted in Protestantism, between them pioneered a model of (relative) pluralism, tolerance, federalism and philosemitism. They reduced the height and scale of human and divine sovereignty and emptied out some of the potency of the sacred concentrated at the heart of the city. Perhaps that weakening of the sacred centre began when the sacred heart of Catholic Amsterdam was forcibly sequestered and turned over to the university. That has to be regarded as a major mutation because it shifted the locale of protected space to university (and eventually art gallery and concert hall) conceived as a new kind of Church. Whether or not that stands up in the academic history of sacred representation, it remains the case that the four cities of Amsterdam, Edinburgh, London and Boston have been historically linked since the later seventeenth century by shared forms of politics, economy and religion, as well as by naval power and global trading empires. They also represent one major linkage and continuity between Europe and North America, just as France represents another. In view of such examples it is not so easy to formulate principles that unequivocally distinguish Europe from the USA. The USA is *not* distinguishable as 'the Other'.

This mapping of the connection between the north-western peripheries of Europe and the north-eastern peripheries of America is really just an extension of the initial map based on such models as Rome and Paris, Byzantium and Florence, and it is one that would reach its term with the sacred field of Washington, DC, representing the final separation of Church and State expressed in purely classical terms. But a second mapping or transparency can be devised, based on the way the historic religious moulds of European societies are mirrored in characteristic secular mutations and transpositions.

For example, the rigorous state monopoly exercised by the Catholic Church in France after the Revocation of the Edict of Nantes in 1685 was transposed into the monopoly eventually exercised during the Third Republic by the omnicompetent secular state. Just as for the Catholic Church error had no rights, so for the sacred Republic Catholic error had no right to acknowledgement in the public realm. The continuation of the French tradition of secular monopoly is perhaps illustrated in recent laws restricting the operation of sects and cults.

Another example of secular mutation is the way the inclusive scope of Lutheran monopoly in Scandinavia has been fused with and replicated by the inclusiveness of Social Democracy and the welfare state. Again, in Germany, Holland and Switzerland religious pluralism is mirrored in the federal character of the state. In England the attempt of the Reformed Anglican Church to accommodate and 'comprehend' an inclusive middle, and the eventual evolution of that into an accepted rivalry of Church–State establishment with religious nonconformity, became mirrored in the flexibility of the political system and its concept of a loyal opposition.

Here another American comparison is useful. England (and Scotland and Ulster) generated a style of evangelical Protestantism based on heartwork which in the USA became a universal devotion to individual sincerity. However, the retention of an Anglican religious establishment meant that England also acted as a hinge turning in one direction towards American inwardness, while in the opposite direction turning towards Scandinavian formality. If these distinctions seem rather marginal to European integration, I hope to illustrate how such cultural characteristics belong among others which separate the Anglosphere from the European continent as well as linking England to the cautious attitude of Scandinavia towards European involvement. For a wide variety of cultural reasons the national traditions of Britain and Scandinavia understand each other while both regarding the mainland of Europe with suspicious caution.

Since the mapping so far has focused to a considerable extent on peripheries and on secular translations, I need now to sketch two supplementary maps, the first identifying the historic European centre for which Britain and Scandinavia are peripheries, and the second tracing the heartlands of secularity and secularism. Secularity I treat as a condition and secularism as an ideology.

The historic centre of the West is arguably in Charlemagne's Middle Kingdom and in the bands of territory either side of Aachen/Aix-la-Chapelle. Looking back even further historically, this is the point where Latinity encountered the German tribes (as Trent was also much later!), and looking forward it gave birth to Schuman and Adenauer, who with Monnet became the architects of the Franco-German compact after World War II. With only a modest extension it takes in Frankfurt, the old imperial capital and the city which hosted the first assembly of liberal Germany, which is now a global financial capital. This heartland makes more sense than Rome, since Rome is really the centre of the Mediterranean, north and south, and one which has lost its southern littoral to Islam.

This frontier area, broadly understood, is one of mixed religion and contains the three key cities of Brussels, Strasbourg and Geneva. Each is symbolically close to the linguistic frontier, which makes them appropriate sites for international coordination and cooperation. The capital of Germany is no longer situated in the frontier area at *gemütlich* Catholic Bonn, but in post-Protestant Berlin. So the heartland of Western Europe *redivivus* is neither in post-Protestant Berlin nor post-Catholic Paris but in between.

Berlin and Paris are the centres respectively of European secularity and European secularism. Increasingly the new Berlin looks like the capital of the whole northern plain, and of a secular landscape stretching from Birmingham to Tallinn. The epicentres of secularity lie in former East Germany and the Czech Republic, in spite of the extraordinary role played by the Lutheran churches of East Germany in the revolution of 1989. The examples of East Germany and Estonia, and to a lesser extent Latvia, suggest that Lutheranism is less able to resist secular persecution in the way Catholicism did in Lithuania and Poland. The crucial point to notice, however, is that a great deal hinges on whether Catholicism or Catholic political powers were hostile to the birth of a modern nation-state: in France and in Czech lands, Catholicism was perceived as hostile; in Poland, Lithuania, Croatia and Slovakia, the situation was quite the reverse; while in Hungary the situation was mixed, given the strong connection between the birth of the nation and the Protestant east of the country around Debrecen.

The countries of East-central and Eastern Europe are all, to this or that extent, characterized by ethno-religiosity, due to a long history of alien domination by Ottomans, or Austrians, or Russians – either Orthodox or communist. Some of the variations in religiosity are not entirely explicable when one compares, for example, the remarkably vital Orthodoxy of Romania and the relatively secular condition of Bulgaria, unless the divisions in Bulgarian Orthodoxy and poor negotiation with the government after the war were serious factors. Certainly Romania, as a country constructing itself in both Latin and Orthodox terms, has a very distinctive national identity nourished by the Orthodox Church.

Serbia is interesting because when at the centre of Yugoslavia under Tito it was highly secularized, yet as the federated state went into dissolution it recovered a strong sense of religious identity, particularly in relation to Kosovo. The recovery in Serbia parallels the religious recovery in Russia after the break-up of the Soviet Empire, and in both cases the framework of Church–State partnership was renewed with perhaps only a minority of the population much engaged by active religion, and a mélange of magical ideas alive and well in the population at large. Revivals also occurred in those parts of the western Ukraine historically linked to Poland and Lithuania. However, the vitality of ethno-religion throughout Eastern Europe has brought about no nostalgia for the restoration of ecclesiastical influence over law and personal conduct. The Polish episcopate tried and failed.

Greece requires some separate comment because it is at the opposite end of the spectrum from the secularism of France and yet remains the historic icon of Western democracy and rationality. Just how far the Church is a powerful presence in the public realm, and Orthodoxy coextensive with citizenship and Greek identity, is illustrated by the fierce controversy over whether the bearer's religion should be noted on the Greek passport. The Greek case also illustrates the vigorous and firm profile of religion brought about by being at a border with Islam in Turkey, by the ethnic cleansings both sides of the Islamic–Christian border, and by a global diaspora on a scale similar to the diaspora of the Armenians and the Irish.

The map of ethno-religion in Eastern Europe overlaps the map of embedded folk religion throughout the littoral of the northern Mediterranean, which is not necessarily marked by conscientious religious practice of a formal kind, but by customs, pilgrimages and festivals. As in much of Eastern Europe and Russia, a confused mixture of magic and paganism, and of ancient and modern notions, lies quite close to the surface.

This kind of religion is rather different from the conscious and socially aware Catholicism that exists further north, especially in countries where practising Catholics are a minority, or where Catholicism itself is only locally the dominant religion. Catholicism in Sicily or south of Ancona is not like Catholicism in either France or Holland. On the other hand, what I have called embedded religion is not only found on the Mediterranean littoral, but in the Alps and various extensions like the Veneto, and in the mountains of the Massif Central, of northern Portugal, Catalonia and north-eastern Spain. There is a further extension here related to various micro-nationalisms that may or may not be shaped by geographical niches like mountains or peninsulas. Galicia, Aragon, the Basque country, parts of Catalonia, parts of the Pyrenees, are often regions of quasi-uniformity with respect to Catholic consciousness in spite of the steep decline of church-going in the Iberian peninsula as a whole. Brittany and Bavaria have been similar areas of intense Catholic consciousness further to the north, even though they also have experienced a marked decline in official practice, and Catholic Ireland may well belong in 'the south' rather than in the north-west. A similar folk Protestantism exists in niches in Northern Europe: the Western Isles in Scotland, and in Jutland, and parts of Norway.

Speculating a little on these regional Catholicisms (often but not always in geographical niches such as highlands, peninsulas and islands), they probably express a resistance to 'the centre', whether the centre is in Madrid or in Paris, though in the case of Italy there are various centres, with Rome virtually in the south and Milan looking northward across the Alps. That fragmentation is part of the 'problem' of Italy: it is nearly all elongated peninsula.

A combination of embedded Catholicism and resistance to 'the centre' gives rise to a distinctive political colouring (southern Italy, Bavaria) and is associated with great pilgrimage centres: Fatima, Santiago, Zaragoza, Montserrat, Rocamadour, Lourdes, Lisieux, the Vierzehnheiligen, Ensiedeln and Medjugorje. Where the Virgin chooses to appear, and when, is not entirely accidental.

The mapping offered so far has covered embedded religion or ethno-religion or some combination, 'conscientious' minority Catholicism and conscientious minority Protestantism, the great centres of northern secularity and French secularism, and it has sketched in some special characteristics of the semi-detached northern and north-western peripheries. What remains now is to fill in some borderlands, enquiring whether the borders are quiet and quiescent or lively and dangerous. Broadly it is all quiet along the old border of the Reformation, except in Ulster: Armagh with its two cathedrals still marks a dangerous transition. As has already been noted, Strasbourg and Alsace have been converted from borderlands into centres of cooperation. However, the old west–east border, at least as you go south and east, is still alive with dangerous tensions. Thus, although Breslau/Wrocław and Pressburg/Bratislava/Poszony are seemingly settled borders, Timişoara, and even more so Sarajevo and Skopje, are not. This is precisely the region of the most intense ethno-religiosity, characterized by dangerous mixtures of majorities and minorities, with consequent danger of ethnic cleansing, for example, the fate of the historic 'seven cities' of German settlement in Romania, and the creation of ghettos such as now exist in Sarajevo and Mostar. The Hungarians of Transylvania, and of areas more isolated and deeper into Romania, feel under pressure, whether they are Catholic or Protestant, and it is significant that the Romanian revolution of December 1989 was sparked off by a Hungarian Protestant pastor in Timişoara. In the whole of this region church leaders may also be political leaders, as Stepinac, Tiso and Makarios were in the mid-twentieth century. Indeed, their representative role needs to be contrasted with the role of church leaders in 'the West'. These Western leaders have mostly ceased to speak for ethnic constituencies and are rather the spokesmen of a liberal middle class within a more conservative active church constituency.

However, it is worth suggesting where other distinctive constituencies may lie, even if not on the strictly political map, and not even overtly present on the ecclesiastical map. Communities can, after all, form around seas, like the Lutheran Baltic and the Celtic Irish Sea. The rise of Celticism around and far beyond the Irish Sea in new spiritualities (or in old spirits in Irish pubs) is phenomenal. It has affinities with other 'constructed' revivals, not only of earlier Christianities, but of pagan roots. In the case of the Irish Sea, it is surrounded by highlands, islands and peninsulas with sacred associations, such as Iona, St Patrick's Mountain and St David's, and these harbour both an ancient Christianity and enclaves for modern spiritual travellers of many kinds. There are links here with folklore and mythological revivals all over the continent, and associated musics.

This area of spirituality is difficult to chart, not only because it is so varied, but because it insists on fragmentation and resists institutions as such. However, I would like to sketch in a mutation of Protestant and post-Protestant spirituality which does to some extent still respect the old border of the Reformation. Its origins lie in the Protestant pursuit of inwardness and in the Protestant desire to internalize the rules, with the result that rules are taken seriously and to heart. In its most developed form this leads to the secular religion of sincerity or authenticity, in particular in the USA. However, sincerity and inner seriousness about the rules leads to an inability to cope with the necessary negotiated compromises, and perhaps the understood corruptions, of politics, and so to an apolitical cynicism about government. What was once a classically Protestant objection to a Catholic theoretical acceptance of rules combined with an understood evasion of them in practice has become an alienation from society as such with strongly religious resonances. Of course, this classically (and stereotypically?) Protestant objection is still present in Anglo-Saxon attitudes towards the EU, and to French, Belgian and Italian politics.

One version of a looser, more spontaneous, spirituality retains links with disciplined lifestyles within a vigorous charismatic Christianity, but the multi-tudinous non-institutional forms defy mapping, except perhaps through the proliferation of holistic therapies and green politics. Concerns over pollution, and demands for pure air and pure food and political correctness, are a version of Puritanism that has relaxed personal responsibility, hard work and self-discipline in favour of complaints about spoliation, war, desecration, and the depredations of global capitalism and misapplied science.

The fundamental shift, present in both the new spiritualities and the shifting psychological landscape within the churches, is (as a very insightful study of Kendal, Cumbria shows) toward subjectivization. Put dramatically, Protestantism destroys its capacity to reproduce and retain its vital memory, not because of some problem with the scientific world-view or rationalization, but by going completely inward, personal and inarticulate. The churches have mostly incorporated this in the USA, whereas in Europe they mostly have not. Subjectivity militates against obedience, group discipline and personal obligation, as well as rejecting authority, in particular patriarchy, religious or otherwise. It therefore overflows into a feminine or feminist sense of 'participation' in the rhythms of the natural world. Nature, human or physical, is good, but sin and evil, sacrifice and redemption are difficult to comprehend, even though evil is readily identified as malignantly present in the institutional and official social order. If one were to identify this complex of spiritualities negatively, it would be as part of the religious hedonism and search for 'goods' of all kinds which has always underlain the more ascetic and indeed Puritanical expressions of both Catholic and Protestant faith. Protestantism has no monopoly of Puritanism, as versions of Irish and Spanish spirituality indicate.

The migration of mostly non-Christian populations is not a focus of this essay except to underline the gulf that separates the Muslim faith in particular from the subjective spiritualities just outlined. In parenthesis Britain is unusual here, partly because some of the migration into Britain comes from the Christian Caribbean and Christian sub-Saharan Africa, but also because it comes, too, from global populations not adjacent south and east of the European continent.

The characteristics of Muslim migrant population are antithetical to the 'advanced' religiosity of much of Europe to the point where assimilation is perceived as death. Muslim communities have learnt how to use a rhetoric of freedom, rights, inclusivity and multiculturalism, while for the most part – whatever their internal fragmentation – remaining integral, organic, monocultural and patriarchal, as well as stirred to some extent by global radical Islam. The relative lack of the religious/secular distinction within Islam has serious consequences. Whether or not there will be accelerating tension along this particular internal border depends on various factors, such as the size, location, and the ethnic and class character of the migrant community. Of course, in this context Turkey as a nation-state seeks a space for neutral civility, rather than for the religiosity of which it has more than enough at home.

That sheer numbers should play a crucial role is obviously a major anxiety with respect to inter-religious tensions and social harmony in general. The official leaderships of the churches mostly express the inclusive sentiments often characteristic of the educated middle classes, while being caught on the classic liberal dilemma as to how far one should include the exclusive. It remains to be seen whether Muslim assimilation will follow the path of Jewish assimilation (bracketing for a moment the horrors of the Holocaust) but there are reasons to doubt it. Nor can one assume the tolerance of even the most multicultural of European societies, as the recent Dutch experience indicates. Even Holland finds that it contains a border.

Summary and Reflection

In this essay so far I have not gone through the standard procedure of recounting figures of variations in belief, practice and religious self-identification, or assessed such indices with regard to secularization. The object has been rather to look at kinds of religiosity and kinds of secularity, or of principled secularism, in the historic French and Russian style, as these might bear on the integration or fragmentation of Europe.

So far as the figures go, what one needs to know is as follows. First that perhaps between one-fifth and one-third of the population has some active engagement with religious practice, depending on the criteria employed, within a range between the former East Germany, low on both belief and practice, and countries such as Ireland, Poland, Greece, Romania and Malta, high on all counts. That list in itself reminds us that Catholicism accounts for a much higher proportion of active, church-related religion than would be consistent with the size of 'Catholic' populations.

However, there is an undeniable secularizing process affecting the capacity of churches to reproduce themselves and their historical memory in the younger generations. This process includes pre-emptive strikes by personnel in the key educational and welfare agencies under religious aegis in favour of secular criteria, as well as the effects of the media. Throughout Western Europe the secularizing process has accelerated since the 1960s, following a post-war plateau, and that has been evident above all in the mainstream churches. The usual caveats have to be entered, of course: the acceptance of a Christian identity, of God, of prayer, of Christian moral maxims, and of 'spirituality'. Protestant Scandinavia ranks low on practice but high with respect to confirmation and, in many areas, it nurtures what is known as 'personal' religion. Britain resembles Scandinavia in terms of indices of practice, yet (in Grace Davie's formulation) Britons believe without belonging while Scandinavians belong without believing. Nearly three out of four Britons describe themselves in a census as Christian, and three out of one hundred as Muslim, even though religious practice in Birmingham is probably more Muslim than anything else, with Catholicism maybe ranking second.

The varied profiles could be amplified, but it is only the broad profile that matters. Clearly, Western Europe has undergone a different experience from Eastern Europe, but secularizing tendencies exist even in Poland and Greece. Also, the decline in church-related religious practice is paralleled by a decline in large-scale voluntary activity *as such*, including political activity, which is sometimes described as a deterioration in social capital, even though partly offset, as the Kendal study suggests, by an increase in the activity of small, intimate groups for self-help, spiritual and otherwise (e.g. Families Anonymous), and mutual support.

How does all the background sketched in so far bear on questions relating to European integration and fragmentation, cultural similarity and cultural variety? To begin with, questions about the role of the religious sphere with respect to European integration are problematic, since one would not put the question in the same way regarding the role of politics, because we all understand that politics is *inherently* about negotiated differences as well as about solidarities. The question is also slightly paradoxical in that one would not pose it were there an implicit consensus. The question suggests there is a problem, and a serious one.

One way of stating the problem is to draw attention to the difference between French laicity and its principled secularism, as contrasted with Anglo-Germanic secularity, and the ethno-religiosity of much of Eastern Europe where churches or religions may be surrogates for nations. There are parallel differences between an actively chosen personal religion on the Protestant model, and embedded religion on the older and more traditional Orthodox and Catholic model. Again, the religiosity of activist and socially concerned Christianity represented by many church leaderships in Western Europe, particularly North-western Europe, differs greatly from religion as cultural resistance, and from the leadership that goes with it. An Anglican archbishop is not remotely like such figures as Archbishops Makarios or Stepinac, or Tiso in Slovakia, or the leadership of the Hungarian minority in Romania – or Ghamsakurdia in Georgia! In terms of spirituality and 'sobornost', Christians in the West reach out to the Catholic and Orthodox world, but in terms of ethno-religiosity, exclusive claims and the ethno-politics of religion they abhor it. (Interestingly, it is that Eastern world, and especially perhaps Poland, now seeking integration in Europe, which most rejects the secularist ideology of France and Russia, and identifies its liberation with the USA and the Anglosphere. After all, there are perhaps nearly as many Poles and Greeks in Chicago as there are in Warsaw and Athens.)

Perhaps this is the point at which to bring out some characteristics of Christian leaderships in Western Europe with regard to European integration. Although such leaderships retain some representative role with respect to religion and nation, more particularly where religion relates to a micro-nationalism, they are likely to be culturally quite close to the secular middle class in modes of expression, attitudes and agenda. That means they are more liberal, ecumenical and European than the rank-and-file active Christian constituency, let alone the average dormant Christian identity in the population at large. The point was aptly put in the USA by whoever it was joked that the divide between Republican and Democrat in the American Episcopal Church ran along the altar rail.

There is a wider issue lurking here brought out by important ethical issues, typically as raised by the advances in the life sciences. In such matters the views of bishops, treated by media as the views of 'the Church' according to traditional Catholic conceptions, are not the same as educated lay views. There is a church view articulated by 'churchmen' and there are any number of informed lay viewpoints held by Christians. So the question is not simply what 'the Church' says or what the pope pronounces.

Indeed, all the evidence suggests that for Catholic identity the pope is a charismatic totem rather than a source of authority on lifestyles, or someone who can prescribe what is appropriate for family organization and sexual behaviour. In the West, church leaderships as such have this totemic quality without exercising what might be called moral jurisdiction, which is an area where they tend to limp painfully behind what lay Christians have already decided to do in practice. The low birthrate of Italy is the most dramatic index of that, and even in Poland and Ireland strong Catholic identity does not imply recognition of ecclesiastical authority or a desire for its embodiment in secular law. Identity is not obedience. Religious identity may and does seek recognition in the public realm, with respect to belief in God and broadly Christian behaviour, but it is decreasingly 'patriarchal' in its attitude to ecclesiastical moral authority, and it looks less than was once the case to exemplary figures and models. Some turn to the Bible or the Church for secure guidance, but most do not. Religious conservatism and secularity therefore increase together.

That in turn is linked to a more general point about Christian morality and secular morality. Christianity is most widely understood as care for neighbour, as reverence for life and as charitable attitudes and endeavours, and in that respect overlaps ordinary secular precepts. However, Christian language concerning moral obligation is expressed in terms of story and image and so has greater existential impact than abstract civic principles. There is a further divide here which relates to what John Paul II has described as a 'culture of narcissism', and it has something to do with the subjective spiritualities (or 'self-religions') already touched on. It relates also to the shift from ethical attitudes expressed in terms of duty and obligation to criteria of happiness, utility, freedom and self-fulfilment. In its extreme form freedom expresses itself as limitless permission to transgress and shock. However, this limitless permission is in no way the final advent of human autonomy but rather the replacement of older exemplars of endeavour and responsibility by peer-group pressure and the often-damaging examples provided by the lifestyles of 'celebrities'.

What is sometimes referred to as consumer hedonism lies behind the American idea of religious preference, and to that extent religion itself is chosen rather than inherited. Once again the difference between Protestant Europe and Islam is maximal. One is talking about different kinds of society, let alone about different varieties of religion.

Such realities pose particular problems for the dominant liberalism of Western societies, more particularly for the dominant liberal élites, Christian or secular, since it is they who hold most firmly that one should respect 'the other' (and indeed feel nostalgia for Catholic, Orthodox and even Islamic communal integrity), and yet most firmly condemn the authoritative deployment of scripture or tradition to inhibit freedom, to limit choice and to maintain patriarchal authority and images of God. The issue could be summarized by asking whether agreement that all the 'children of Abraham' believe in *one* God is the same as agreeing that all believe in the *same* God. No doubt the polite and politic fiction 'Judaeo-Christianity' has served a purpose in obscuring serious differences in angle of vision, however closely affiliated Christianity may be to Judaism. But just how far such ecumenical concepts can be extended to Islam is a moot point, more especially because of the difficulty Islam has in recognizing the autonomy of the secular in relation to the religious when it comes to law and the boundaries of social belonging. Conscientious choice in religious matters is inadequately developed. This is an area where contemporary liberals are no more inclined to grant rights to egregious error than Catholics were to concede such rights in the past.

At this point one comes to issues that trespass awkwardly beyond the remit of sociology. Such issues turn on the specificity and particularity of religious forms of association and language. They are brought out most clearly with respect to the role churches often play, locally and nationally, as foci of communal grief and rejoicing, as for example at the death of Princess Diana and the sinking of the *Estonia*. Here religious solidarity, the commonalities of sacred space, and the depth and range of religious language take over where secular talk and utilitarian venues have little or nothing to offer.

Religious association has traditionally been expressed through communities of obedience, discipline (internal and external) and sacrifice, based on cumulative reference to deposits of tradition and/or canonical scripture. That is still a crucial aspect of the specific difference exemplified in most forms of contemporary European religion. Religious language also exemplifies difference through being rooted in narratives bearing images of transformation and deformation, transcendence and immanence. It points 'beyond' in a vertical as well as a horizontal direction: it aspires, and its grammatical tense is not only the past but the perfect in the future. It conveys solidarity in hope rather than facilitating negotiation over rival interests, as political language does. Of course, it may be that religious hope and aspiration lose some degree of purchase as the consumer society offers an interim satiation of human wants, except that satiation is not satisfaction.

'European' principles, such as the dignity of the individual, human rights, equality, solidarity, the primordiality of reason and the rule of law, function at a different level of abstraction from that of religious language, and to an important extent cover a different spectrum of concerns. There are, indeed, mediating concepts, like subsidiarity or the autonomy of the secular, which can be fed into secular discourse; and governing concepts like liberty, equality and fraternity can be viewed as translations of St Paul respecting the unity and equality of humankind in Christ. But religious language is embedded differently and in a different range of concerns. That human beings are made in the image of God can be translated into such terms as 'All men are endowed by their Creator with certain inalienable rights'. But the priority of faith, hope and love, above all love, cannot be translated in civic and constitutional terms. Such priorities are laid on human beings by religious commitment in a manner which cannot be articulated as constitutive of the state or as a matter of policy in the public realm. No more can incarnation and redemption be reduced to secular discourse, or churches converted into art galleries and concert halls, or into civic spaces, without remainder. Such space is *there* not for particular social functions but for the specifically human, and for griefs and joys, unmet and unconsidered by other kinds of meeting place. How you treat that specificity and acknowledge it as a presence in the public realm is partly a matter of whether you view religion as archaic survival condemned by social evolution to continuous erosion, or as a constitutive language as primordial in its way as reason, and with its own coherence and continuing relevance. Beyond that basically philosophical divide, the question is how far and in what manner you do or do not explicitly acknowledge the religious presence. Empirically it is there; but is it a private or a public fact? Historically, after all, without the prior existence of Christianity, in successive mutations of Reform, Humanism and Enlightenment, the 'West' and Europe are little more than geographical expressions, or congeries of economic convenience.

This chapter is a think-piece not needing academic reference except in its citation of the Kendal, Cumbria, study by Paul Heelas and Linda Woodhead with Benjamin Seel, Bronislaw Szersynski and Karin Tusting, entitled *Bringing the Sacred to Life*, Oxford: Blackwell, 2004. I have also drawn on Grace Davie, *Religion in Britain since 1945: Believing without Belonging*, Oxford: Blackwell, 1994; *Religion in Modern Europe: a Memory Mutates,* Oxford: Oxford University Press, 2000; and *Europe: the Exceptional Case,* London: Darton, Longman and Todd, 2002. There is further empirical detail in Andrew Greeley, *Religion in Modern Europe at the End of the Second Millennium*, London: Transaction, 2003. There is a discussion of neo-classicism and its secularization in Robert Rosenblum, *Transformations in Late Eighteenth Century Art*, Princeton, N.J.: Princeton University Press, 1969.

CHAPTER 6

Canada in Comparative Perspective

Clearly, someone from outside Canada asked to comment on religion inside Canada has no new data to offer not already better known to Canadian scholars. The only tactic available to the outsider is a novel theoretical perspective or else comparisons with other countries. My specific tactic depends on those comparisons in particular as they are informed by the perspective of my *A General Theory of Secularization*, published over two decades ago.

Most of my comparisons will turn on about a dozen key questions, but there is a prior question to be asked about which countries offer the most fruitful comparisons. My first supposition is that comparisons arise most obviously in relation to those societies recently settled by people of mostly European descent in the ambit of Anglo-American culture: Britain, Canada, Australia, New Zealand and the USA. At one end of the spectrum presented by these societies is Britain (the original source, with Holland, of voluntarism) with a residual state church and regular practice in the region of 10 per cent. At the other end is the USA, with no state church and regular practice in the region of 40 per cent. Canada and Australia, with their history of shadow establishments, have figures of about 30 per cent and 20 per cent regular practice respectively, though I am surprised to see how very high Canadian practice is in the first half of the twentieth century. That raises a question about the different times at which the Victorian boom in religion ceased in each of those countries. Or, to put it another way: why did the boom end first in Britain?

Apart from these five closely related societies there are two other sources of comparison I want to deploy. One is found in those North-western European states, notably, Holland, Germany and Switzerland, where there are two (or three) main religious traditions, each rooted in different parts of the country. The other is found in former British colonies, such as Jamaica, which reproduced variants on the British pattern. Jamaica exhibits a residue of the Anglican establishment and a large sector of what was once called 'nonconformity', but that sector has been inundated with Pentecostalism. It is from these societies that I draw the bulk of my comparisons.

I begin with a group of questions, roughly hanging together, which have for the most part only to be raised in relation to Canada to be answered. Are there founding cultures and what is their relative size, power and territorial distribution? Clearly, in the group of Anglo-American societies cited earlier, Canada is the only one with two, or possibly three, founding cultures, of which one has a demarcated territorial base. The nearest comparison here would have been South Africa, which also had two or three, indeed several, founding cultures, each with territorial linkages; but in other respects South Africa is too different to deploy. Of course, in the Northern

European set both Protestant and Roman Catholic cultures have territorial bases, although in the case of the Catholic culture it is much more demarcated. That in itself is suggestive: where a Catholic culture has a territorial base in a Protestant society it is more clearly bounded and internally integrated. It is marked out in a way the Protestant culture is not, either because the Protestant culture does not need to be or because Protestantism produces a less organic connection. Moreover, such Catholic cultures have invariably retained a higher level of practice for longer into the modern period, until going into sudden crisis in the 1960s. There is a world of comparison to be exploited here, above all between the crises in Dutch and Quebecois Catholicism; this is worth further consideration before going on to the next question.

Catholic practice has been higher in Protestant countries where Catholics are a minority than where they are a majority and politically and/or socially dominant. That is because they form a carefully defended subculture, defining identity over and against a state perceived as alien or, at any rate, as populated by, non-Catholic élites. In such situations Catholics seek parity of esteem and may sometimes align themselves with other movements that seek to displace those élites. However, once that is achieved or is well in train, the religious bonds and boundaries that helped bring it about are more constricting than enabling. At that point it only needs a rupture somewhere in the protective dyke of symbolic practices for major parts of the culture to give way and the level of pressure behind the dyke to fall dramatically. Furthermore, minorities often latch on to aspects of their distinguishing characteristics so as to define them as essential – in these cases all the paraphernalia of the sacerdotal system. Once the Second Vatican Council shifted some of the markers of difference, many of the other markers collapsed at the same time. There was, therefore, a crisis in mass-going and above all a crisis in vocations. In Québec and in Catholic Holland this was greater than in England, Australia or the USA, because a territorial base created the sense of a complete subsociety. Everything was thrown into turmoil, and not just the sector of everyday living defined as religious. Religion then became a cultural colouring and ritual recollection rather than a militant practice, and in Quebec that role was carried by politics and language as much as by faith. It might also be that the extension of the welfare state pre-empts the role of the Church more comprehensively where the Church has been standing in for a complete subsociety (or stateless nation).

The next related question has to do with the degrees of dominance achieved numerically and/or socially by the founding cultures in particular areas, which may be provinces such as Alberta, but might be larger, like the Atlantic region of Canada, or smaller. The reference point here is Britain, or rather England and Scotland, since both England and Scotland have had churches that were numerically and socially dominant, although neither has been as socially dominant as Catholicism in French culture or as numerically dominant as Catholicism in Irish culture. What we have, then, in Canada are residues of Scottish and English established religion, free from the anchors of social and numerical dominance, but still bearing status and vaguely connected with overall 'Anglo' cultural dominance in North America, and specifically in Canada. That diminishing aura stands over and against a French Catholic tradition deprived of its original anchor in the pre-revolutionary French state, and the Irish Catholic tradition set free from direct English political hegemony to encounter a vaguer cultural hegemony. (Of course, the two Catholic traditions are as incompatible as the Irish and Italian, and Polish and German Catholic traditions were in the USA.)

What one would expect to happen is something as follows. The Catholic Irish and Catholic French struggle between themselves, but are united in their ultramontane devotion to Rome, which is the linchpin of their several identities. The Anglican Church, without the social supports of its home base, faces a vigorous Methodist movement competing for the same ethnic constituency. This Methodist movement runs parallel to American Methodism, though unaided by the desire in America to desert a church associated with the pre-revolutionary colonial power. Anglicanism thus inevitably becomes a minority, though not as small a minority as in the USA, and its established pretensions lack a sufficient numerical base, even in Newfoundland.

In any case, the Scots are relatively numerous and in some of the western provinces are the closest approximation to a numerical or social establishment. However, the approximation is not all that close, and in any case the two ex-establishments of England and Scotland are often mixed rather than segregated as in Britain, and so cancel each other out to some extent. So the Scots do as they do in England: gravitate towards their nearest Protestant neighbours, notably the Methodists and Congregationalists, and the bulk of them eventually formed the United Church in 1925. In this respect Canadian developments parallel Australian ones, including the emergence of a largish residue of conservative Presbyterians reluctant to merge their theological (and social?) identity. This pan-Protestant sector then becomes the largest single group within the more or less dominant Protestant culture. (I presume this argument, if correct, might apply also to the Scots Irish, who had their own local dominances early on, for example in Toronto.)

At this juncture some comparisons need to be made with the USA, Australia and New Zealand. Of course, in all four countries there are local dominances, but in the USA they are checked by the total separation of Church and State, and by a genuine federalism that assists continuous fragmentation as well as making the voluntary association normative. Thus, in the USA the initial dominance of a few Protestant founding cultures (English, Scots, Scots Irish and Dutch) fragments into cultural variants, each counterbalancing the other even where one or the other is relatively more numerous. The increased opportunity for subcultural formation and maintenance, and the relative weakness of state provision, makes for a very wide range of competitive religious agencies operating across the board. In Canada, by contrast, there remain shadow establishments rather as in early New England, on the 'mosaic' model rather than on the 'melting pot' model. No doubt that standard contrast of mosaic with melting pot can be pushed too far, but it presumably retains some leverage. In other words, in Canada there are identifiable, though modest, hegemonies that have a link to distinct institutional churches rather than to an overall Protestant tone. Of course, in both societies the culture most strongly attached to a distinct church is the Catholic one, but that is not initially well placed to combine institutional presence with social dominance, except in Québec, and (to some extent) in New Orleans.

If we turn from the comparison with the USA to that with Australia and New Zealand, there are, once again, local concentrations of socio-ecclesiastical power, for example, Anglicans in Christchurch, South Island, and Presbyterians in Otago and Dunedin, South Island. The differences between Australia or New Zealand and Canada seem to lie in the relatively greater number of Anglicans in the former two societies (about one in four), and in New Zealand the greater number of Presbyterians (about one in five). Thus in New Zealand there has been a dual shadow establishment institutionally defined: practice is about 15 per cent. In Australia there is a greater degree of pluralism, and a Catholic Church which even in bare numbers, let alone practice, is marginally larger than the Anglican Church. Practice there is about 20 per cent. The net result of this is that if we were to abstract Québec from Canada, then the three societies are strikingly similar, apart from the smaller proportion of Anglicans in Canada.

All three societies have experienced declines since the 1960s, roughly along the same lines, with the Catholic Church and the liberal Protestant Anglican churches taking the main impact and the conservative evangelical churches (or evangelical sectors of other churches) holding their own or expanding. However, this relative evangelical success does not place evangelicals on a par with co-believers in the USA where, by comparison with all the other societies, there is a higher degree of overall practice within a totally voluntary system, which is further associated with a proportionately much larger evangelical sector, able to take advantage of the opportunities for subcultural institution building. Britain, in particular England, is at the other end of the spectrum, with relatively little opportunity for subcultural institution building, although even in England the evangelical sector is the most lively.

Here perhaps is the right place to introduce the Jamaican comparison, with a sidelong glance at South Africa. Jamaica offers a massive contrast with all the other societies cited, in that a combination of Anglican 'emplacement', indicated by a central location in townships, with adjacent Methodist and Baptist churches, has been overtaken by a Pentecostal inundation of about one person in three. Likewise in South Africa, Pentcostally derived churches may account for up to one in five. By contrast, Pentecostalism in Canada and Australia, though expanding, only accounts for some 1 per cent. Plainly, societies like those in the West Indies, sub-Saharan Africa and Latin America are much more open to Pentecostal inundation, though one would expect charismatic manifestations of various kinds to emerge from the Roman Catholic fallout in Québec. Indeed, in Quebec one has an interesting combination: quite high levels of serious alienation and of Pentecostalism.

The next question is a very important one, although not permitting a clear answer, and it has to do with the role of élites, especially those in the so-called knowledge class, concerned with the manipulation of symbols. What strikes one in the USA is the inability of this class, though clearly dominant in the upper echelons of education and in the TV media, to overwhelm and erode the religious subcultures. Perhaps this is because there are so many élites in the USA, and so much fragmentation of control. By contrast, in England the élite has substantial levers of control and successfully radiates out secular impulses. It is as if the monopolistic power once invested in the Church has been transferred to secular élites. Presumably, Canada and Australia exist somewhere in between on the spectrum, between the USA and Britain.

Of course, one of the most important subcultures in the USA is the South, and that represents a defeated nation whose identity is nourished in evangelical faith. One might describe the South as a vast periphery larger than most autonomous states. Canada, however, has no equivalent (unless there is a partial analogy in Quebec), but it does have a relatively isolated and relatively practising region – in the east. That generates the obvious question as to where resistant peripheries lie in relation to centres, and what are the relative strengths of peripheries *vis-à-vis* centres. Clearly, in Britain the peripheries are weak, just as the subcultures and religious counter-élites are weak, whereas in the USA peripheries, subcultures and counter-élites are strong and can defend their own space. Once again Canada, Australia and New Zealand have their resistant peripheries, and also, in the past, have been peripheries of Britain and the USA, with the balance of power slowly slipping from the former to the latter. (I have never forgotten the symbolism in Canberra of a set of British bells placed symmetrically over against an American eagle.) At any rate, London is a strong centre, whereas Canberra, Ottawa and Washington are weak centres when considered against their vast hinterlands.

There is one further question that this time sets the USA and Britain (or rather England) together against Canada and Australia, and that is the strength and coherence of the national myth, as New Israel and New Jerusalem as well as the socially progressive Light of the World, and as New Athens and New Rome. England passed its messianic and millenarian myth over to the USA, and both nations mingled Christian light with secular enlightenment, providence with destiny. Caught between such powerful grand narratives, Canada, Australia and New Zealand have struggled to create secondary variants. Canada seems to have generated the idea of 'His Dominion' in awkward lock step with French Catholic projections, and that seems to have mutated towards a social gospel of international good works alongside the innocence claimed by Scandinavia. It is almost as if a post-Protestant virtue wells up in the everlasting pine forests and the vistas of virgin snow. Yet there is not enough 'dynamic density' to support it, especially in a nation strung out along the longest undefended frontier in the world. It follows that a 'civil religion' is a possibility frequently canvassed but not achieved. Order and continuity and a scepticism towards expansive revolutionary enthusiasms of the

American kind characterize an upright nation, but you cannot make fire out of driven snow.

Two other questions are inevitable in any comparative analysis of religion and culture. They concern, first, the pattern of migration and, second, the distribution of native peoples or peoples of another colour likely to be exposed to prejudice, forced segregation or coercive assimilation. With regard to the pattern of migration, it has not yet converted Canada from a bicultural to a multicultural society. The arrival of Asians in British Columbia, or of Ukrainians in Ontario, or Greeks in Quebec does not in that respect add a new dimension – yet – beyond maybe giving a further thrust to the privatization of Christianity.

If Protestant and Catholic Christianity possess both a public face and a political voice, the emergence of a significant non-Christian sector hastens the occlusion of face and voice. In the USA that is coped with by adding one more voice to numerous other voices. In Canada, however, the Christian voice spoke for a community nearly coextensive with active or nominal Christian identity, and when that ceases to be the case the voice is muted or else fixated on intercommunal relations. The greatest problem is likely to emerge where a foreign religious body, such as Greek Orthodoxy, inserts itself in the heartland of a culturally 'integral' Quebec. The majority community suspects a logic whereby all of the out-groups ally together to counterbalance the in-group. That is an obvious source of interreligious tension that is rooted in ethnic tension. Here I make a tentative query about a contrast between Quebec and Ontario. The exuberant ethnic and religious variety characterizing Toronto seems not a problem, whereas major increases of minorities in the heartlands of Quebecois nationalism and semi-monopoly Catholicism might well become so.

With regard to Native American or Inuit peoples a rather similar consideration applies in that tension arises where they claim large segments of a territory also claimed by an embattled nationalism. However, this again is much more an ethnic and cultural tension, and only marginally religious. In large parts of Latin America subordinate native peoples have been disproportionately drawn to Protestantism, but in Canada there seems little disposition to find counter-definition through a distinctive faith. In any case, conditions are relatively benign. (In Russia, where they are not benign, militant paganism is a real option.) Proportions of native peoples in the region of 1.5 per cent in both Canada and Australia have not been large enough for massive tension, although recent political events in Australia illustrate how volatile such situations can become. By contrast, a population of about 10 per cent of Maori descent in New Zealand now represents a serious political problem.

A final set of comparisons relates to those North-western European countries with a bipolar religious difference rooted in a (very rough) north–south territorial split. All of these have similar characteristics to Canada in that the Catholic areas are more practising and Catholic voters likely to support parties well disposed to Catholic and regional interests, for example, the Christian Social Union in relation to Bavaria. However, the Catholic minorities have not shown any inclination to support a separated nationalism such as from time to time emerges. Perhaps the lack of a linguistic reinforcement for Bavarian or South Dutch distinctiveness has something to do with this. The nearest analogue may be Czechoslovakia, now the Czech Republic, and Slovakia. Here the difference was between Catholicism in Slovakia and indifference in the Czech Republic, and in the upshot, the resentments in Slovakia over supposed Czech misdemeanours in relation to economic assets led to a separation in which the Slovak politicians were exerting more pressure than the population was for independence. Nevertheless, it went through without violence, and such a scenario may be quite possible for Canada.

Perhaps one might conclude by a brief comparative glance at the problems of the United Church, as these compare with the problems of the parallel body in Australia, and comparable denominations elsewhere. Here it is not possible to say much that adds to work done by Roger O'Toole and others, but it is worth underlining widespread similarities across several societies. If we take England first, it is abundantly clear that denominations like the Methodists (and to a lesser extent the Presbyterians) are prone to ecumenical unions and that these in no way seriously bolster their resistance to decline. In England the Methodists and the United Reformed Church, both products of earlier unions, have continued a steep decline. Many of those who have 'ceased to meet' have relocated themselves in the Church of England, and perhaps most dramatically in its ministry. Decline breeds decline, both in terms of the possibility of living a full life within the group, including marriage partners in the same denomination, and in terms of lower morale. That situation also characterized the United and Uniting churches in Canada and Australia respectively, although both are larger than their British counterparts and can still pull themselves round. The Methodist and Presbyterian churches in the USA have declined, and the Methodists (and even the Baptists) of Jamaica have also done so. So this is a widespread phenomenon clearly illustrated in Canada. It is as if the voluntary bodies, whose ethos has been so congruent with (and so productive of) democratic and participatory modes in the Anglo-American world, have no resistance to their environment and simply leak into it. By the early years of the twentieth century they were shifting towards liturgical styles and social service, and their distinctive call for the circumcision of the heart and complete revision of life was blunted. The latent power built up by evangelical fervour was now being expended without renewal so that conversion was translated into decency. In so far as they adopted formal styles of worship and its furnishings there were others to whom that came more naturally, and in so far as they no longer preached for a decision, there were others who moved into the vacated space, notably the Pentecostals. The institutions they helped create for education and welfare were gently secularized, leaving only an aura of piety, and their functions were replicated or improved upon by state provision. They provided the motivation for innumerable conscientious citizens who staffed the social and educational services and were active in good causes, yet somehow this credit account with society at large was almost invisible. Their children acquired mobility through these virtues but felt no special religious call to stay in the institutions that had fostered them. In Canadian society or English or Australian society they were simply part of unnoticed normality, the religious form of the good character of the culture.

Moreover, the increased openness to the world, especially the world of education and social service, meant that the cultural wars that emerged in those worlds flooded back into the Church. The result was that churches that helped form the image of a caring service for others and of mutual help were themselves reformed in the image of what they created. The churches divided into politicized and evangelical wings tugging in contrary directions under the aegis of leaderships and teachers in denominational colleges for whom political correctness was as salient as Christian values, and who indeed saw little difference between the two. The churches were ripe for demythologization and the emptying out of the original generating power into what used to be called, in Christian parlance, 'the world'. The world used up their virtues of duty, service and commitment to others, and then proceeded along its own calculating and utilitarian course, while every now and then regretting the loss of social capital, because it was so inconvenient. Only their decline in Anglo-American societies makes clear the nature of the contribution that the churches made to the social and political fabric.

Perhaps (in the cultural context of Ontario where Methodism has been important) I can conclude by a programmatic extension, still focused on the problems of a liberalized evangelical Christianity in Anglo-North American society as illustrated throughout the twentieth century. I have already mentioned the failure of this kind of religion to hold on to the institutions it initially inspired, whether we are talking about the Young Men's Christian Association (YMCA) or universities with religious foundations or large associations for youth work, such as the Methodist Association of Youth Clubs in England. Those who founded and initially ran such institutions had a vision rooted in faith to which they gave social and charitable form, but the justification they offered for God became, in time, the good consequences of their own activity: a sort of social works righteousness. The New Testament became a charter selectively deployed to legitimate and motivate that activity, but there was no particular reason why those they served should share those motivations. Again, all kinds of agreeable and harmless social interactions could occur within the ambit of the church, but their connection with the Church was quite contingent. The drama committee of the Wesley Guild and the Epworth Choral Society, let alone the badminton club, were simply moderately equipped competitors for people's time.

In approaching this slackening of the specifically religious as it embeds and embodies itself in social activity, I suspect we need to integrate our sociology, and our social history of institutions, with what people feel able to say about God and Jesus and what selected aspects of the Christian Gospel they feel able to preach. In other words, we need to integrate the kind of social history dealing with the local evolution of religious institutions with the content of Christian messages and especially teachings about God and redemption. The decline of preaching presumably has something to do with a diminishing stock of things to say. What brought about the collapse of the great preaching stations in this tradition? Or to put it another way: why should people seek out a folksy psychotherapy in the context of hymn singing on Sunday mornings? What powerful interpretation of the wider culture, its directions, events and concerns, could this subculture offer out of its own unique resources? Why should the cosmopolitan world and its media listen to analyses more professionally available elsewhere?

To ask that last question is ultimately to raise the question of content and thus the presentation of the nature of God and the role of Christ. Thomas Jenkins, in his *The Character of God* (1997), analyses that presentation in Protestant culture over the past century and a half in such a way as to challenge sociologists to integrate it with their empirical analysis and social historians to incorporate it with their accounts of institutional change. The question is: what follows from an uncertainty about sin, redemption and the meaning of the Cross as it plays into an etiolation of the vocabulary and of the phraseology of faith as well as into the emptying of God into politics, communal celebration and history? The question that Jenkins raises relates to our quest for sociological understanding: what roles have the churches assigned to Christ, what emphases and what silences about the peculiarity of the Gospels, what characterizations of the agency, being and character of God?

CHAPTER 7

The USA in Central European Perspective

The background to my argument is provided by the location of this presentation in the centre of Munich, in the Amerika Haus, close to the Königsplatz. I want two comparisons to lie at the back of our minds. One comparison is between the ecology of sacred space in Munich and in Berlin, considered as rival poles in a federal country with two principal and numerically balanced versions of Christianity, covering some two-thirds of the population. The second comparison is between sacred space in Germany and the varied sacred spaces of the USA, another federal country with numerous versions of Christianity, but bound together by a common myth called by Harold Bloom *The American Religion*.[1] That myth overlaps Robert Bellah's *Civil Religion* but can be expressed in more directly theological terms.[2]

I begin with the myth, not the comparisons lying in the background. This myth generates a Haggadah commemorating the recovery of original innocence following an exodus from the wickedness, cynicism and corruption of Europa, or 'old Europe'. Once safely installed in the Paradise Garden of a new world, after hacking a path through the wilderness and overcoming some scattered Canaanites, the infection of sin became 'Unamerican'. This had some awkward consequences: a dangerous self-imputed innocence requiring a principled ignorance of cults and cultures outside the garden, and a combination of generous intent and *realpolitik* in dealing with them. Following in the steps of Moses and ringing the Liberty Bell around the globe entails Rousseau's famous paradox whereby we are forced to be free.

Given this combination of Rousseau and Joshua, Jeshua (or Jesus) is required for personal redemption but not the collective advancement of the people. Purgation and suffering are no longer strictly necessary, and Christianity – or rather God – provides a way of naming what works, above all what works for America and Americans.

Americans are empowered by a God in whom they trust – not having been let down like the rest of us – to arrive directly at the sincere and heartfelt spirit of their universal Pentecost without passing by Golgotha. Europe, however, France perhaps excepted, is a land of failed gods in whom therefore we do not trust. Europe has reworked the Passion too many times, but with no redemption, and a most uncertain resurrection. Europe cannot agree on its myth of origins, whether it is a Haggadah based on God or a rather murky Haggadah appealing to civilization and humanist civility. Some European countries regard themselves as essentially martyr nations, for example, Poland and Serbia, whose God is their support in time of trouble rather than in time of triumph.

All the same, Europe has bit by bit achieved a modest post-imperial innocence which European leaders can use to criticize America's more assertive mythology. America's performance can be judged by its own myth in the light of 'European values'. A Kantian ideal of 'perpetual peace', mostly achieved under the umbrella of America's imperial power, can be contrasted with America's Hobbesian relationship with the rest of the world.

The problem with Europe's uncertain and disputed myth of origins is that Europe remembers too much. The anamnesis of Europe treats its faiths as ambiguous goods. The problem with America's all-embracing myth is that it requires amnesia, and therefore treats its faith as straightforwardly virtuous. Europe forgets too little; America forgets too much.

This America, based in European eyes on a backward religion, but in American eyes seen as a faith at the leading edge of providence and progress combined, was the first country to send a man to the moon. Contrary to all the assumptions of civilized Europeans, America views successful faith and successful science as part of the same providential and progressive package. Americans do not think of religion and science as different modes of apprehension, but as aspects of the same common-sense reality: hence an exacerbated problem over evolution. However, in paradise, alias god-land, progress ensures there are no insoluble problems. As Charles Wesley wrote, quoting Paul: 'all things are possible to him that believes'. Europeans have never believed 'all things are possible' – not for good, anyway.

In sum, then, America may have its cultural wars over religion, but the wars are between rival versions of the American faith, and above all between rivals in righteousness. America is a religious country: Hebrew and philosemitic, progressive and providential, enlightened and pious, religious in its secularity, secular in its religiosity, this-worldly in its apocalyptic, Protestant in its Catholicism and offering immortality not so much by faith as by natural right.

I realize that mapping myths in this way is even more dangerous for an academic than 'helicopter history'. It smacks of essences, and goes one further than analysis by 'ideal types'. So, in the spirit of living dangerously, I compound the offence by embedding comparison between rival myths in a further comparison between rival triumphal ways, European and American. By triumphal ways I partly mean the cultural style known as 'triumphal*ism*', but I also mean monumental architecture such as we find in Munich and Berlin, or in Vienna, Madrid, Rome, Paris, London and St Petersburg, or in Washingston, DC. Much of the time I contrast the failed triumphal ways, and therefore the failed gods, of Central Europe, whether Christian, revolutionary or neo-pagan, with the triumphal ways of the contemporary USA as prefigured in the layout of Washington.

I suggest that London, Paris and Rome are special cases. London is special because its triumphal ways never came to fruition. What was implicit in London became explicit in Washington, because America was the realization of possibilities frustrated in Britain. Paris is special because it embodies a secular religion that sees itself as the rival universalism to American universalism. Paris represents laicity militant and triumphant over Catholicism. Rome is special for the opposite reason. Its secular religion was based on a fascist restoration of the Roman empire, and so offers another example of a god that failed. But the other Rome of Roman Catholicism still celebrates the universalist myth of the universal Church. Rome and Paris have, therefore, been rivals for the allegiance of Latin Christendom, and beyond, including Latin America and parts of francophone Africa. Both Paris and Rome are still guardians of viable myths and plausible public gods. Nevertheless, the long shadow of 1789 throughout the world is being overtaken by the long shadow of 1776, just as Paris after 1940 gave way to New York as global capital of art.

We have to keep in mind rival faiths with their rival triumphant ways, in Paris and Rome, in Paris and Washington, and in Washington and Rome. These are not the only players, but London is to some extent a base for Washington on an offshore island that now fosters geopolitical links with the outer rim of European capitals. The other capitals, Vienna, Madrid and St Petersburg, are scarred by a historical caesura, and Berlin in particular is doubly scarred by experience of the failed gods of Nazi neo-paganism and communism. No wonder the former GDR is the most dispirited region of Europe, following successive recessions of Christianity, neo-paganism and communism. No wonder the former western Germany, following a post-war Christian rally against communism, is now host to a fragmented 'spirituality'.

I hope you can now visualize the historical and sociological theses I am proposing as to the contrast between failed gods and successful gods, and the way these failures and successes bear on the indices of faith in various countries, whether it is the secular religion of France, the failed religions of Germany, the slack uncertainties of ex-imperial England, or Russia between a failed new faith and a partly resurgent faith in Russia as a Third Rome. I could go through the numerous objections to theses of this kind, such as the temporary stabilization of Christianity after World War II under Christian Democratic aegis. But that is not really necessary. I am simply highlighting a theme that is too often underplayed, which is the way religious vitality either thrives on success, whether understood as progress or providence, or provides a last resort when all else fails as, for example, in the messianic martyrdoms of Poland.

So far I have not mentioned the Enlightenment except by way of oblique references to the cooperation between progress and providence in the USA, and the triumph of progress over providence in France. I want now to complicate matters by reviewing my chosen countries, represented by my chosen cities, considered as instances of different concordats between the myth of Enlightenment and the myths of faith. Let me illustrate. The gods represented by the triumphal ways of Paris are Roman or Graeco-Roman at the expense of Roman Catholicism. The god represented by the triumphal ways of Rome, beginning with the Bernini colonnade, is Christian but arrayed in ancient Roman, or renaissance, vestments. In Rome resurrection and renaissance collude, and the big break does not come until the Risorgimento. While Paris might be symbolized by Napoleon as painted by Ingres, Rome might be symbolized by a pontiff (or Pontifex Maximus) as painted by Titian.

It is not difficult to call to mind all the various concordats arrived at between the Enlightenment and faith, all the way from St Petersburg to Washington. They are each of them resolutions of the ancient question 'What has Athens to do with Jerusalem?' Since the focus here turns on a contrast between the failed gods of Central Europe and the gods currently flying high in Washington, I begin in Washington.

Washington was, of course, designed on a vast scale by a Frenchman, and seems to represent the most complete triumph of Enlightened order and Graeco-Roman ideals. The British initially laughed at it as a ridiculous piece of grandiosity; and at first glance it seems there is not a hint of Jerusalem anywhere. In reality, however, the separation of Church and State enabled America to combine the public face of the Enlightenment, embraced by its élite, with the faith (or rather faiths) increasingly embraced by its people. Washington (like Boston with its gold-leaf Senate House, recalling the Dome of the Rock) is a city set on a hill. It is both a light to lighten the Gentiles, and the heavenly Jerusalem of the philosophers. After all, in the Book of Revelation the heavenly Jerusalem has no Christian temple, because it is illuminated by the Lamb alone.

In *The American Religion* Harold Bloom suggested that America was post-Christian and gnostic and had, therefore, forgotten that redemption came through the suffering of the Passion.[3] He was writing as an agnostic Jew, or maybe a gnostic Jew. Building on that, I suggest instead that America is Jewish with a profound Christian resonance. America is Jeremiah's law written on the heart as transcribed by Luther and Wesley. It is Hebraic in its collective consciousness as the New Israel, while cherishing a Christian inwardness in any number of mutations of second birth and the new spiritual fire of Pentecost. It is naturally philosemitic, in a tradition also transmitted by the feeder-nations of Holland and England, and the only problem is whether it completes the Old Israel or supplants it.

Of course, the cross was central to the great transactions in the American soul: ''Tis done, 'Tis done, the great transaction's done'. Crux probat omnia. If you know the book of 'Sacred Songs and Solos' produced by the Chicago evangelists Dwight L. Moody and Ira D. Sankey, you can hardly miss the centrality of the cross. 'At the cross, at the cross, where I first saw the light, and the burden of my heart rolled away; it was there by faith I received my sight, and now I am happy all the day'. That unites Moody, Wesley, Bunyan and the pursuit of happiness.

I want it to be clear that I am talking about Jerusalem as a *city*, as a civic reality, and about America, the subject of perpetual invocations led by its high priest, the President of the United States. The ritual intonation 'God bless America' refers to the Israel of the Solomonic Kingdom, not of the Babylonion exile, let alone the Christian Passion. Where else in the world could legislators gathered at a

Washington prayer breakfast listen to an invocation beginning 'We are met here today in the presence of Almighty God and of the President of the United States'? Conor Cruise O'Brien tells the story in his book *God Land* and it out-Solomons Solomon.[4]

If you want an example of genuinely Christian heartwork you can find it in the occasion when Bill Clinton repented in tears before a large company, including his wife, and was tearfully forgiven. From the Solomonic pretension we derive a *realpolitik* as ruthless as any; from the Christian heartwork we derive kindness, acceptance, forgiveness, openness, hospitality, neighbourly generosity and public philanthropy on an unexampled scale. America represents an empire pursued in all Christian sincerity for our own good. The desire to do good justifies the *realpolitik*.

I saw both together in a service following 11 September in St Paul's, London. A vast concourse, including much of the American community, stretched beyond the cathedral and down Ludgate Hill. The American ambassador read, movingly, from Isaiah, chapter 61, about building up the waste places of Jerusalem, and then the congregation sang the 'Battle Hymn of the Republic':

> In the beauty of the lilies Christ was born across the sea,
> With a glory in his bosom that transfigures you and me,
> As He died to make men holy, let us live to make men free,
> While God is marching on.

But what has the battle-hymn of the Republic to do with the warfare of the cross? Is God really marching in lock step with the American Republic?

I do not apologize for that question because it is as much a sociological and historical question as a theological one, and it picks up yet again the issue of what Jerusalem has to do with Athens or Rome, whether in the USA or Europe. Every imperial nation in Christian history has converted the contrast between the triumphal ways of Rome (or Greece) and Christ's triumphal way into Jerusalem into a complementarity. The Hebraic Joshua has been reconciled with the Christian Jeshua. It may be more blatant just at this moment in the American New Israel, but every triumphal way in European Christendom, now in evident dissolution, embodies some variant of the tension between Jerusalem and Rome, the Hebraic and the Christian, the Enlightenment and faith.

The pre-eminent triumphal way in Europe is located in Rome itself, creation of the Renaissance popes, and such brutal old roués as Leo X and Julius II. We can visualize the relation between Rome and Washington architecturally by placing in apposition the vast pilgrimage temple of the Universal Church in Rome and the crowds streaming below Capitol Hill in Washington.

The difference is partly a different balance of Enlightenment and faith, particularly in Catholic Europe, but partly also a difference between triumphal ways that have failed and those that have not yet failed, though there are plenty of prophets around to predict the decline and fall of Washington – or Rome, for that matter. We in Europe trusted in God that He would deliver us, and He did not. God was not 'with us', any of us, though in our different ways we survived.

There was a time when we in Europe believed otherwise, and were all too ready (except for intermittent alarms over divine judgement for backsliding) to accept a triumphalist reading of the Scriptures. Part of the horror of Islamic militancy for us lies in the discovery that there exists a world religion still programmed for success. We have learnt, at least in some degree, that the sacrifice of the warrior differs from the redeeming Passion of the crucified. On the front of war memorials we may place the dead warrior and the dead Christ together, but in so far as we recognize an essential difference, we remain 'Christian' whatever our individual beliefs. Clearly, the performances of Islam and Christianity *in power* are strikingly similar, given the ineluctable imperatives of politics, but they differ markedly when disembedded by modernity. The politicization of a disembedded Christianity most often resembles the action of a voluntary and peaceable pressure group, whereas the politicization of a disembedded Islam is organic and intermittently violent. We somewhat chastened Europeans are bound to be anxious bystanders when the world-winning ways of the American religion meets the violent version of a triumphalist Islam trying to engineer a return to global power and imperial hegemony after two centuries of stagnation.

I can now survey in turn some of our failed European myths, with an eye to their attempted amalgamation and resuscitation by the European Union. I say resuscitation rather than Renaissance, Risorgimento or Resurrection, because that would be pitching it rather high. All the while I am implying a contrast with the single-minded myth of America, and I begin in a surprising and perhaps provocative place: Northern Ireland or Ulster, though I could have chosen Scotland. At any rate, I'm talking about egalitarian and Protestant peripheries of the British Isles, above all the New Israel of Ulster, known to Americans as the home of the Scots Irish.

The New Israel of Ulster is the failed version of the American project. The plantations of Ulster and Massachusetts occurred about the same time, and led to the same tally of massacre and counter-massacre. The history of Ulster combines the Reformation and the Enlightenment in just the same way as the history of British North America does. Dublin was very much a creation of the Anglo-Irish Enlightenment. Equally, Edinburgh New Town was a creation of the Anglo-Scottish Enlightenment, and the Scots actually started to build a new Parthenon on Calton Hill above the city. The orderly lines and classical temples of Hanoverian Britain, after the Union of 1707, can be traced all over the eastern seaboard of America.

The North American plantation of the early seventeenth century aroused an enthusiasm the Ulster plantation did not. In the 1620s the priest–poet George Herbert went so far as to declare (in lines from 'The Temple'):

Religion stands atiptoe in our land
Ready to pass to the American strand.

It is this trajectory that makes plausible the idea of England as a half-way house to America, and the English Civil War as the first round of the American Revolutionary War. The British and the American colonists could together crush the rival empire of France in what was perhaps the first global conflict of 1756–63. Things went very differently in Ulster, where the Protestants faced a Catholic majority composed of Irish, Anglo-Normans and old English, and invasions by Spain and France in succession. At the same time, the American revolutionaries sought to make common cause with sympathizers in Ulster and Scotland, and it was descendants of Ulster people and Scots who had gone to North America rather than endure Anglican dominance who made up a disproportionate part of the revolutionary army. That is why Jonathan Clark can describe the war of 1776–83 as the last war of religion, and why seventeen American presidents were of Scots-Irish stock compared with one Catholic.[5]

So, the Ulster experience shows the American project in semi-defeat. It has the same Hebraic spirit under the influence of an evangelical revivalism, and it created a genealogy in British military history traceable to the present day. On D-Day 1944, General Montgomery not only said 'The Lord sent his winds and scattered them', but was also known to have addressed his troops with the words 'Jesus Christ said, and I agree with Him …' Could an American president say more? When British soldiers went to Iraq, Prime Minister Blair was prevented from saying 'God bless you' by a Downing Street *apparatchik* who explained 'We don't do God.' But a northern Irish commander told his men they were entering Bible lands and should show their respect. President Bush was sufficiently moved by his words to have them placed in front of him in the Oval Office. The speech contrasted with another by an American commander: 'Our God is bigger than your God.'

My argument here, stripped down, is that so far as politics goes, you either believe in God as a 'man of war' who overwhelms the horses and chariots of Pharaoh in the Red Sea, or in a God who is your sole resort and comfort when Jerusalem has been taken and you have to sing the songs of Zion in a strange land. Babylon (and exile) is always the typological contrary of Jerusalem (and home). Initially, of course, the English and others in North America were in exile, except for those who returned expecting Cromwell to usher in the millennial reign of King Jesus. The nostalgia of exiles for homelands is patent in all the scrambled maps in North America of the old countries (Holland, France or England) from Haarlem to New Orleans, and from Rochester to Boston. But once the shock of experience in the wilderness was over, they settled down hopefully in their Promised Land, their Providence or Hope Valley or Philadelphia or Bethlehem. Eventually they saw themselves as mankind's 'last best hope', providentially undefeated in war. There was no more need for exile to teach them about being the saving remnant of an apostate nation, or the precarious state of the world, or redemption by suffering, or frustration through the cunning of history. They could celebrate Thanksgiving in a Haggadah of liberation with none of the irony of Jewish history. 'Next year in Jerusalem' is not a sentiment voiced by those already in Jerusalem, and to this day most American Jews have good reason to stay in their New Israel rather than return to the Old Israel.

Europeans, especially the British perhaps, lament the disappearance of irony from the American view of the world. Using Swiftian irony simply goes astray, and maybe that is because irony depends on a big gap between aspiration (including Christian aspiration) and performance. Americans may feel they have closed the gap just sufficiently to keep irony at bay, whereas we know all about it, especially since 1914. In Rumsfeld's 'old Europe' we devise tropes on the irony of American history to prick the Solomonic pretension, but only succeed in sounding peevish. The pretensions are ridiculous, as when the younger Bush claims America has never intervened elsewhere except in the cause of freedom, or when the older Bush told the Republican Convention, 'We have whipped the world with our culture', but it all ends in mutual incomprehension. We accuse them of Christian Zionism and they accuse us of anti-Semitism. What we have never understood is the cooperation in the USA between Enlightenment and faith, Athens and Jerusalem. Perhaps, as Jonathan Clark argues, we have not adequately recognized how far the Enlightenment retained the idea of providence, and in the USA retains it to the present day.[6] (As a famous Catholic intellectual put it to me 'You believe in God. Why do you not believe also in the USA?')

What now of the failed gods of old Europe and their partly disused triumphal ways? In what different ways are these gods Janus-faced, looking both to Graeco-Roman civilization and to Jerusalem? One way to begin is to take the Greeks and the Jews, Athens and Jerusalem, in turn, before contrasting the failed gods of Russia with the failed gods of Germany, and looking at the different ways in which both Russia and Germany have revived. The special historical relation of faith and Enlightenment in Germany will then allow one to pass to Britain as a mediator of the pietist impulse through the evangelical revivals of Britain and the awakenings of North America. I shall be arguing that the pietist impulse in Germany as mediated by Methodism in England and by the Awakenings, is the clue to the unique collaboration of Enlightenment and faith in America and to the formation of American culture in the early nineteenth century. So my basic contrast between Europe and the USA is still in play.

The Greeks and the Jews are special cases, partly because they are the joint sources of European and American civilization, partly because, with other nations in diaspora, like the Armenians, they survive by adapting to special niches in the social system. Yet there are marked differences. Though Greeks and Jews exist in the USA in similar numbers, the Greeks are far less visible than the Jews. And they have very different relationships to the Enlightenment. The Greeks saw themselves, and were seen by most Europeans, as the primary source of the Renaissance and the Enlightenment. France, Germany and Britain all had love affairs with Hellenism, prolifically illustrated in nineteenth-century painting, but the contribution of Christian Byzantium was largely ignored. For Greeks the Hellenistic heritage and the Byzantine heritage *together* provided the foundations of the modern nation.

Athens barely needed to enquire too deeply into the question 'What has Athens to do with Jerusalem?' In that respect Athens was like Washington. The tale of two cities was one tale.

For the Jews matters stood very differently. They had their 'Jerusalems' in the ghetto, for example, the Jerusalem in Vilnius, Lithuania. But they could embrace the Enlightenment as a release from the ghetto which enabled them to turn the tables on Christian universalism and become agents of secularization.[7] The scandal of particularity was only recovered with the advent of Zionism and the establishment of Israel under American protection – Israel today is a modern equivalent of the Latin Kingdom of Jerusalem. Both the Greeks and the Jews are at a crucial border between the West and Islam, but they have very different relations between Enlightenment and faith. (In Salonica they shared a border.)

Russia, after 1917, represented a militant and historicized version of the Enlightenment equipped with far more persecutory zeal than France even during the period of maximum tension between 1870 and 1905. The persecution of Christians and Jews lasted seven decades, but the discontinuity with the Orthodox past was so massive it had to be ameliorated in the Great Patriotic War 1941–45. And when the new gods finally failed in 1989, Orthodox Christianity was resurgent, partly as the remaining link with the historic past. Almost all the cathedrals in St Petersburg, the great city of enlightened absolutism, are now restored to Christian use. It was President Vladimir Putin, ex-head of the KGB, who said Europe was rooted in Christianity, not Chancellor Schröder. The same resurrection is visible in Romania and even in Bulgaria, showing what happens when religion codes the historic core of ethnic identity.

Finally, then, we come to the centre of Europe, here in Munich, capital of Catholic Bavaria, sometimes called 'the Rome of the North', and also to Berlin, not only the resurgent capital of Germany but of the whole of post-Protestant(?) northern Europe. The Amerika Haus where we meet now has until recently been the chosen location for today's imperial superpower, and it lies close by the Königsplatz, a parade ground and triumphal way first for the German empire and then for the Nazis. It has an almost Egyptian monumentality. Just off the Königsplatz lies the Evangelische-Kirche of St Mark, representing only a minority locally, but by its position symbolizing a closeness to power in the German Reich as a whole. The Catholic cathedral, representing the majority, stands in the ancient centre quite close to the old emplacements of civic power in the Marienplatz. The terrible caesura in the German myth is invoked by the spot where the first deaths took place in the failed Nazi *putsch* of 1923.

Berlin, with Potsdam and Sans Souci, provides the rival pole, as the classical capital of Protestant imperial absolutism in Prussia. This was to have been another new Rome under another Kaiser. The caesura in the German myth is marked in Berlin by the Gedächtniskirche, once an imperial memorial, now a witness to the ruination brought about by twelve brief years of Nazi neo-paganism. The Protestant cathedral is a disused sacred space, full of imperial tombs and haunted by memories of its occupation by the 'German Christians', while the later Catholic cathedral only represents the minority. If there is a Christian sacred in Berlin you would perhaps find it in the hall of the meat-hooks where Bonhoeffer was strung up, but equally the effective and material sacred may be the K.K.D., or the other great temples of shopping in the Kurfürstendamm. Berlin still retains its impressive triumphal ways, for example, the Siegessäule, which the Nazis planned to extend on an even grander scale, but the myth has fled to be replaced by a resurgent city, dedicated to commerce and finance.

At the same time, it is here in what is now post-Protestant northern Germany that you pick up the trails leading to the inwardness of faith in the USA, in Wittenberg, of course, but more proximately in the Pietism and social conscience of Francke. Yet Pietism was coopted as part of the discipline of enlightened absolutism of the Prussian state, before partly mutating into German Romanticism. So the spirit underwent an institutional confinement, reinforced by a compromising proximity to power, as it did not where it energized an oppressed national consciousness in Eastern Europe, or where it animated purely voluntary denominations as in the USA. The debates about the role of faith and Enlightenment were carried out by state-bearing élites, above all in the universities.

In Britain evangelicalism had its links with Pietism, particularly through Wesley, and it grew within an established Church infiltrated by the Enlightenment as well as in the nonconformist denominations which expanded with industrialism far more than they did in Germany. As in Germany, so in Britain, the conflict between Enlightenment and faith was contained, though in both countries, as Hans Kippenberg has shown, moves were made to tap new sources of religious dynamic outside an over-moralised and intellectualized Christianity.[8] The retention of an overarching religious establishment led to the emergence of a philanthropic Christianity supplementing the welfare state and eventually to the churches mobilizing as voluntary pressure groups as well as replenishing depleted reserves of ethical community and social capital.

Though in both Germany and Britain there were stabilizations of the Christian religion after 1945, the trauma of 1914–18 undermined faith in the old gods of nationhood. The communication lines of the Protestant faith had run between Britain and Germany, though mostly from Germany to Britain, but a common confidence collapsed in the nightmares of Flanders. You can trace the transition in Max Beckmann, in Lovis Corinth's *Crucifixion*, in Stanley Spencer's piled-up crosses in Burghclere chapel and in the contrast between the initial war poems of Rupert Brooke – 'Now God be thanked who has matched us with this hour' – and the later war poems of Wilfred Owen, set by Benjamin Britten in his pacifist *War Requiem* (1962).

The year 1918, and even more 1945, left the USA, as a late entrant into both world wars, the one remaining inheritor of an optimistic myth, combining Enlightenment with the pietistic impulses of the great awakenings in the immediate pre-revolutionary phase and the early decades of the Republic. What passed from

Halle and Franke to Wesley and Whitefield, and found its final flowering in the open social and geographical spaces of the Republic and the frontier, became the faith informing the nascent American character. We have only to compare the confident prose of the Declaration of Independence with the bureaucratic fumblings of the Preamble to the new European Constitution to gauge the difference between the confident ethos of the Republic and the uncertainties of even a resuscitated Europe. Beneath the deistic affirmation of the Declaration of Independence lay a reformed evangelical faith, providing the collective solidarities and affective ties needed to support the Enlightened framework.

There is a musical version of this spiritual genealogy stepping westward from Halle (and Leipzig) to Boston, Massachusetts, or Bethlehem, Pennsylvania, via Huddersfield and Manchester. It begins with Luther, Buxtehude, Bach and Handel (to return *ad fontes*), and is realized in the popular choralism exported from England and Wales to America, as well as in the American spiritual, in gospel and in soul. It was entirely natural for Michael Tippett in his pacifist oratorio *A Child of our Time* (1941) to replace chorales with spirituals. If Bach is the stream at the beginning, it flows all the way to the black music of America.

Once in the USA, evangelical doctrine underwent numerous secular translations without collapsing into secularization as such. A version of the sacred–secular dynamic was retained. The offer of redemption to all could become the offer of citizenship to all and the Calvinist Elect could evolve into the electors and the elected. The commonsense perspicuity of scripture could mutate into the right of individual judgement (as it did elsewhere) while the beatitude of conversion allied itself to the pursuit of happiness whereby each and all 'had a nice day'.

In a similar manner a reverence for the body as the 'temple of the Holy Ghost' could be reinterpreted as the need to have a nice body, keeping it out of harm's way by the pursuit of 'wellness'. At one stage you might stuff it with 'good' food, at another cosset it and keep it trim by making sure the food was truly good and really pure. (Health and wealth, hele and weal, have long linguistic roots in the Anglo-Saxon world.)

Christian liberty from sin and death is easily translated into liberty pure and simple, just as righteousness through faith can be translated into mere righteousness. The trust that 'all things are possible to him that believes' turns into a belief in infinite possibility, while 'blessed assurance' turns into secular confidence.

John Wesley said, 'Is thine heart as my heart? then give me thine hand.' America is the land of fraternal heartwork and mandatory sincerity. But the most extravagant realization of the American Dream is Mormonism, issuing from the burnt-over soil of evangelicalism. The Mormons became a separated people who once again faced a wilderness and a desert to seek a city and raise a temple. Their Kingdom of God really is expected to come on earth as it is in heaven, because in that day you shall eat chocolate and not grow fat, bear children and feel no pain.[9] Paradise Regained.

Notes

1   Harold Bloom, *The American Religion*, New York: Simon and Shuster, 1992.

2   See entry on 'Civil Religion' (Robert Bellah) by R.K. Fenn in *The International Encyclopedia of the Social and Behavioural Sciences*, Oxford: Elsevier, 2001.

3   Bloom, *American Religion*.

4   Conor Cruise O'Brien, *God Land*, Cambridge: Harvard University Press, 1988.

5   Jonathan Clark, *The Language of Liberty*, Cambridge: Cambridge University Press, 1993.

6   Jonathan Clark, 'Providence, Predestination and Progress', *Albion*, Vol. 35, No. 4 (2004), pp. 559–89.

7   David Hollinger, 'Jewish Intellectuals and the Dechristianization of American Public Culture', in Harry Stout and D.G. Hart, *New Directions in American Religious History*, Oxford: Oxford University Press, 1997, pp. 462–86; Mark Mazower, *Salonica*, London: Harper Collins, 2004.

8   Hans Kippenberg, *Discovering Religious History in the Modern Age*, Princeton: Princeton University Press, 2002.

9   llustrations taken from Fenella Cannell, 'The Christianity of Anthropology', unpublished Malinowski Lecture, 20 May 2004.

CHAPTER 8

Central Europe and the Loosening of Monopoly and the Religious Tie

I begin my discussion with the example of Hungary, not just because this presentation is being given in its Houses of Parliament, but because it is a country in the centre of Europe illustrating most of the major themes of this chapter, and very much in the middle range according to recent statistical enquiries into European religion. My most important single theme is the individualization of contemporary spirituality as compared with the more organic ethical communities of Catholicism and Protestantism. The latter retain institutional links with the state or, at least, have a recognized presence in the public square, whereas contemporary spirituality does not. Instead it generates diffuse moral passion directed against capitalism, the state, or whatever. It has no permanent representatives to promote a view, no corporate ethical discipline and little interest in self-discipline. It is an extreme version of Protestant inwardness often mixed with an antinomian dislike of rules and authority.

If Hungary is in the middle religiously as well as geographically, secular France and Holland are at one extreme and the ethno-religion of Poland, Romania and Serbia at the other. Hungarian roots lie in a union of faith, monarch and nation, and like much of Europe north of the Alps it was divided at the Reformation. To the west of Budapest lies Eztergom, a Hungarian Rome (or another Rheims) representing the old unities, and in the east is Debrecen, a Hungarian Geneva. Hungary's experience of the Enlightenment differed both from the partial alliance of faith and progress found in Northern Europe and Anglo-America, and from the clash of principles characterizing Latin Europe. Instead it came in the form of enlightened absolutism and with that the kind of tolerance found in the multi-ethnic empire. That history is mirrored in the architecture of Budapest. The hill of Buda is almost entirely Catholic, while Pest is more pluralistic. This historic pluralism is not individual but communal. In Pest you see the sacred buildings of juxtaposed communities, Jewish, Calvinist and Lutheran. Moreover, while other nations became more multicultural after World War II, Hungary, like Poland and Lithuania, became less so following the fate of its diaspora and its German and Jewish communities. The difference has implications for loosening monopoly and a loosened religious tie.

Like many parts of Europe, Hungary has passed through a semi-fascist phase, a communist phase (or occupation) and partial Americanization. The result is ambivalence all round, for example, disputes about what holidays or holy days the nation should celebrate. A police building in Budapest commemorates separately victims of Nazism and communism; and the decapitation of the Catholic Church in the course of its struggle with the communist dictatorship is also memorialized. However, the struggle between Church and State in Hungary was not quite like the struggle in Poland. The internal divisions just mentioned weakened the unity of Church and people as they did not in Poland. For the same reason the Church could not really make the strenuous but mistaken efforts of the Polish Church to resume the moral guardianship of the nation through collusion with the State. Even in Poland identification cannot be translated into obedience, and solidarity fragments with the end of polarization and oppression.

I am summarizing this well-known history partly because it offers an example of a more general European experience, and because it illustrates the variability of outcomes all the way from eastern ethno-religion (a term I borrow from Attila Molnar) to French laicity. Just these differences have recently emerged in debates on Christianity and the European Constitution.

With the end of the polarization created by communism, ethno-religion slackens and a space opens up for individual spirituality. Here a comparison with the USA is useful because the USA was created by a combination of individualism and pluralism, Enlightenment and religion, which made easy and necessary the separation of Church and State. In Hungary these factors did not cooperate but ran in opposed directions, and the decapitation of the Church by the state was an act of external force. Perhaps the Faith Church in Budapest approximates the American situation, with its combination of voluntary bonds, individualism and entrepreneurial activism. Like American influence generally, it both attracts and repels.

I now turn directly to individualized spirituality, and the way it separates religious solidarity from national solidarity, and the memory of the national past from the memory of the religious past. Those who wanted to avoid any reference to Christian roots in the international debate over the European Constitution were clearly anxious to uncouple the national past from the religious past, and represented countries where secular or multicultural influences (or both together) were powerful. In contrast, people in countries where ethno-religion was strong and multiculturalism weak were unhappy about this. Hungarians do not forget the battle of Mohács in 1526 or the expulsion of the Turks from Budapest in 1686, the Irish (whether Catholic or Protestant) do not forget the battle of the Boyne in 1690, the Greeks still lament the loss of Constantinople in 1453 and their expulsion from Turkey in the 1920s. These are historic markers and traumatic events which unite national and religious identity over centuries. They also show that too much memory has its problems as well as too little.

England provides an example of the advanced separation of religious identity from national identity, even though its wars with France and Spain were between a Protestant nation and Catholic opponents. There was no trauma of defeat and occupation, and Admiral Nelson and the Duke of Wellington do not figure as religious heroes, which is just as well given their lifestyles. The same is true for much of Western Europe, even allowing for El Cid and Joan of Arc. Indeed, there is a serious loss of memory in Western Europe, in part created by an alliance between teachers, the metropolitan intelligentsia and the secular media, as well as by the reality and the propaganda of multiculturalism, and the reduction of active Christians to a minority. What remains are the shared rituals provided by the largest of the historic churches in times of national mourning, such as the death of Princess Diana in Britain, or in Sweden the loss of the *Estonia*. Even as the words of faith have grown unfamiliar, its gestures seem to emerge naturally, many of them with a quasi-Catholic resonance. The ceremonies of massed candles and flowers can either be seen as a post-modern mix or the return of syncretic Catholic symbolism in contrast to Protestant wordiness.

Another shift in Western Europe concerns the new way in which the Church addresses the nation once no longer coextensive with nationality or integrated with secular élites and state power. Traditionally the Church saw itself as moral guardian of the nation, able to address state and nation from that vantage point. Christian morals provided the acknowledged reference point which people in practice selectively ignored. The Catholic Church well understood the difference between law and actual practice, and this understanding still defines a different attitude towards corruption between Northern Protestant Europe and Latin Europe. The Catholic Church wanted its rules acknowledged not followed, whereas Protestant Churches unrealistically linked theory and practice together. So they were more ready to give up the role of moral guardian once it was obviously just a façade. In any case, they couldn't propose the Blessed Virgin as patroness of the nation, or erect statues and crosses overlooking capital cities. St George doesn't overlook London as St Gellért overlooks Budapest, or Christ Rio de Janeiro, or the three crosses Vilnius. Protestantism lacks visible eminences, including cardinals, to objectify its guardianship. It is the disadvantage you suffer if you embrace the invisible Church in the heart rather than the hierarchy. Being invisible does not help when the media want to take pictures.

However, the invisible Church in the heart has now taken root far beyond the historic borders of Protestantism, and has mutated into the authenticity promoted by contemporary spirituality. In Western Europe the voice of the Church has become the voice of a voluntary pressure group using its remaining vantage points to address the nation. It speaks for human and humane values and stresses the intrinsic rather than the instrumental and the utilitarian. The incarnation of the human face is, after all, its *raison d'être* once no longer guarantor of state legitimacy and moral conformity. The State now represents a contrast to the Church, because it is subject to pressures, abstract forces and the logic of *realpolitik*. The social characters of Church and State have become strikingly different; though that difference is greater in Western Europe than in much of Eastern Europe; and, of course, the Vatican itself is a major geopolitical player, fully conscious of the dynamics of international and national politics. The Catholic Church or, for that matter, the other Churches, cannot be entirely indifferent when it comes to the politics of institutional survival, so as voluntary pressure groups the Churches speak in the public square both from the perspective of values and of interests, including material interests that bear on their spiritual tasks. I mean such material interests in education, welfare and prosperity as bear simultaneously on their role as philanthropic institutions and on their capacity to reproduce themselves and socialize the next generation.

Here I have to stress a three-sided relationship between the increasingly distinct social characters of Church and State, consequent on the process of structural differentiation, and the social or asocial character of an individualized spirituality, not to mention sheer apathy. Since the 1960s there has emerged a major fault line in the sphere of social and moral consciousness, based on the symbiotic relation between psychic liberation in the cultural sphere and liberalism in the economic sphere. They may appear different and opposed, but they also cooperate, especially in the commercial media. Individual rights, above all automatic rights to happiness, increasingly take precedence over communal, neighbourly and national duties. People demand more respect than they give, especially with regard to the law. Moral rules are decreasingly based on duty, sacrifice and long-term commitment, and more on a short-term hedonistic calculus indifferent to costs. This affects religious, political and national mobilization alike, and politicians are as worried about indifference to democratic duties as priests are worried about indifference to religious ones. This has its good side in that people demand more care be taken of their environment and are reluctant to be mobilized for sacrifice in dubious causes or, in the case of women, to bear all the responsibilities of familial and social cohesion. But in so far as respect and obligation give way to cultures of victimage, complaint and litigation, there is a problem for both State and Church. The situation is paradoxical because contemporary inwardness is partly a mutation of the Christian (above all the Protestant) stress on direct experience, sincerity and authenticity at the expense of external acts and public ritual. Again, antinomian attitudes to rules were originally related to a Protestant reliance on faith alone rather than works, because sinful creatures could not hope to meet the demands of the Creator. So you might expect contemporary individualism and antinomian attitudes towards rules to assist the Protestant cause. Not so, however, because in practice Protestantism rapidly reinforced the tie between religious works and work, discipleship and discipline, striving and reward. All the Protestant virtues are now condemned as vices, because striving to fulfil a rule is proof positive of inauthenticity, whereas the dissenter and the victim are always in the right. That in itself is yet another mutation of Christianity.

Victims and dissenters are full of moral passion about pollution and other good causes, but these issues concern the responsibilities of *others*, not their own. Moreover, the costs of alternatives are not adequately canvassed because prosperity has deprived the idea of cost of its bite. These developments should not be construed in classical terms as rationalization or the retreat of faith before science. It is rather the loss of *telos* and historical purpose, understood either as progress or providence, in favour of magical thinking, conjuring, an ancient fatalism shuffling off responsibility to circumstances or genes, and the giving up of natural law in favour of the rotations, rhythms and impulses of nature. Both the State and the Church as ethical communities find themselves in difficulty given that no sense of communal or personal obligation can be conjured from the contemplation of nature, whatever some Romantic poets may say. Indeed, our current condition is simply the Romanticism of earlier élites transferred to the population at large through the revolutions in consumption and the alliance of the teaching and welfare professions with sections of metropolitan intelligentsia. It is the ideology of Dahrendorf's 'knowledge class'.

Let me put it this way. The sense of obligation, membership one of another, and of sacrifice and self-discipline, built on to religious understandings, has slackened enough in Western Europe for the functional requirements of civility to be under threat. As a result the State either seeks to help faith communities regarded as threatened sources of social capital, or attempts to resocialize people in respect, obligation and responsibility through education in citizenship. The State has even cast a more friendly eye on religious schools as sources of intellectual and social capital.

Catholics as well as Protestants are affected by the partial uncoupling of guilt and reparation from salvation. That unhinges the practice of confession, and devalues the Church's treasury of grace. The implications for authority, both in Church and State, are clear enough, because authority is a functional necessity of any viable organization, but lacks plausible justification. The pope may act like an authority but in practice he is a totem. It is not that the motifs of guilt, reparation and redemption have disappeared, because in film and literature they have a myriad analogues, but they float free of their historic institutional channels.

I am discussing the situation of Catholicism and Protestantism, the two historic faiths of Hungary, each with rival claims on the national myth, and I am comparing them with regard to the partial separation of faith from nation and State, from the people and authority. This frees the Catholic Church to be centralized and visible above the nation-state and a harbinger of internationalism. It frees Protestantism to be decentralized and invisible below the level of the nation, and so realize its latent capacity for voluntarism. Inevitably that loosens religious monopoly (or duopoly) and the religious tie is further weakened by the fragmented spirituality or apathy I have just described.

The relation of Protestantism to voluntarism introduces my final theme, which is the way voluntarism as pioneered in Holland, Britain, and realized in North America, relates to the distinction between Church and State, God and Caesar. Historically this distinction has bolstered Catholic claims to be above the state, but the more profound implications have to do with the creation of autonomous space for the individual conscience and for voluntary institutions between the individual and the State. It is here that we gain some insight into the special, perhaps unique, character of secularization in 'old Christendom' and 'old Europe', by way of contrast both with the USA and contemporary Islam.

In the case of the USA, the federal, decentralized nature of the country, its variety of peoples and faiths, its origins in Protestantism, including the voluntary form of Protestant dissent, and the separation of Church and State, have meant that religious socialization has been a central element in socialization *as such quite apart* from the education system. The USA rests on subcultures which make up its *raison d'être* rather than offering a threat to centralized religious and social power. Religion adapts to its varied constituencies and includes an overall religion of America itself, under the joint aegis of enlightened progress and providential faith.

By specifying these foundations of American religiosity, I specify what is absent in Europe, which has had a system of centralized social and religious power in necessary conjunction with religious monopolies. With the fragmentation of spirituality, and the emergence of subcultures for which religion as such can be seen as associated with class, hierarchy and preponderant power, the old system slowly collapses. The exceptions are to be found where external oppression has fostered the union of faith and nation as in Ireland and Poland, but even in those countries the strains caused by any association of the Church with power and moral conformity are evident.

It takes time for the Church to move from a situation where it occupies an eminence from which it addresses the nation as acknowledged spiritual and moral guardian, to one where there is no single spiritual or moral reference point, and where the Church is one voice among a number of voluntary pressure groups. Indeed, though the media take advantage of the visibility of the hierarchy to talk of *the* voice of the Church, in fact there are many different Christian voices. The voice of the Church on disputed moral matters in the end exemplifies the logic of Protestantism, since there are many voices each informed by faith and reason in different ways. That really is the end of religious monopoly, either in society or within the Church itself.

The situation of old Christendom is also thrown into high relief by the comparison with Islam, which is the polar opposite to the USA, especially when we consider the raised profile of religion brought about by Muslim migration into Europe. Though Islam is split into numerous subgroups, it is by nature organic, advancing education, law and religion as an indissoluble unity. In Europe and North America, Muslims seek to use the logic of multiculturalism to create a miniature version of just the opposite. One can assume the tenets of liberals will be stretched to the limit should they attempt to respect the autonomy of subcultures at the same time as they respect the autonomy of law and education, and the rights of women and homosexuals. Liberalism claims to be the universal language into which all other claims have to be translated, and since the universal Church has largely granted that claim, that has worked reasonably well. The challenge of Islam, however, is precisely to this translatability and the terms of the debate, and if it had a centralized magisterium we might anticipate another Syllabus of Errors very soon.

Contemporary Islam in Europe, as well as in Islamia generally, represents the most militant version of what Charles Taylor calls a neo-Durkheimian religiosity.[1]

That is contrasted with what he calls a palaeo-Durkheimian religiosity represented by the union of monarch, people and faith, such as was set up in Hungary a millennium ago. Greece provides an example of a neo-Durkheimian country, given that Church and nation define themselves as coextensive. In Greece the socialization of the next generation includes induction into the national religious inheritance of the Orthodox Church regarded since independence as pre-eminent guardian of the national myth. It is significant that a similar situation exists in Turkey, where the army acts like the Church in Greece. The army guards the national myth of laicity as established by Ataturk in his revolutionary programme of modernization after defeat in World War I.

That reminds us that the neo-Durkheimian mode of solidarity does not have to be religious, and that in countries like France, Turkey and the Czech Republic the guardians of the national myth are lay and secular. The overarching myth of progress and providence built into the shared religion of America, as distinct from the varied forms of American religion, provides an example of the modern version of Durkheim in a Protestant context where individualism and spiritual fragmentation are otherwise far advanced.

That means that in contemporary Europe the fragmentation of spiritualities proceeds alongside situations varying from the kind of union of people and faith found in Greece, Romania, Serbia and Poland to the devotion to laicity found in Belgium, France, Turkey and the Czech Republic. There are also intermediate cases, such as Scandinavia, where Church and Social Democracy together provide one single sacred canopy. In Hungary there are rival claims on the national myth, with perhaps the Catholic Church claiming the largest single segment of the sacred canopy.

Clearly, there will be a variety of constitutional arrangements between Church and State corresponding to these varied situations and histories, within the limiting liberal premiss mandating freedom of choice. Perhaps the main exception here is Greece since Church and state argue – and collude – about a quasi-homogeneity resistant to liberal pressure.

In any case, the social differentiations associated with modernity reduce the social coverage of the Church, though education is always likely to be a contested sphere with respect to issues such as the equality of citizens, and social cohesion, especially when the Church can throw its political weight about, as in Greece. Elsewhere the Church deals with a specific sector of humane concerns. It develops niche markets for those attracted to its spiritual provision, and contributes to public debate as a voluntary pressure group without overt political affiliations.

From time to time, I have pointed to mutations of Christianity rather than repudiations. My final example may serve to show how a mutation of Christianity based on an attempt to raise the level of commitment may result in the secularization of the average sensual man. The secularization of the average sensual woman is rather different, since it comes about through a change in the balance of advantages, given that until recently women paid the costs of patriarchy in return for security and stability.

With the ending of the Constantinian establishment, and as a further contribution to its dismantlement, Christians have raised the bar about what it means to be a Christian, and so inhibited the take-up. Even the Catholic Church has reduced the distance between average attainment and what Weber called virtuoso performance, and so helped reduce the apathetic middle to a secular condition. Evangelicals, who are currently growing, increase secularity by their stress on genuine experience and change of life, whereas Catholics, especially since Vatican 2, stress devotion and commitment to the Eucharist. So the more devout Christianity you have the more difficult any attempt at any general re-Christianization of society becomes. In its self-understanding Christianity returns to what it originally aspired to be: the leaven in the lump, the salt that has not lost its savour.

Note

1   Charles Taylor, *Varieties of Religion Today, William James Revisited*, Cambridge, MA: Harvard University Press, 2002.

PART III
NARRATIVES AND
METANARRATIVES

CHAPTER 9

Secularization: Master Narrative or Several Stories?

I need to begin with comments on what is known as 'the standard model' of secularization, because however battered by four decades of critical pressure, it still holds the field. And that is because it is not straightforwardly untrue. In any case whatever sophisticated reservations are entertained by sociologists of religion, in the world at large secularization, in more or less simple guise, is implicitly assumed. However, once 'the standard model' has been briefly handled I revert to my usual tactic, which is to turn the 'hermeneutic of suspicion' against the taken-for-granted. I point to the number of possible stories about secularization, allude to the infiltration of ideological, philosophical and theological influences, and draw out the paradoxes and ambiguities deflecting or blurring the trajectory of secular advance.

Since secularization stories are so numerous, even if they intersect and overlap, I select just three of major importance which bear on what many, and José Casanova in particular, regard as the most workable form of secularization theory: social differentiation, meaning by that the increasing autonomy of the various spheres of human activity.[1] Once welfare and education (let's say) were under ecclesiastical aegis and the governing modality of thought was theological. Now welfare and education are independent spheres and theology has become a delimited sphere of our thinking. That was the approach adopted in my own *A General Theory of Secularization*.[2] It goes back to Talcott Parsons and I now extend it to the spheres of nature, of nation and of religion itself in the form of evangelicalism.

However, when I was setting out that 'General Theory' and trying to integrate empirical trends in belief and practice with the increasing autonomy associated with social differentiation, I found it very difficult to absorb approaches to secularization based on the history of ideas. I could do little more than indicate how different historical patterns of secularization, Anglo-American, Latin or whatever, cast national intelligentsias in very different roles with respect to religion.

At the same time the history of ideas is important and has been very broadly based on the notion of the avant-garde, whereby what the intellectual élite propose today the mass will accept tomorrow. That means it has organized history to pick up successive and crucial advances on the intellectual front line, such as the advocacy of a separate sphere of civil government by William of Ockham or Marsilius of Padua, or the secular consequences of Puritanism, or the moment in the mid-nineteenth century when the cooperation of religion and science collapsed in a phase of hostility.

It is perhaps this kind of history which serves to lodge simple secularization stories in educated minds, and my treatment of nature, nation and evangelicalism seeks at least to make matters more ambiguous and complicated. My linking thread still remains the increasing autonomy of spheres, so that what was united in social organization and thought has broken up into semi-independent realms. The coping stone has come down.

The Standard Model

What then of the standard model? You find it laid out with maxium simplification in the kind of sociology textbook chapter briefly dealing with religion and perhaps mostly given over to ethnic minorities. The focus is on empirical trends in belief and practice, and these are handled with what I once called a handy historical tripod, one leg in the high-Victorian period, another in the high Middle Ages, from which to measure the advance of secularity. The governing frame is modernization, based either on the contrast between medieval society and today, or on downward trends since the time of high Victorianism. At this point I pause only to recollect that the year 1870 in both England and France can be regarded as the peak of re-Christianization after the inroads made over the eighteenth century. However that may be, at some point or other, variously determined between 1880 and 1960, trends start to turn decisively down, though there are temporary plateaux and some upturns on particular criteria.[3] What had been massive practice, even quasi-uniformity in some regions, supported by social sanctions, becomes the purely optional leisure activity of a decreasing minority. Western Europe becomes the most secular place on the globe.

Inevitably there are debates about what these trends mean and their relation to other relevant trends, by such well-known scholars as Grace Davie, Steve Bruce, Rodney Stark, Robert Wuthnow, Peter Berger, Callum Brown, Hugh McLeod, Wade Clark Roof and Robin Gill. Whereas Rodney Stark has argued for persistent renewals of religious activity, especially where there is competition rather than monopoly, Steve Bruce has argued for steady irreversible decline.[4] Whereas Grace Davie has suggested religious decline is part of downward trends in voluntary association as such, Steve Bruce argues the loss of appeal affects religion quite specifically.[5]

There are two wider issues, the first of which has to do with what has been identified as 'European exceptionalism': is secularization in Europe due to factors not present elsewhere? The second concerns the impact on participation both of the Victorian domestication and feminization of Christianity and of the changes in women's roles, more particularly since the mid-twentieth century. Peter Berger, David Martin, and Grace Davie in her *Europe: the Exceptional Case* (2002) have argued that secularization in Europe has been exceptional due to factors not necessarily present elsewhere, for example the USA, while for others, Steve Bruce included, the problem is rather 'American Exceptionalism'.[6] Both Grace Davie and Linda Woodhead have examined the question of female participation, which has been for a long time considerably greater than male participation, and Callum Brown, in his *The Death of Christian Britain*, has dramatized what a changing female role has meant in terms of the overall decline of the churches since the 1960s.[7]

Those who believe Europe is exceptional and those who believe it is the test-bed for a secular future watch the USA with care. In the USA participation increased during the nineteenth century and up to the mid-twentieth, and though there has been a levelling off and downward slopes visible in younger age groups, both participation and belief are greatly in excess of what one finds in Europe. There are important debates about Robert Putnam's thesis as to the relation between religious decline and a more general decline in social capital, for which Nancy Ammerman's documentation of the continued vitality of American religious groups is a major marker, as well as some continuing debate about the theses of Thomas Luckmann and Will Herberg concerning the internal secularization of religion in the USA.[8] Harold Bloom, in his idiosyncratic, *The American Religion*, suggests that we are now dealing with post-Christian and gnostic spirituality.[9] Few doubt that popular religion in America, as everywhere and always, has a somewhat 'flakey' character. After all, it is just as 'flakey' in contemporary Italy or Brazil.

These, then, are just some of the issues, and I want now to illustrate the contrast between explicit sociological theories based on fundamental processes and crucial transitions associated with modernization, and the kind of implicit assumptions which I suggest undergird cultural history. I choose Scandinavia to bring out the approach of cultural history, partly because it has long been a prime exhibit (with France) in the straight case for secularization, and partly because a recent book on Scandinavia, *The Soul of the North* by Neil Kent,[10] touches on my three secularization stories about nature, the nation and evangelicalism (or Pietism).

It is not generally realized that much of Northern Europe, and even more so North-eastern Europe, was not Christianized until well after the millennium. However, once established, often by warfare and the monarch's decision, the Roman Catholic Church became a pivot of ideological, economic and political power. As a result the Reformation was not only motivated by spiritual protest but (in Sweden at least) by aristocratic and monarchical desire to strip ecclesiastical assets. As Lutheranism supplanted Catholicism, the Church retained its monopoly and its obligatory character until the rise of a more individual, experiential and (to some extent) voluntary piety. Evangelical Pietism based on feeling overlapped both the rise of Romanticism, with its reverence for nature, and the rise of nationalism, with its cult of national symbols, the language and a semi-mythic history. In Denmark, for example, there was a cult of the nation both in a religious form, as promoted by Grundvig, *and* also quite independently. The nation, like nature, had become an independent object of worship, even though religion *might* still include both nation and nature.

The crucial underlying contrast Neil Kent draws is between the Middle Ages and today. Once the Church was pre-eminent, and the main source of legitimation, whereas the Lutheran Church of today, while retaining the passive adherence of an apathetic majority, is now a voluntary organization appealing to people of a charitable and liberal disposition. Even the revivalism of the nineteenth century tended to peter out in the twentieth. Adding a further gloss, one might say Scandinavia has moved from a communal and binding faith to an individual and optional spirituality.

How does this compare with a sociological approach based on fundamental processes and crucial transitions? The umbrella term is the process of modernization, under which head are a group of cognate terms such as rationalization, bureaucratization and disenchantment; urbanization and industrialization; individualization, privatization and liberalization. All these processual terms are adjuncts of secularization and together they frame the analysis of empirical trends in belief and practice.

There are also large-scale dramas of fundamental transition, specifying *the* great transition (or transitions) cutting us moderns off from the past. Such dramas of discontinuity may be based on one stage, as for example in Ernest Gellner's *Thought and Change*,[11] or on two stages, as in a recent book by John Gray entitled *Straw Dogs*.[12] Ernest Gellner not only posited a great gulf fixed between all previous modalities and modern ones (nationalism included), but specified the different elements. In a discussion of French eighteenth-century materialism he pointed to various shifts initiated by the Enlightenment, such as the rejection of 'supernatural' or spiritual explanations of phenomena in favour of the structure and activity of matter; determinism and relativism; empiricism in epistemology; hedonism and/or egoism in psychology; belief in reason as the arbiter of existence; utilitarianism in ethics; utilitarianism and/or democracy in politics; pragmatism in the theory of truth; and a belief in the power of education to improve the human condition. Gellner also suggested that what was once the duality of nature and supernature had become the duality of subject and object.[13]

I cite John Gray in his *Straw Dogs* because he offers a two-stage transition, and because it contains somewhat different elements, though his position and Gellner's need not be contradictory. The first stage is represented by the secular humanism still widely represented in the educated classes, but that, in Gray's view, is only so much theology in disguise. Belief in progress is millennial expectation transmuted, while the unique status of man is a version of the *imago dei*. It is time now finally to jettison these theological residues and to enter a stage of realism, facing the reality of our true status as animals who are not going anywhere. That, it would seem to me, implies a post-modernist understanding of the petering out of all master narratives. Parenthetically, Charles Taylor gives a very different account of the humanist dependence on an unacknowledged Christian ontology in his seminal *The Sources of the Self*.[14]

The point is that master narratives *should* peter out, and it is worth noticing just how often philosophical accounts include a prescriptive as well as a descriptive element. That is particularly obvious in the case of secular theologies, where prescription virtually overrides description. In Harvey Cox, Christianity provides a long prologue to the advent of the secular city while in Don Cupitt a linguistic analysis of contemporary expressions purports to reveal Christian notions emptied out into mundane reality. The 'sea of faith', itself one of those dramatizing master metaphors, is not so much at very low tide as resurgent and once again 'at the full' in the resonant way we talk about everyday experience. Unlike George Herbert, who saw another world 'as through a glass', we have a single eye for a single reality.

So, then, we have grand schemes, multitudes of them in fact, including the post-modern scheme to end all schemes. However, not only are the various scenarios apt to combine philosophies with expectations, but inherently related to theories of religion and what it is 'essentially' about. It is not that such linkages undermine an argument *per se* but we are certainly dealing with organizing frames which – as is usually the case – leap beyond what can be inferred from observation. As to master metaphors such as the ebbing sea of faith, the most pervasive of them contrasts faith in the childhood of humanity with secular reality in its maturity.

Two organizing frames of increasing contemporary importance are evolutionary psychology (or cognitive science) and 'rational choice' theory. The expositions I select are Pascal Boyer in his *Explaining Religion*[15] and – of course – Rodney Stark and his associates in *Acts of Faith*.[16] The model for the first is sociobiology, and for the second economics, and it is interesting how trenchantly both deal with earlier theories of religion. Evolutionary psychology is, of course, notorious for reductionism, and especially for reducing other subjects to its own level of understanding.

Rodney Stark in his *Acts of Faith* (written with Roger Finke) argues that religion arises from perfectly reasonable calculations (allowing for the level of knowledge) with respect to what is incalculable and intrinsic to the human condition. There is, therefore, a built-in limit to secularization, though religious vitality is more likely to manifest itself where there is competitive pluralism rather than established monopolies. Pascal Boyer, in contrast, sees no evidence of 'rational choice' because concepts fostering religious notions are delivered from the mental basement where they were laid down long ago under the exigencies of survival and selection. An example of such a concept would be the attribution of agency to spiritual entities. Only members of intellectual élites can expect to escape their power, and so once again there is a limit to secularization. Clearly in both cases the theory of secularization complements the theory of religion. Reductionism has no necessary connection with confident predictions about a secular future.

In summary, then, we have here two powerful illustrations of what I have been suggesting so far. The frames which govern our understanding of secularization are the frames which govern our understanding of religion. They reflect contemporary world-views, including concepts of human nature. In the two cases just cited the world-views are choices on a competitive market and the unconscious structure of our animal nature. Both go beyond mere observation and both are comprehensive in that they exclude each other and a very wide swathe of previous theorizing, all of it equally confident and comprehensive. So let us just for the moment bracket the question of validity to say with modesty and simplicity that there is enough circumstantial evidence for a hermeneutic of suspicion.

Differentiation: Autonomous Nature

Here I extend an approach based on increasing differentiation to the increasing autonomy of nature, before looking at the autonomy of the nation, and at evangelicalism as that kind of religion which *in principle* represents increasing autonomy with respect to nature and nation. As will be illustrated in each case, there is a dialectic of secularization and sanctification, so that the sanctification of nature, or of nation, or of religion in evangelical form, while it becomes a matter of *choice* rather than necessity, increases in emotional potency. All three can be recombined, and very often are, but a break has been made which cannot be unmade. Thus, to take the example of nation, the separation of Church and State, and the separation of communities of faith from the processes of secular government, is unlikely to be reversed. To that extent secularization theory is endorsed.

Historically, attitudes toward nature have been grounded in imaginative visions of the world. That argument is eloquently advanced and illustrated in Mary Midgeley's *Science and Poetry*,[17] but there are many earlier versions of it, such as Burtt's exploration of the metaphysical foundations of modern science, or the quite contradictory views of Robert Merton and Lewis Feuer on the role respectively of ascetic Protestantism and hedonism in fostering the investigation of nature. Mary Hesse has stressed the role of metaphor in theories of nature (and society); and a revisionist historiography of science has challenged notions of a cumulative displacement of religion by science, and documented periods of cooperation between religion and science, as well as phases of conflict dramatized and sometimes misrepresented by secular ideologists. The well-known struggles in the late nineteenth century were about professional power as well as truth, and varied greatly in length and vigour according to social, religious and national context.

The emerging autonomy of nature includes both a disenchantment rejecting the operation of occult forces and a rational religiosity complemented by a rational atheism. Perhaps one should pause at this point to distinguish this rational atheism from the practical atheism of (say) Samuel Pepys or William Petty. A rational religiosity has now become an *option*, and if one adopts the terms used by Roy Porter, it was based on an admiration for order, unity and intricate mechanism.[18] Perhaps one sees its spatial manifestations in the geometrical organization of city and garden. God himself is Divine Architect and Great Mathematician, and from Newton and Priestley to James Jeans and Paul Davies admiration for the mind of God revealed in nature has constituted a continuing genealogy of rational religion.

Just how dangerous that could be when deployed out of context is clear from Newton's attempt to understand and organize the Bible along similar lines. Such a religion requires little or nothing by way of institutional or clerical mediation, and is likely to view miracle as arbitrary interference with law. But it is not merely a transitional phase en route to atheism, such as secularization theory might lead one to suppose. Fundamental kinds of faith exist in their own right, not as interim modes. Moreover, evangelical Christianity itself, whatever its stress on redemption rather than natural theology – Wesley, say, rather than Watts and Cowper – often propagated common-sense views in the philosophical meaning of the term. It admired the rational goodness of creation, and was reinforced in that by the Hebrew Scriptures and the Wisdom tradition. Evangelical scientists, including a great if tragic figure like Philip Gosse, traced the intricacy of nature up to, and back to, nature's God.

The alternative genealogy, rigorously articulated by D'Holbach, does not *need* the hypothesis of a divine originator or sustainer. As a *hypothesis* God is otiose, especially if the order of nature is reduced to an atomized and closed collocation of components. Again, one has to stress that the social distribution of scientific atheism is related to a national, cultural and religious context and to cultural struggles over the governing definition of 'the real', so that English responses tended to be less thoroughgoing than was the case in France.

The opposition to a mechanized, disenchanted world came from various sources, such as Blake and Swedenborg, but above all from the holistic re-enchantment of nature sought by Romanticism, which stressed reverence, awe and participation, rather than 'measurement and line'. As in rational religiosity, so in Romantic religiosity one might *choose* either a theistic or an atheistic response, and Christianity and Church and religion were not even residually coextensive. I mean that for Keats an intense response to nature stood in sharp contrast to the dispirited condition of the Established Church. Some poets such as Wordsworth might adopt a panentheistic philosophy, or like Shelley turn to Neoplatonism, but Richard Jefferies could celebrate a purely naturalistic ecstasy. One has only to compare Goethe with Blake and Swedenborg to see how variously a personal gnosis could treat the Christian repertoire.

When Keats writes about the sea as employed in its 'priest-like task of pure ablution round earth's human shores' or Wordsworth of a mountain pass in the Trossachs as 'an apt Confessional', one sees how metaphors have been taken from ecclesiastical ritual into the open air, and how Catholic ceremonial and imagery provide a richer resource than the radically reduced rites and imagery of Protestantism. It is as if Catholicism has undergone a translation outside the frame of institution and creed to serve and feed a personal religious apprehension.

Wordsworth is especially interesting because he created a mode of personal faith which (eventually) reintegrated nature, nation and even Church in a manner still quite influential. He united a nature mysticism celebrating moral impulses 'from a vernal wood' with a biblical sense of awe in the high and holy place, as well as with an evocation of the sacred edifice set in the particular landscape of England. The same evocation is present in Constable, while in the later Gainsborough one sees a further linkage between evangelicalism and Romantic 'sensibility' about place which includes the poor who inhabit the place. Gainsborough himself was a Methodist, but what we see germinating here are divergent as well as intersecting streams of personal piety, including an autonomous invocation of nature entirely outside the confines of creed or institution.[19] These potent intersections and major divergences have been immensely influential and are a part of our religious repertoire utterly opaque to the interview schedule or questionnaire.

Something of the impact of cultural context can be gained by comparing how the differing elements combine and diverge in different national contexts. In Germany a devout Christian such as Caspar David Friedrich represents a rich strand of connection in his representation of the soulful Romantic standing in the high and solitary place or set against a background of evocative landscape and Gothic sacred edifice. Here we see one major source of a whole genre of country and mountain mysticism. In Germany, as in Scandinavia and Britain, the evocation of nature, of country – in the widest sense – and of sacred edifice has been potent, and probably remains so. In the USA the paintings of 'The American Sublime' suggest an interesting mutation in that the strong religious connotations, for example in Frederic Church, turn on Bible and Creation rather than on Church.

The 'history of religions' movement, as recently explored by Hans Kippenberg, could offer further illustration of how the themes of the religious repertoire were variously inflected in Britain, Germany and France.[20] But crucial to the whole movement in Kippenberg's view is a *religious* frustration with an over-intellectualized and chronically moralistic Christianity, all the way from the wistfulness about a lost pagan world expressed in 'Schöne Welt, wo bist du?' to the recovery of myth and ritual. That this lay more in a Catholic ambience than a Protestant one is obvious, and its reworkings in symbolist painting make this abundantly clear.

In these reworkings elements from the Christian repertoire might reappear as universal types, including the outsider and the victim cast against seascape and landscape, as in Crabbe and Melville. Landscapes and seascapes contain significant figures. Analogues of ancient dualisms might also reappear in a revived sense of the hostile, ferocious and recalcitrant character of the natural environment. Today we are still inheritors of all these shifts of repertoire and register. We have, for example, to ask ourselves just how far language about the 'rape' of the natural environment or about the intrusion of evil into the innocent paradise of Bali is extravagant metaphor or massive echo of a Christian repertoire.

Differentiation: Nation as Autonomous Icon

Nationalism as conceived by some, for example, by Ernest Gellner,[21] is part of the project of modernization, specifically, in the view of Anthony Smith,[22] related to the aspirations of intellectuals who present themselves as an avant-garde awakening the true spirit of the nation. It is here that one sees how the reconstitution of the Holy Church as manifesting the authentic national *Geist* runs alongside reconstitutions of Christianity as a source of civilization or vanguard of progress. A national *Heilsgeschicte* is created with accompanying genealogies devised to provide legitimation, especially through invocations of antiquity, and in this one recognizes a simultaneous secularization and sanctification of both history and nation. Just as the Bible sets up genealogies reaching back to Adam or Abraham, and monarchies devise genealogies reaching back to the Bible and the figures of classical or local antiquity, so the nation invents its succession and mythic self-presentation. One of the attractions of Mormonism is to provide a third testament for the Americas and even to create a new nation for those who otherwise might feel they had missed out. If the Scottish kings made it up, why not the Mormons?

Just as, in relation to nature, there is a shift from admiration of mechanism to holistic participation, so in relation to the nation there is a shift from contractual notions of membership to concepts of a sacred and integral bond. The Catholic definition of heresy becomes a national definition of treachery, and the all-inclusive and automatic inheritance of baptism becomes an all-inclusive inheritance in the holy spirit of the nation and its sacred emblems. Whether the Church itself plays a role in the creation and sustaining of this spirit, or some more general invocation of Protestantism or Catholicism, or some reference back to 'pagan' pasts in Nordic, classical or native American myth, is a matter of national trajectories. Poland, as a Catholic nation under occupation, emerged as a suffering Messiah, whilst France as a revolutionary nation switched from eldest daughter of the Church to first standard-bearer of liberty, equality and fraternity. Britain and the USA deployed biblical ideas of the 'other Eden', of New Israel and New Jerusalem.

The USA as the first new nation and first unchallenged superpower traces genealogies designed to paint an icon of America as the abode of persecuted innocents who have turned the wilderness into a Promised Land of milk and honey, as well as successor to republican Rome. In the course of this idealized self-presentation God has been put on contract to deliver by ensuring victory in war, prosperity in peace and provisional immortality for every citizen. It is this postulate of New Israel or the *Novus Ordo Seclorum* which helps explain the language of fractured and violated innocence following the events of 11 September. That the attack was wicked and appalling is clear, but the blowing out of city centres has been a regular experience in Britain and Europe. More generally (and not in the context of 11 September), it is as if the biblical model of judgement as well as promise has in God's own country shifted decisively to promise.

Peace is one of the great biblical visions, and both the USA and Britain have felt that the peace and prosperity promised to Jerusalem have been partially or wholly extended to them, in a protected continent and a protected island respectively. In Europe, however, violation, destruction and intrusion have been so endemic up to the mid-twentieth century that the stark reality of political imperatives is frankly accepted, and the likelihood of an unhappy outcome fully canvassed. Innocence and virtue are less frequently claimed by continentals than they are by Anglo-Americans. Yet by a curious reversal, ever since Europe has been shielded by American power, Europe has begun to see itself as the abode of Immanuel Kant's 'perpetual peace' and the USA as still in a Hobbesian situation of inevitable war. Something approaching complacent innocence has begun to emerge in Europe with the slow recession of inveterate war though, of course, French *realpolitik* never wavers.

The literature on nationalism frequently distinguishes between a civic variety based on universal citizen rights and more organic varieties basic on the mythic spirit of the people (or even their biological constitution). Organic nationalism may combine ethnicity with religion (as in Greece where precisely that combination is now fiercely debated, or as in most of the countries of Eastern Europe and the Middle East). Civic nationalism is by definition more open to a multi-ethnic, multicultural mix, but even those countries exemplifying civic nationalism retain ethnic, cultural and maybe religious markers in reserve. These come out under pressure of mass migration, particularly when the migrants are at some cultural distance from the 'home' population, for example, Islamic migrants from North Africa attempting to stay in the countries of the northern Mediterranean, or Hispanic migrants crossing to the USA from Mexico.

There are many points on the spectrum from civic to organic nationalism of which England offers an example close to the civic and Spain and Ireland examples closer to the organic, at least until recently. England has historically understood itself as a Protestant and progressive nation apart from its Church, whereas imperial Spain and an oppressed Ireland centred their identity both in ethnicity and the Roman Church. Of course, civic nationalisms still invoke the spirit of the real nation while organic nationalisms shift towards notions of citizenship, law and education divorced from religion.

It is worth stressing the extent to which civic nationalism in practice requires assimilation to the national totems and ethos on the part of sub-communities bound by ethno-religious bonds. In Britain and the USA at the present time the official public doctrine of multiculturalism is proving difficult to sustain when challenged by quite different forms of ethno-religious solidarity and popular resistance to them by the majority population. The current tension focuses for obvious reasons on Islam, but a particularly interesting earlier example is provided by the Jewish community. When Jews were confined to a ghetto they retained their ethno-religious identity over against hostile pressure from the ethno-religiosity of the majority, for example in Poland and Russia. However, in enlightened nations like post-revolutionary France they were invited out of the ghetto on condition they accepted the universal criteria of citizenship. Several consequences followed. One was an embrace by many Jews of enlightened universalism based on humanity as such as a way to outflank Christian universalism. Jews, particularly Jewish intellectuals, became part of the advance guard of secularization, challenging the ethno-religious understanding of the majority behind the banner of a civic definition of national identity. A typical example would be the late nineteenth-century clash in Denmark between Brandes as a secular Jew of germanophile sympathies and cosmopolitan provenance, and those followers of Grundvig who viewed the Danish nation in terms of its authentic religious spirit.

Just as there is a variable admixture of the civic and the organic, so there is a variable balance between a national project framed in terms of a manifestation (or fount) of civilization and one framed as vanguard of progress. In the USA religion is closely aligned with a national project leaning towards the idea of progress, which has something to do with its vitality, whereas in Victorian Britain religion was aligned with a combination of civilization and progress, which may have something to do with its subsequent declining vitality given that both the Christian Churches and the nation lost confidence in civilization and progress after 1914. In France there emerged two nations, one Catholic, leaning towards the French role as the heart of civilization; the other secular and republican, relating French civilization to progress. Paris was the artistic capital of the world up to the mid-twentieth century, since when claims to progress and to civilization have been defensive rather than confident.

In short, in considering the state of religion one has to take into account how far it is or is not aligned with the national project, and how united or divided the nation is with respect to what lies at the heart of that project. One has to ask what are the consequences of French Catholics blaming secularists for the defeat by Germany in 1870, and of secularists blaming Islam (or at any rate the Caliphate and failure to westernize) for the defeat in 1918–19. Again, one has to enquire into the consequences for the Russian Orthodox Church of the collapse of the communist version of progress and of the national project in 1989. This is not an area in which one can propose straight correlations, because of the many factors involved and because both failure and success are capable of reinvigorating national aspirations. It is all much more complex than the relatively simple relationship discernible between suppressed nationhood in Ireland, Croatia, Slovakia, Lithuania and Poland, and the degree of religious vitality. That kind of relatively simple relationship may also be seen in the remobilization of Islam under pressure from the West, as well as in Hindu and Buddhist nationalism. Will it be Islamia *contra mundum*? The obvious question which follows in that context is whether this global rise in religious nationalism will follow the European sequence of rise followed by fall.

A final question to be asked is whether Catholicism, having felt the hostile pressure of movements for national independence, may not benefit from the contemporary slackening of national identity, if indeed that is actually happening. International Catholicism might find itself consonant with modern internationalism, while at the same time reconceiving itself as the largest voluntary denomination and making an implicit alliance with evangelicalism – the pioneer of voluntarism. That might lead progressive Catholics to link up with liberal Protestants over against conservative Catholics and evangelicals.

Seamus Heaney offers a comment relevant to the future role of Catholicism, more particularly with regard to Ireland now it has become a consumer nation on equal terms with others rather than a frugal republic. In *The Independent* for 31 October 2002, he says that

> some kind of metaphysic has disappeared from the common life. The inner ethic that came from this authoritarian Church, which gave so much of its character to Irish life – its puritanism, but also its sense of service and readiness to go on missions and so on … I think we are running on an unconscious that is informed by religious values, but I think my youngsters' youngsters won't have that. I think the needles are wobbling in that way.

Differentiation: The Autonomy of Religion Itself

The paradox of evangelicalism (in which Pentecostalism is included for present purposes) turns on the way it both embodies secularity and seeks a more thorough sanctification. Evangelicalism is the most expansive element in contemporary Protestantism and yet as it seeks this deeper appropriation of faith at the individual level it erodes the idea of a Christian society by dismissing the uncommitted majority as not Christian. Given that the democratic state increasingly reflects the comparative indifference of the majority, evangelicalism in principle abandons it, except in the USA, where it has devised a myth of a Christian Constitution about as ill founded as the opposing myth of militant secularists. That leads to forays into the 'naked public square' from which it retires frustrated and bruised, wondering why a 'moral majority' makes comparatively little effective impact. Whether the Bush presidency is altering that remains to be seen.

The 'ideal type' of evangelicalism has to be constructed in terms of the restriction of religion to a voluntary sector unable and unwilling to propose norms governing the autonomous sectors of law, business, politics and foreign policy. These sectors follow their own rules. Given the voluntary group has to survive in the religious market, everything except personal piety turns on instrumental and pragmatic criteria as to what works, including objective ritual and the location of the sacred. The public forum and public face of religion have been subjectivized *in foro interno*.

Of course, evangelicalism seeks to Christianize society, as it attempted to do in the late nineteenth century in Britain and America; and as a moral interest group it seeks to influence law and public policy to favour its agenda. It may even, in certain circumstances, revert to notions of theocracy or embrace neo-Calvinist ideas of a comprehensive Christian understanding of culture. But in logic and in practice it jettisons birthright membership in the community or neighbourhood for a second birth within the voluntary religious group, and reduces comprehensive political concern to a limited moral agenda. If politics is somehow to be redeemable, that depends on the personal virtues of those in public life, not on some overall social vision.

None of this is invalidated by an evangelical ambition to Christianize a whole country, such as Simon Green outlines in his study of part of northern England between 1870 and 1920 entitled *Religion in the Age of Decline*.[23] In fact it is in part the over-extension involved in such an ambition that is a factor in decline. Evangelicalism as a faith based on choice and mobility stands in contrast with socially comprehensive faiths based on birthright membership and territorial location, and it is part of the process whereby parishes cease to be foci of local community. Territorial parishes retain some relevance, of course, because even voluntary groups are based on proximity, and there are elements of local belonging even in the most mobile sectors of society. There have to be places for communal mourning and celebration, as for example assemblages at Trinity Episcopal Church and St Patrick's Cathedral in New York after 11 September and parallel assemblages at St Paul's, London. There is, therefore, a continuing dialectic between the principle of mobility and second birth and the principle of settlement and generational transmission. One correlate of mobility plus generational transmission is the increase in faith-based rather than community schools. Where school, community and peer groups subvert rather than support learning, discipline and virtue the remedy is obvious.

Evangelicalism can also be understood as part of a long-term process of individualization and interiority rooted in Christianity itself, and in Judaism for that matter, with varying expressions in Augustine, Cistercian spirituality, the Reformation and pietism. Here lies part of the rationale of its relative indifference to objective ritual, sacred objects, liturgical language, credal formulas and the mediations of clerical hierarchy. All such elements, while retaining a place as part of necessary structures of ecclesiastical and social order, are undermined by heartwork and by the pragmatism about forms that so easily goes with it. Such pragmatism opens the way for a persistent adjustment to new conditions, which actually means that evangelicalism can be trapped and immobilized by the culture into which it initially enters as an agent of change. Though the evangelical spirit restricts the individualistic motif somewhat in order to sustain solidarity and mutuality, all the same the emphasis on inwardness and the good feelings consequent on faith leads to persistent adjustments to cultural demand such as one sees in the churches of the 'New Reformation' like the Calvary Chapel: transparency, secular-looking facilities, minimal clerical mediation.[24] In the case of evangelicalism, one possible adjustment is a therapeutic view of religion consonant with wider therapeutic culture, or a consumerism based on catering for post-modern eclectic preference with a vaguely Christian ambience and vocabulary. Whether such consumerism is new or just more explicit than before is a moot point, but it is interesting that in a theologian like Don Cupitt consumerism is actually validated. However, in Britain the likely consequence has been a refusal to 'consume' institutional Christianity based on a culture (particularly among young males) of inarticulate interiority, or else the spectacle of ex-evangelical denominations operating as declining clubs for religiose entertainment.

In this sphere of entertainment the prime tactic of evangelicalism, at least initially, is to bring all aspects of Christian living under supervision of a sanctified spirit. It provides leisure facilities like the YMCA or Seamen's Missions or Temperance hotels or sports venues or Christian television to show how the spirit can animate all aspects of leisure. But in entering the consumer market it is bound to be in competition with secular rivals to provide a rather similar product. In the USA, where evangelicalism is more pervasive, it may have the resources to compete, at least in the provision of an acceptable ensemble of services in the context of mutual solidarity; in Britain it does not, and the Salvation Army (for example) formed originally to sanctify 'the world' becomes internally secularized and without sufficient religious distinctiveness. Society proves yet more individual, mobile and competitive than evangelicalism. Here the contrast between Britain and the developing world is stark because throughout the continents of Africa and Latin America, and in parts of Asia, versions of Pentecostal and charismatic Christianity can provide comprehensive environments far more all-embracing than alternatives subject to the corrosions of a chaotic and secular world. Pentecostal and charismatic religion becomes the presenting edge and avant-garde of social and geographical mobility. It is in the lead rather than reacting to what is happening elsewhere. The inevitable question is for how long, or is this a phase on the way to the condition of developed society? Will that developed society be on the US or the European model?

So, the paradox of evangelicalism is a simultaneous claim over the whole of personal life accompanied by a diminution in range as the once-established national churches cease to provide religious cover for a whole community or to put forward regulatory social principles about usury or family or sexuality. In this, evangelicalism contrasts sharply with the churches descended from the Radical Reformation for whom the regulatory principles of the Gospel are at the heart of a social project, and who stress obedience to the requirements of the Kingdom come on earth rather than transactions in the individual soul. The paradox of simultaneous secularization and sanctification central to my argument is here truly dramatic, because one either extends a claim over the whole secular society, which is bound to fail, or one withdraws into a carefully bounded enclave. Moreover, this radicalism also swings between setting up the Kingdom by violence, taking God's providence into one's own hands, and pacific withdrawal. In religious terms the long-term consequence is a pacific and utopian communtarianism, leaking radical reforms into the wider society. However, in S.N. Eisenstadt's view, the long-term consequence of sectarianism is found in the tradition of apocalyptic revolutionary politics, and in the rule of the pure which in turn leads either to the dissipations of anarchy or to authoritarian corruption as the pure try to drive society through a forcible transition to a qualitatively better world.[25]

That, however, is a counterpoint to evangelicalism too large to pursue here because it raises the vast question of secular religions and ideologies reproducing the morphology of religious forms in immanent formats. More germane here is the problem for sociological hermeneutics posed by an evangelical attempt at sanctification which can mutate into internal secularization. Evangelicalism is persistently inventive, altering and renewing itself in capturing the world for Christ. It is, for example, simultaneously implicated in scaling religion down to family values and domesticity, with consequences in terms of the feminization of religion, and in seeking to create masculine versions of Christianity to compensate. Something similar is true of evangelical music, which is a major medium of conversion: the impulse to sanctify seeks to rob the devil of all the best tunes by almost giving up the religious register of the sacred to embrace whatever works and attracts. The result is that the higher reaches of the aesthetic remain the potent resource of older churches still retaining a sense of 'the sacred' and the register appropriate to it.[26]

The hermeneutic and methodological problem is clear enough. Given the background assumptions derived from the master narrative of secularization, does one treat new initiatives as creative restatements or as responses to secularization based on a compromise with 'the world' which is bound eventually to fall on bad times and evil days? When an interpretation based on compromise is adopted, the notion of 'traditional religion' is often called upon to provide a historical baseline, without a time and place being precisely specified or the content of traditional religion itself fleshed out. Nor does one enquire whether analogous if not identical compromises with 'the world' have not occurred many times before. Thus if a sociologist identifies a serious fragmentation in contemporary American religion, one does not ask just how far a similar situation existed in 1850 or in 1750. The possibility of a partial rotation in types of religious situation should at least be accorded the same right to consideration as a straight line (with intermittent wobbles) to a secular terminus.

That same query about baselines and the persistence over centuries of a 'secular practice' can be extended much more widely because so much standard historiography elides the underlying questions, preferring to proceed *ad hoc* and reaching for such crude organizing metaphors as come to hand. The lack of comparison between the type of pluralism found in classical antiquity and contemporary pluralism provides one illustration, but on a less extended timescale one might ask how one assesses the Catholic and evangelical revivals of the mid-nineteenth century against the antecedent baseline provided by the courts of the four Georges, and such figures as Lord Melbourne, Charles James Fox, the Duke of Wellington, Lord Nelson and Beau Brummel. Even with respect to the immediately pre-modern piety so eloquently evoked by Eamon Duffy and others, how does one assess what Joel Rosenthal called *The Purchase of Paradise*[27] in terms of consumerism? May not the consumerist attitude be rather more persistent compared with the well-publicized forms of clerical asceticism, just as *realpolitik* is a persistent feature of society before as well as after Machiavelli scandalized

'Christian' Europe? The modalities differ, but the structures of desire and power persist.

Some of the worst distortions derived from the master narrative of secularization occur in relation to Puritanism, supposing one still feels able to use that label with any confidence. In the sociological literature trailing in the wake of Weber's master work, we often do not bother to ask when 'Puritanism' existed, or how many people were involved and how it eventually turned from a conservative to a radical force. Instead we focus on a trail of consequences for science, democracy, individualization or capitalism under the joint head of secularization and modernity. Puritanism in its own right barely figures and yet it serves effectively to blot out vast and significant movements like the Counter-Reformation and enlightened absolutism. The trajectory of history moves forward on an erratic course determined and distorted by the problematic of modernity and what are identified as its potent anticipations. The French Revolution and the American duly appear, but all other enlightenments except the French are elided as sideshows to the real story. Thus we acquire a quick fix on what Tennyson aptly called 'the ringing grooves of change'. History, it seems, is a train on a railway line to a terminus, and 1642, 1776 and 1789 are stations en route to *the* future, rather than history being full of cunning alleyways, and the future prone to turn whimsical or unexpected. And the reason we tidy up history in this intolerable manner is because we are still thinking through the lens provided by the semi-mythic horizons which carried the forces behind 1642, 1776 and 1789 to victory. *They* have constructed the way we see *them*. As Patrick Collinson commented with respect to the English Revolution, the developmental processes discussed by scholars all the way from R.H. Tawney to Christopher Hill may not correspond to any notion of modernity likely to appeal to the twenty-first century.[28]

I am not implying that modernity is other than distinctive or that the modalities of society since the Enlightenment and the Industrial Revolution are not very different. I am saying, however, that our observations are inflected and selected according to semi-mythical frames associated with crucial and successful social groups, and that our key metaphors and master narratives have philosophical links which include recommendation as well as documentation.

The trajectory derived from the French Revolution has been vastly influential through its dispersion among intelligentsias as a track along which history is destined to proceed. At the same time, it is supplemented by Anglo-American traditions of utilitarianism, so that a composite picture is built up of an advance guard proceeding either on a mainly revolutionary or a mainly evolutionary trajectory. In the early stages religion is allowed to be part of this advance guard, but then it not only falls behind but falls out with the advance guard, and engages in successive rearguard actions or suffers successive translations. Among these translations might be the shift from personal faith to sincerity (that is, from a theological to a natural virtue) or from the genuine instincts of the assembled chosen and godly to the genuine instincts of *all* the chosen people in God's own country ceaselessly invoked by American political leaders. The batons switch with different runners but the goal remains the same: the secular version of that 'one far-off divine event' at some secular end to history. Perhaps instead these are phases of secularization and sanctification such as I have described.

Notes

1   José Casanova, *Public Religions in the Modern World*, Chicago: Chicago University Press, 1994.

2   David Martin, *A General Theory of Secularization*, Oxford: Blackwell, 1978.

3   Robin Gill, *The Myth of the Empty Church*, London: SPCK, 1993.

4   Rodney Stark and Roger Finke, *Acts of Faith*, Berkeley: University of California Press, 2000; Steve Bruce, *Choice and Religion. A Critique of Rational Choice Theory*, Oxford: Oxford University Press, 1999.

5   Grace Davie, Steve Bruce and Robin Gill: articles on 'The Putnam Thesis', *Journal of Contemporary Religion*, Vol. 17, No. 3, October 2002.

6   Grace Davie, *Europe: The Exceptional Case*, London: Darton, Longman and Todd, 2002 and 'Europe – the Exception that Proves the Rule', in Peter Berger (ed.), *The Desecularization of the World*, Grand Rapids: Eerdmans, 1999, ch. 5; Peter Berger, *The Secularization of the World*, Grand Rapids: Eerdmans, 1999; David Martin, *Pentecostalism – The World Their Parish*, Oxford: Blackwell, 2002.

7   Grace Davie and Tony Walter, 'Women's Religiosity', *International Encyclopedia of the Social and Behavioral Sciences*, Oxford: Elsevier, 2002, pp. 16532–4; Callum Brown, *The Death of Christian Britain*, London: Routledge, 2001; Linda Woodhead, 'Sex and Secularization', in Gerald Loughlin (ed.), *Christianity and Sexuality*, Cambridge: Cambridge University Press, 2003.

8   Will Herbert, *Prostestant–Catholic–Jew*, rev. edn, New York: Doubleday, 1960; Nancy Ammerman, *Congregation and Community*, New Brunswick, NJ: Rutgers University Press, 1997; Thomas Luckmann, *The Invisible Religion*, New York: Macmillan, 1967; Robert Putnam, *Bowling Alone*, New York: Simon and Schuster, 2000.

9   Harold Bloom, *The American Religion*, New York: Simon and Schuster, 1992.

10   Neil Kent, *The Soul of the North*, London: Reaktion.

11   Ernest Gellner, *Thought and Change*, London: Weidenfeld and Nicolson, 1964.

12   John Gray, *Straw Dogs*, London: Granta, 2002.

13   Ernest Gellner, 'French Eighteenth-Century Materialism', in *A Critical History of Western Philosophy*, ed. D. O'Connor, London: Routledge, 1965, pp. 278–84.

14   Charles Taylor, *Sources of the Self. The Making of Modern Identity*, Cambridge: Cambridge University Press, 1989.

15   Pascal Boyer, *Explaining Religion*, London: Heinemann, 2001.

16   Stark and Finke, *Acts of Faith*.

17   Mary Midgley, *Science and Poetry*, London: Routledge, 2001.

18   Roy Porter, *Enlightenment: Britain and the Creation of the Modern World*, London: Penguin, 2000; Robert Wuthnow, *Communities of Discourse*, Cambridge: Harvard University Press, 1989.

19   William Vaughan, *Gainsborough*, London: Thames and Hudson, 2002.

20   Hans Kippenberg, *Discovering Religious History in the Modern Age*, Princeton: Princeton University Press, 2002.

21   Ernest Gellner, *Nations and Nationalism*, Oxford: Blackwell, 1983.

22   Anthony Smith, *The Ethnic Origins of Nations*, Oxford: Blackwell, 1986.

23   Simon Green, *Religion in the Age of Decline*, Cambridge: Cambridge University Press, 1996.

24   Donald Miller, *Reinventing American Protestantism*, Berkeley, CA: University of California Press, 1999.

25   Schmuel Eisenstadt, *Fundamentalism, Sectarianism and Revolution*, Cambridge: Cambridge University Press, 1999.

26   David Martin, *Christian Language and its Mutations*, Aldershot: Ashgate, 2002

27   Eamon Duffy, *The Stripping of the Altars*, New Haven: Yale University Press, 1992; Joel Rosenthal, *The Purchase of Paradise*, London: Routledge, 1972.

28   Patrick Collinson, *English Puritanism*, London: Historical Association, 1983, p. 6.

CHAPTER 10

Pentecostalism: A Major Narrative of Modernity

When I initiated the critique of the concept of secularization in 1965, I suggested that it had roots in rationalist and historicist ideology which needed to be exposed. By way of a concluding rhetorical flourish I even suggested that the word 'secularization' be expunged from the sociological dictionary.[1] Later, over the period 1969–78, when trying to give an account of secularization within the limits of social differentiation and in the context of varied historical patterns, my object was not so much to expunge a word as to render a more modest account of secularization shorn of wider resonances.[2] It seemed to me that one could indeed trace certain systematic changes over the periods of time we label modernity, long in Holland (say) and short in Albania, but one had to be cautious about herding all such changes under grand theories like rationalization and privatization.

That in practice was the implication of my approach, though for a magisterial account of the varied processes embedded in the grander theories of secularization, and their attendant metanarratives, one has to turn to José Casanova's *Public Religions in the Modern World* (1994).[3] In particular that work cast doubt on the privatization of religion under modern conditions, and gave concrete evidence of its active public role in several countries.

My own concern since 1978 when *A General Theory of Secularization* first appeared has been to pursue lines only lightly touched on or omitted in that work, in particular the mutation of the Latin European pattern evident in Latin America since the mid-twentieth century. The initial focus was on the onset of competitive pluralism in Latin America, principally in the form of Pentecostalism, as discussed in *Tongues of Fire* (1990), but that has gradually broadened into an account of Pentecostalism as a global option as set out in *Pentecostalism – The World Their Parish* (2001). In the course of this extended enquiry certain basic problems emerged, in particular whether Pentecostalism was a harbinger of modernity throughout the developing world, or part of its 'fundamentalist rejection'. I embraced the former option. Overall my analysis both treated Latin America as a hybrid combining the North American and 'Latin' modes of secularization through the introduction of competitive religious pluralism on a massive scale, and espoused Pentecostalism as a major metanarrative of global modernity. That is the core concern of what follows, drawing on the publications just mentioned and on a future publication *Betterment from on High*, written with Bernice Martin, the argument of which has been prefigured by her in three major articles.[4]

The analysis now offered lies athwart the conventional paradigm of secularization, because whereas that tends to view religion as inhibiting modernity, apart from the role of Protestantism in easing its earlier phases, religion is treated here as offering more than one alternative route to the modern. Clearly a metanarrative of modernity based on Pentecostalism as a viable global option continues the problematic of Protestantism, but it does so in relation to Halévy rather than to Weber,[5] to Methodism rather than to Calvinism. The metanarrative of Pentecostalism is not based on rationalization and bureaucracy but rather on story and song, gesture and empowerment, image and emobodiment, enthusiastic release and personal discipline. One has to view this potent combination of empowerment with release as just as viable in terms of advancing modernity as rationalization. There are alternative logics besides those of rationalization which are not just evident in interim phases of development but through other ways of 'being', and of being modern. That implies that one's mode of understanding secularization is related to one's understanding of the status and staying power of varying modes of being. One is offering an alternative to that classic mode that conceives of religion as simultaneously a set of empirical mistakes, a malignant influence and an interim barrier to modernity doomed in time to be swept away in the light of scientific day (or existential autonomy).

To introduce a metanarrative based on Pentecostalism as a global option one needs first to present a model of the way religion relates to society and culture. If one understands any given religion as a linked repertoire of themes and motifs constituting an approach to 'the world' in the terms originally set out by Max Weber, then the issue of religion in relation to modernization becomes one whereby the absences and presences of certain themes resonate with particular developmental possibilities. Furthermore, if each religion emphasizes particular themes at the price of significant absences and lack of coverage elsewhere, then one needs to say how these play into openings on to modernity, and indeed shape and mould those openings in characteristic ways. Absences may be as significant and helpful as presences. New Testament Christianity, for example, offers scant coverage with respect to law, war and political action generally, while at the same time providing scope for increased subjectivity. These particular absences and presences can be exploited in concert with processes of individualization and the secularization of law and in the context of social differentiation.

In the more solidary types of society most characteristic of pre-modern times, established power and the sacred are sufficiently intimate and mutually supportive for the radical motifs even of Christianity's core repertoire to be reduced to projections carried forward 'on the books'. Yet because they participate in the sacred and carry authority and legitimacy, they can be realized in social practice given the right cues, especially once literacy makes them generally familiar. They are potentials already written in, with the absences leaving room for manoeuvre and the presences positively opening up the new and playing into processes of social change.

Some examples may help. Just as the themes of sacred monarchy and divine legitimation are selected from the original repertoire for magnification in the more solidary and hierarchical kinds of society, so the themes of individuality, voluntarism, pluralism, lay participation and inward 'faith' are selected as appropriate accelerators of incipient social differentiation. How fast matters may move is suggested by the kind of changes fast-forwarded in the brief reign of Edward VI from 1547 to 1553 as delineated by Diarmaid MacCulloch in his *Tudor Church Militant* (1999).[6] Of course, there are blockages, stabilizations and reversals, but retrospectively one can see the English Republic of the mid-seventeenth century already implicit in the new monarchy of the mid-sixteenth century. Or again when John Penry and others envisaged voluntarism and an end to state religion in the 1590s, the First Amendment of 1788 was already in the sights.

When these revolutionary changes occur, some kinds of religion will continue to embody the old communitarian, heteronomous and hierarchical modes, along with their appropriate images, and not just as resistances either, but as potentials temporarily recessive and available for revival in fresh forms. Changes will occur covertly within the old forms parallel to the kind of changes overtly present in the new ones but within a different frame of meaning. Stabilizations, resistances, conservations and alternative potentials will be held together and impacted, sometimes by way of a 'reaction formation' so tight that religion itself is perceived as a mainstay of resistance to change. That was conspicuously the case with regard to the Catholic response to an aggressive Enlightenment, especially in France, and thereafter the multiple resistances became so tightly bound together that they did not break up and reform until the mid-twentieth century. One result was precisely the antagonistic metanarrative of secularization and modernity which linked religion inherently to the darkness of the past and to its inadequate grasp of reality.

Such an account of how religion relates to culture leans on a standard version of the difference between a Catholic, communitarian, organic and heteronomous relation to modernity and a Protestant relation rooted in voluntarism, individualism and autonomy, though in fact the communitarian and the heteronomous are always present. However, both Catholicism and Protestantism have also had to encounter another form of organic community and heteronomy in the form of nationalism and the nation-state. In the Catholic case the encounter has often been antagonistic, as in Mexico, Brazil, France and Italy, whereas in the Protestant case the relation has been mostly positive, as in Britain, Holland, Norway and the USA. The antagonism of Catholicism to nationalism involves a clash of the national with the international, and of clerical élites with secular ones.

That conflict also illustrates how a temporarily recessive religion may conserve possibilities for the future, since the transnationalism of Catholicism may achieve a fresh relevance in the post-national phases of late modernity, leaving established Protestantism over-identified with the nation–state in its period of decline. Protestantism and Catholicism exploit, and are indeed defined by, different elements in the Christian repertoire, so while Protestantism can be tuned to neo-liberal motifs in contemporary North America and Europe, Catholicism can be tuned to transnational and communitarian motifs.[7] It is as if different religious themes take turns to partner the processes of modernization, lending them depth and also providing checks and visible alternatives, keeping older potentials in reserve.

That, then, is the necessary background for what follows, which is a metanarrative tracing the emphasis on individuality and inward faith from its nurseries in Lutheranism and Pietism to its realization in Anglo-American voluntarism, and in its massive Pentecostal/charismatic dissemination throughout the world since the mid-twentieth century. In due course one will have to show how the lineage running from Pietism to Pentecostalism is linked positively to modernity in respect of the domains of gender, secular law, transnationalism, voluntarism, pluralism, the nuclear family, peaceability, personal release and personal work discipline, consumption, modern communication, social and geographical mobility – as well as changes in mediation, authority and participation.

In tracing Pentecostalism back to Pietism, one needs to sketch a historical genealogy beginning in Germany with figures like Spener and Francke, which then spreads to England and to the nascent USA. This westward trail is at the same time a process moving from participatory cells within an established national Church to the kind of mixture of internal reform of the establishment and the emergent voluntary denominations that characterized England from 1750 to 1850, to the complete voluntarism devoid of all state connection in the USA. It is this voluntarism and pluralism that then takes off and rapidly indigenizes in the developing world, partly on account of its astonishing combination of motifs from both black and white revivalism. And since Pietism is prone to be understood as culturally narrow and socially passive, it is as well to remember that its roots were not only in a deepening of inner life but in the founding of schools, orphanages and missions.[8]

Perhaps the Pentecostal metanarrative of modernity can be thrown into high relief by contrasting it with Islam, which is its main contemporary revival outside Christianity. Islam and Pentecostalism are even more sharply different than Pentecostalism and its main Christian rival, Catholicism. That is because Islam embodies to an even greater degree than Catholicism the realities of organic community, located in territory and uniting religious with social identity. Interestingly those respects in which Islam differs from Pentecostalism are precisely those in which it resists modernity, notably pluralism, voluntarism, individualism, inwardness, secular law and (though this is more complex) patriarchy.

Where Islam resembles Pentecostalism it is compatible with modernity, notably egalitarianism, personal work discipline, transnationalism and contemporary modes of communication. That means that Islam enters the modern world through the mobilization of whole populations, whereas Pentecostalism enters it through the mobilization of subcultural and individual self-consciousness. Moreover, colonial experience at the hands of the West has ensured that compared with Europe secular nationalism in Islamia has been less influential than ethno-religion. Pentecostalism only overlaps ethno-religion when it gains access to minority peoples at the periphery, and even then contributes more to their fragmentation than to their unified mobilization.

Buddhism is capable of generating both national self-consciousness and a voluntaristic subculture, such as one finds in the neo-Buddhist new religious movements of Japan and Taiwan. Its inwardness also enables Buddhism to appeal to élites in the West as well as in the East. Not only is Buddhism compatible with modern pluralism, but arguably provides a prime instance of privatization.

Parenthetically with respect to comparisons between Catholicism and Pentecostalism, they are, of course, not entirely self-contained entities. Catholicism has produced its own 'functional equivalent' of Pentecostalism in the Catholic charismatic movement, while Pentecostalism exhibits quasi-sacramental characteristics, for example in the use of holy oils and blessed substances. Where Catholicism has been rationalized from the centre at the expense of local tangible presences, Pentecostalism can move into the vacated space, whether in Guatemala or East Africa.

If we now turn directly to Pentecostalism as offering a major metanarrative of modernity in relation to the domains listed earlier, it may be useful to begin with the two domains where the relation is ambiguous: authority and gender (or patriarchy). Much depends here on whether you understand modernizing potential in terms of a confrontation with resistances across the board or in terms of ambiguities which assist undramatic subversions and local stratagems. Liberal ideology demands a full agenda of political rectitude across the board without recognizing adequately how limited and ambiguous gains are in practice or how 'authoritarian' and non-participatory are even the most conspicuous examples of liberal Western institutions, such as the British Labour Party and its continental equivalents. Practice and theory sharply diverge in the 'lead societies'.

Routinely Pentecostalism is accused of authoritarianism and there is no more pejorative label in the critical lexicon. One therefore has to enquire into the paradoxical nature of authority in Pentecostalism since it is exercised in an organization which is lay and participatory. A good example of an authoritarian personality cult might be Ezekiel Guti in the Zimbabwe Assemblies of God.[9] The Pentecostal movement exhibits one of the major paradoxes of freedom, which is that autonomy depends on heteronomy if it is not to disintegrate, while participation depends on boundaries and rules. Within Pentecostalism the injurious hierarchies of the wider world are abrogated and replaced by a single hierarchy of faith, grace and the empowerments of the spirit as mediated by the pastor. Mediation is radically reduced and concentrated in charismatic leadership.

This paradox of authority and mediation, most evident and necessary where groups gather on rafts to take them through the turbulence of the great journey from extensive rural networks to the mega-city and the nuclear family, is not confined to Pentecostalism. It is found in other movements helping people to cope with the major transitions of modernity, and provide them with purpose, meaning and an interim stabilization. The Tzu Chi movement in Taiwanese Buddhism and the New Religions of Japan exhibit exactly the same paradox of authority and participation.[10] Authority is both reduced and concentrated.

What, then, of gender, and what Bernice Martin has called 'The gender paradox' of Pentecostalism?[11] It is interesting that so much of the research and interpretation of data serving to undermine the facile association of Pentecostalism with fundamentalism and with patriarchy has come from women, especially female anthropologists. It is women who understand the difference between formal arrangements conceding headship to the male and informal realities conceding effective power to the female, and engendering mutuality rather than subjection.[12]

For Western feminists in general the main objective has been to release women from the weight of family responsibilities, including the linked trio of cooking, children and church, whereas in the developing world today the main objective is to bring the man back into the family in order to take up his responsibilities. Desertion, violence, promiscuity and alcoholism are the main factors militating against the survival of women and children, and Pentecostalism is very much the trade union of the women aimed at a different and more beneficent regime within the home. As in the home, so also in the church the male is not threatened by loss of respect and status but accorded a recognition of status provided it is earned. There can be no double standard allowing men the right to roam and engage in macho mayhem while the women defend hearth and table against the depredations of the street.

Perhaps this is the juncture at which to introduce a further paradox, which is that of work discipline and religious consumerism. There are many forms of Pentecostalism on the contemporary market of faiths, and the form which most promotes the consumerism of a health and prosperity gospel takes up rather more academic attention than its actual importance warrants,[13] mainly because its relative expansion has been recent. Nevertheless, what one observes is a continuum running from a severe work ethic operating in humble circumstances with some suspicion of the seductions of riches to a more expansive and world-affirming faith often exercised in a mega-church and anxious to advertise the happy union of virtue with the acquisition of bodily and material goods. In a rather Jewish way God wants His people to be righteous and prosperous. From the viewpoint of a contemporary capitalism appreciating both good workers and discriminating consumers, the combination is indeed benign, which is precisely why it appears so problematic to critics of global capitalism. An earlier critique of Methodism's contribution to social harmony and work discipline has been revived, but it has no serious bearing on the issue of contribution to modernity. Indeed, as it has turned out, it is the Marxist critics who backed the losing horse in terms of long-term modernization. In terms of the old debate about Methodism versus Marxism, it is the latter which represents a failed modernity.

Most of the moral characteristics of Pentecostalism revive those of the 'Protestant Ethic' modified for the difference between Weber's Calvinists and Halévy's Methodists. Apart from work discipline and rejection of romantic revolutionary violence, Pentecostals exhibit such traits as honesty, fair dealing, responsibility and trustworthiness. Those in the developing world running moderate-sized enterprises or seeking reliable personal and domestic service depend on trust, and trustworthiness is also desirable in the vast informal economy.

Bernice Martin has given an account of these moral traits in her article 'New Mutations of the Protestant Ethic', showing how the self-motivation, initiative and discipline fostered in the Church assist survival, or advancement and betterment, in niches in the post-industrial economy where flexibility is highly desirable. Among Pentecostals there is a continuum of attitudes towards prosperity from an emphasis on humble accumulation with suspicion of materialism to a frank acceptance of the bounty attendant on faithful confidence in the Lord.[14] It is perhaps worth adding that the peaceability of Pentecostals does not mean they are oblivious to the injustice of their situation or incapable of protest.[15] They simply refuse supinely to accept the way liberals cast them as victims. On the contrary they prove what can be done by energy and agency.

Where they diverge most from the profile of the classical Weberian Protestant is in their embrace of a religious version of the 'Expressive Revolution' which they anticipated by over half a century. They 'let go' in their services just as they also exercise control in earning their living. They also anticipated later developments (as well as picking up and conserving an older tradition) in their holistic approach to healing. Healing is of body and mind simultaneously and is fostered in the community.[16]

Particularly with regard to their capacity for expression and release as well as for discipline, Pentecostals and charismatics could be regarded not only as the inheritors of Methodist 'enthusiasm' but as peculiarly adapted to the expressive modes inherent in the contemporary ethos. Yet it is this very adaptability which leads them to be characterized as irrational or even hysterical, and thus atavistic and orgiastic, when such manifestations outside the religious sphere do not attract these hostile sobriquets. One does not find the *théâtre de complicité* written off as a throw-back. Nor is alternative medicine dismissed as pre-scientific.

A crucial group of characteristics has to do with their break with the rural past and with the extended familial relationships and community responsibilities embedded in it. They demonize the past while at the same time accepting the continuing reality of its coercive powers.[17] In a literal sense they represent a re-formation or conversion, meaning by that a turning in a new direction. That new direction is global modernity.

To be on the move from the rural to the urban and from the old to the new is to constitute a kind of protected caravanserai, with the churches as depots or reception areas. Thus West Africans on the move about the globe may find reception areas among the brethren in Amsterdam or London,[18] as well as channels of communication back to the home base. The chill threat of anonymity and *anomie* is fended off in the warm fellowship of a welcoming fraternity. (It is interesting that the recent edited volume by André Corten and Ruth Marshall-Fratani *From Babel to*

Pentecost (2001) is entirely given over to the transnational scope of Pentecostalism.)

Most characteristically, Pentecostalism fosters a regional awareness across the borders of ethnicity and nation. Television and radio ensure that the church is not just a local place of meeting but an 'imagined community' of fictive brothers and sisters in the faith.[19] Even in apartheid South Africa, charismatic fervour could cross racial barriers, and in Brazzaville after the breakdown of the social fabric in the Civil War, Pentecostalism succeeded in crossing the partitions of tribal and racial enmity.[20]

Conventionally the Protestant Ethic is associated with individualism, but the believing individual is always part of a community and the disciplined raft the church offers for mutual support and survival. Personal discipline depends on group discipline, especially with regard to young males tempted by the fiesta or the weekend spree. Thus the theme of individualization can be over-emphasized, as Harri Englund has argued, on the basis of data collected in Malawi.[21] There is an internalization of norms as part of the continuing process of conversion but not atomization.

One of the 'notes' of modernity is pluralism, and in this respect Pentecostals represent the full fissionable potential of Protestantism. If the local church and its pastor do not suit them, they find another more to their liking. Many of the myriad churches honeycombing the poorer areas of Seoul or Santiago are simply small family firms. This is unhampered competition pursued in the free spirit of outrageous religious entrepreneurs, and since those who join the church expect to participate, one has a kind of analogue of democracy. That is not to say that all Pentecostals are *ipso facto* democrats, but rather to indicate how religious competition and participation have an elective affinity with democratic organization and ethos.

What most militates against the concrete realization of that and against the virtues nurtured in the protected enclave is the neo-patrimonial character of environments based on clientship and corruption. Once you leave the protected enclave to assert yourself politically and raise your new-found voice, you encounter centripetal social forces drawing you back into a culture of political corruption and nepotism.

It follows that there are also kinds of Pentecostalism which as much mirror as they challenge the cultural environment. To indigenize rapidly and to 'acculturate' is an ambiguous process, and in the case of 'The Universal Church of the Kingdom of God' one finds a theology promoted by holy hustlers which in some respects mirrors the random donations of economic fortune. Paul Gifford has shown how in Ghana the popular mega-churches promoting prosperity are infiltrated by magical powers dispensed by recent mutations of the traditional 'Big Man'. In his view it is rather too easy for the big men of the church to collude with the big men of politics, so that the democratic and populist potential of conversion is sucked back and reassembled in yet another neo-patrimonialism.[22] Indeed, the reading of the Hebrew

Scripture can even yield ideas of Christian theocratic governance. Change can be bent back into spirals of corruption and nepotism. Thus there are always limits set on democratic potential, such as are persuasively documented in Paul Freston's *Evangelicals and Politics in Asia, Africa and Latin America*.[23] It is even possible to read Pentecostalism more as a recrudescence of older forms of spiritual animation rather than an instalment of the new.

Though from my standpoint this reading leans too much on a Weberian metanarrative requiring a classical Protestant rationalization of the world, it serves to underline how Pentecostalism unites ancient and modern just as it combines motifs from the culturally despised among both black and white. The result is a potent ambiguity dramatically realized in an ability to catch fire among marginal peoples at the periphery of major civilizations, whether we think of the gypsies of Europe or the Maya and Aymará in Latin America, or groups in Central Africa and remote Nepal. Pentecostalism and other similar movements enable marginal people to divest themselves of backward and dissolute stereotypes and leap over the local national environment to embrace a global modernity.

In spite of the reservations of those who regard Pentecostalism as a reconstitution of folk religiosity, there is massive evidence to hand to sustain the argument that Pentecostalism, in company with evangelicalism and its charismatic penumbra, within as well as outside the mainstream churches, mobilizes against the horizon of modernity and offers one of the major options before contemporary global society.

The fact that perhaps only a quarter of a billion people are directly affected does not really count against this claim given that changes are rarely carried by the majority. It is the active minority which signals the movement of change. Again, the argument construing Pentecostalism as a blind alley, evading the pressing need for structural change in an orgy of irrationality and hysteria,[24] ignores the way in which the future can be prefigured and anticipated at the level of culture, as well as ignoring the failure in practice of so many of the proposed structural changes.[25] Whether we think of Blair in Britain or Cardoso and now Lula in Brazil, the shift to pragmatic solutions is clear enough. For that matter, it is not only the proposals of the left that have failed in the developing world, but the proposals of neo-liberalism have also encountered a deep recalcitrance, as indicated in De Soto's *The Mystery of Capital*.

The spread of Pentecostalism goes hand in hand with the spread of an American pattern of competitive religious pluralism[26] and planetary English.[27] That means that the trajectory of 1789 based on a conflict over lay or clerical dominance in a monopolistic system gives way to the trajectory of 1649 and 1776, and that includes francophone countries such as Haiti, Congo, Benin and Burkina Faso.[28] That means that for intellectuals who have invested in the metanarratives of 1789, or even of 1917, the present course of events is either alarming and malign, or else invisible, usually the latter. Quite contrary to the standard metanarrative of European intellectuals, it is not the pattern of 1789, with its transition from religion to politics that overtakes the Anglo-American pattern, but the reverse, and one marker of that is the massive indigenization of Pentecostalism in three Latin languages, French, Spanish and Portuguese.

Inevitably the mainstream churches are also alarmed by Pentecostalism, because their position is being undermined among the younger generation in the developing world and because Pentecostals are mostly outside the ecumenical consensus. As a result Pentecostals may not be as invisible as they are to the secular intelligentsia, but they are dismissed as 'fundamentalist' when in truth their real appeal derives from their ability to empower and offer a voice.

Empowerment through Pentecostalism is also threatening to those Christian intellectuals who made a major investment in the appeal of liberationism. The poor have clearly taken up their own options in Pentecostalism and (whatever one's moral judgements about the base communities) liberationism is in decline, even where not positively inhibited from Rome. It is Pentecostalism and charismatic Catholicism that make the running, and the liberal Christian metanarrative drops behind along with the metanarrative deriving from 1789.[29]

There is, however, one further metanarrative produced by Anglo-American secularization theory, whereby the United States for all its vibrant religiosity is still destined to secularize, though behind in the queue, on account of the long-term impact of hyper-individualism and atomization. The lively religion of the developing world is not one of several alternatives based on social and historical specifics, but a phase undergone by peoples even further behind in the queue.[30] It is also argued that even the relative rise of evangelicalism in the developed world precedes a fall, and that just as an earlier evangelicalism peaked as part of a phase in industrial development, so Pentecostalism in the contemporary developing world will peak and then recede.[31] So the empty chapels of the Welsh revival that once brimmed with life early in the twentieth century are harbingers of the empty chapels of Manila and São Paulo at the conclusion of the twenty-first. However, since this metanarrative tells a story yet to unfold, we can only wait and see.

It is interesting, parenthetically, that one does not raise the same questions about the contribution of Pentecostalism to post-modernity as one raises with respect to modernity. This is not because there is no connection, particularly with regard to neo-Pentecostalism. Rather it is because post-modernity is not as all-inclusive a concept as modernity, dealing as it does with cultural changes, especially through modern communication, and thus resting on the prior achievement of modernity. While, as Bernice Martin has argued, Pentecostalism can emerge in societies moving directly from pre- to post-industrial, it is difficult to conceive of a post-modernity not based on modernity, even where that is imported.[32] The modern is never displaced, only developed.

I can now summarize the metanarrative of Pentecostalism as a major mode of entry into modernity as presented in *Tongues of Fire* and *Pentecostalism – The World Their Parish*, and set in the context of *A General Theory of Secularization*. That 'General Theory' took off from a critique of the ideological foundations and incoherence of the concept of secularization to devise a *limited* account of the secular and the modern in terms of social differentiation, in particular as pioneered by Talcott Parsons.[33] It turned on the variety of paths to the secular deriving from certain crucial historical events, in particular 1642/1776, 1789 and 1917 as proposed by S.M. Lipset.[34] Above all, it rested on a dramatic distinction between the 'Latin' trajectory following from 1789, with extensions in Latin America and the Russian revolution, and the Anglo-American trajectory based on the successive and related revolutions of 1642 and 1776 in a manner argued by Jonathan Clark.[35] The former trajectory illustrated a political messianism with roots in Christian sectarianism as recently analysed by S.N. Eisenstadt.[36] The latter trajectory also exhibited messianic characteristics, but was relatively pragmatic and untheoretical, with roots in a semi-Christian enlightenment and resting on a social base of Protestant piety. In terms of continental intellectual expectation, the crucial trajectory was supposed to derive from 1789, with history beginning again at year one, but in practice and in the long term the crucial trajectory has been Anglo-American, spread by the successive (and different) empires of Britain and the USA, and associated with the adoption of English as the global second language.

As already suggested, Pentecostalism (which here includes the wider universe of evangelicalism and charismatic movements) lies within the ambit of the Anglo-American trajectory, in particular its competitive pluralism and 'enthusiasm', though there are further roots in Dutch pluralism and German Pietism and their associated 'modest' enlightenments.[37] There is thus a movement westward from Halle to Los Angeles, even though the origins of Pentecostalism are worldwide and multicentred, including India in the mid-nineteenth century.

As the current of enthusiasms moved westward and into open plural and competitive spaces, it became a movement at the level of culture rather than politics. Culturally it combined black and white revivalism, with the powers of the Holy Spirit and of the shaman, enabling it to cross the cultural species barrier, initially to Latin America, then to Africa and parts of Asia.[38] In innumerable contexts it proved capable of rapid indigenization in a manner hitherto eluding the mainstream churches and the classic missionary. Though missionaries were involved, the main mode of communication was along personal networks all over the globe, through which the culturally despised were able to appeal to the culturally despised, above all the women of the developing world.

Millions of people from rural China to the Andes and Zimbabwe have been on the move, above all to the mega-city and, to this or that degree, breaking with their embedded links and their ancient continuities and local hierarchies.[39] For these Pentecostalism provided an internal compass and a portable identity, a protected environment for revisions of consciousness and social organization, including the nuclear family. It offered way stations en route for those on the move, and by reviving the full range of original Christian contents, above all the empowerments of the spirit, it was able to package the ancient elements of the inspired world within the format of the new. At the same time it was accompanied by parallel charismatic movements in the mainstream churches, often at a level above the culturally despised, which could serve as vehicles for socially mobile Pentecostals, and for members of transnational business, academic or other groupings among the vast new middle classes from Brazil to West Africa to Seoul, Singapore and the Chinese diaspora.[40] One further reinforcement of these Pentecostal-charismatic impulses derived from the emergence into modern self-consciousness of marginal peoples or peripheral ethnicities from Ecuador to Burkina Faso and from Jamaica or Haiti[41] to Nepal. These threw off old stereotypes and embraced identities with transnational horizons.

Whether in Africa or 'Latin' America, Pentecostalism is a harbinger of the pluralism initially established in the USA, and prefigured in Britain and Northern Europe. In Britain and Northern Europe, however, the impact of populist religion and pluralism was restricted by establishments now in decline, so that Methodism as the main progenitor of Pentecostalism achieved its real expansion on the American frontier, and the British imperial frontier.[42] In America populist religion worked through competition and religious entrepreneurship to achieve multiple cultural adjustments which now prove their viability and flexibility in the developing world. Thus whereas the dominant patterns of Hispanic and French civilization combine militant religious monopolies with militant and revolutionary secularism, these yield place to pluralism, especially since the collapse of the revolutionary secular project in 1989. The French revolutionary trajectory, so widely exported, with its revision of consciousness in the hands of secularist élites, gives way to pragmatism and the analogues of participatory democracy and global capitalism promoted by populist religion, protected as they are by strong boundaries and structures of authority.

This is in no way to predict the demise of Catholicism as the main rival of Pentecostalism within Christianity, but it is to suggest that Catholicism will be less associated with ethno-nationalism and emerge more as a paradigmatic transnational competitor within an increasingly multicultural framework. If we leave China out of the frame, as potently ambiguous, the main alternatives to these Christian metanarratives are some variant of Buddhism, or liberal secularity or Islam. The metanarrative of Islam is precisely the reverse of the metanarrative of Pentecostalism: increasingly ethno-religious and monocultural.

Notes

1   David Martin, 'Towards Eliminating the Concept of Secularisation', in Julius Gould (ed.), *The Penguin Survey of the Social Sciences*, Harmondsworth: Penguin, 1965.

2   David Martin, *A General Theory of Secularization*, Oxford: Blackwell, 1978.

3   José Casanova, *Public Religions in the Modern World*, Chicago: Chicago University Press, 1994.

4   David Martin, *Tongues of Fire*, Oxford: Blackwell, 1990 and *Pentecostalism – The World Their Parish*, Oxford: Blackwell, 1991, and with Bernice Martin, *Betterment from on High*, Oxford: Oxford University Press, forthcoming. The argument of this book is available in the articles by Bernice Martin referred to later in the text on new mutations of the Protestant Ethic, on the move from pre- to post-industrial, and on the Pentecostal gender paradox.

5 Elie Halévy, *History of the English People in 1815*, Book III, *Religion and Culture*, Harmondsworth: Penguin, 1938.

6 Diarmaid MacCulloch, *Tudor Church Militant*, London: Allen Lane, 1999.

7 These misalignments are discussed in Martin, *Pentecostalism*, 2.

8 Gary Sattler, *God's Glory, Neighbor's Good*, Chicago: Covenant Press, 1982.

9 David Maxwell, *Christians and Chiefs in Zimbabwe*, Edinburgh: Edinburgh University Press, 1999.

10 Yu-shuang Yao, 'The Development and Appeal of the Tzu Chi Movement in Taiwan', Ph.D., King's College, London University, 2001.

11 Bernice Martin, 'The Pentecostal Gender Paradox', in Richard K. Fenn (ed.), *The Blackwell Companion to the Sociology of Religion*, Oxford: Blackwell, 2001, pp. 52–66.

12 Two distinguished and pioneering works here are Elizabeth Brusco, *The Reformation of Machismo*, Austin, TX: University of Texas Press, 1995, and Diane Austin-Broos, *Jamaica Genesis*, Chicago: Chicago University Press, 1997.

13 Much recent work focuses on neo-Pentecostalism, for example David Lehmann's *Struggle for the Spirit*, Cambridge: Polity Press, 1996.

14 Bernice Martin, 'New Mutations of the Protestant Ethic', *Religion*, Vol. 25 (1995), pp. 101–17.

15 John Burdick, *Looking for God in Brazil*, Berkeley: University of California Press, 1993.

16 Andrew Chesnut, *Born Again in Brazil*, New Brunswick, NJ: Rutgers University Press, 1997.

17 Birgit Meyer, *Translating the Devil*, Edinburgh: Edinburgh University Press, 1999.

18 Rijk van Dijk, 'The Ghanaian Pentecostal Diaspora', in André Corten and Ruth Marshall-Fratani (eds), *From Babel to Pentecost*, London: Hurst, 2001, pp. 216–34.

19 See David Maxwell, 'Delivered from the Spirit of Poverty', *The Journal of Religion in Africa*, Vol. XXVIII, No.3 (1998), pp. 350–73, and Rosalind Hackett, 'Charismatic/Pentecostal Appropriation of Media Technologies in Nigeria and Ghana', ibid., pp. 259–77.

20 Elizabeth Dorier-Appril, 'The New Pentecostal Networks in Brazzaville', in Corten and Marshall-Fratani, *From Babel to Pentecost*, pp. 293–308.

21 Harri Englund, 'The Quest for Missionaries', in ibid., pp. 235–54.

22 Paul Gifford, *Ghana's New Christianity: Pentecostalism in a Globalising African Economy*, London: Hurst, 2002.

23 Paul Freston, *Evangelicals and Politics in Asia, Africa and Latin America*, Cambridge: Cambridge University Press, 2001.

24 Paul Gifford, *African Christianity: Its Public Role*, London: Hurst, 1998.

25 Edward Thompson, *The Making of the English Working Class*, Harmondsworth: Penguin, 1968. For a critique of Thompson see David Hempton, *The Religion of the People. Methodism and Popular Religion c. 1750–1900*, London: Routledge, 1996.

26 Martin, *Tongues of Fire*.

27 Martin, *Pentecostalism*, and Alister McGrath, *The Future of Christianity*, Oxford: Blackwell, 2001.

28 Several articles in Corten and Marshall-Fratani, *From Babel to Pentecost*, including Cédric Mayrargue, 'The Expansion of Pentecostalism in Benin', pp. 274–88.

29 Andrew Chesnut, *Competitive Spirits: Latin America's New Religious Market Place*, New Brunswick, NJ: Rutgers University Press, 2001. For an analysis of liberationism from a rational choice perspective see Anthony Gill, *Rendering Unto Caesar*, Chicago: Chicago University Press, 1998.

30 Steve Bruce, *Choice and Religion*, Oxford: Oxford University Press, 1999.

31 Callum Brown, *The Death of Christian Britain*, London: Routledge, 2001, and Simon Green, *Religion in the Age of Decline*, Cambridge: Cambridge University Press, 1996. For varying approaches to the history of secularization see numerous works by Hugh McLeod including *Piety and Poverty. Working-Class Religion in London, Berlin and New York 1870–1914*, London/New York: Holmes and Meier, 1996, and Steve Bruce (ed.), *Religion and Modernization*, Oxford: Clarendon Press, 1992. I am grateful to Steve Bruce for sight of his paper (Lausanne, October 2001) 'Evangelicalism – where the U.S. goes will Europe follow?'

32   Bernice Martin, 'From pre- to post-modernity in Latin America: the case of Pentecostalism', in Paul Heelas (ed.), *Religion, Modernity and Postmodernity*, Oxford: Blackwell, 1998.

33   Talcott Parsons, 'Christianity', in David Sills (ed.), *The International Encyclopedia of the Social Sciences*, New York: Macmillan, 1968.

34   Seymour Martin Lipset, *Revolution and Counterrevolution*, London: Heinemann, 1969.

35   Jonathan Clark, *The Language of Liberty*, Cambridge: Cambridge University Press, 1993.

36   Schmuel N. Eisenstadt, *Fundamentalism, Sectarianism and Revolution*, Cambridge: Cambridge University Press, 1999. See also Adam Seligman, *Modernity's Wager,* Princeton: Princeton University Press, 2000.

37   For an account of the origins of the Enlightenment in the Netherlands see Jonathan Israel, *Radical Enlightenment*, Oxford: Oxford University Press, 2001.

38   Harold Bloom, *The American Religion*, New York: Simon and Schuster, 1992.

39   For a critique of the individualization theme see Harri Englund and James Leach, 'Ethnography and meta-narratives of modernity', *Current Anthropology*, Vol. 41, No. 2 (2000), pp. 225–48.

40   With regard to the massive middle classes of Brazil, see Brian Owersby, *Intimate Ironies. Modernity and the Making of Middle-Class Lives in Brazil*, Stanford: Stanford University Press, 1999.

41   Diane Austin-Broos, *Jamaica Genesis: the Politics of Moral Order*, Chicago: Chicago University Press, 1997.

42   David Hempton, *The Religion of the People. Methodism and Popular Religion c.1750–1900*, London: Routledge, 1996.

PART IV
COMMENTARY

CHAPTER 11

Mission and the Plurality of Faiths

There are two relevant kinds of religious pluralism, both massively present in the world today. The first and historically the earliest is communal pluralism, which consists in the more or less tolerated propinquity of faiths, usually within a larger social unit, and where for the most part one community is superior and central and the others inferior and peripheral. However, straightforward competition is unlikely except in so far as people in the inferior communities find it advantageous to assimilate to the superior. The second kind of pluralism is relatively recent unless we count the kind of shopping among the gods in the Roman empire or, indeed, in some traditional oriental societies. It consists in the open competition of life-worlds and styles, each with a stall – more or less centrally placed – in the supermarket of beliefs. We have to look at both these kinds of pluralism as they contract and expand in the contemporary world.

With respect to the tolerated propinquity of communal faiths, the historical example most familiar to us is provided by Islamic empires, and their acceptance of the two religions of the Book but with second-class status and only conversion to Islam permissible. This really has little to do with mission or conversion in the modern Protestant sense since it is a change of an inferior for a superior social identity, such as occurred in Albania, in Tunisia and Nubia, though many converts to Christian missions have also had such a change as part of their motivation.

At any rate, adjacent communal faiths allowed everyday encounter across religious lines, and even some overlap of cults such as occurred in parts of the Balkans and Middle East until quite recently, and still occurs at the shrines to the Virgin at Ephesus and Fatima, and at the shrine of the Velankanni Virgin in India. Rival faiths in practice recognize varied sources of spiritual power. Parallel examples are available in the multi-ethnic Russian and Austro-Hungarian empires under enlightened autocracy, in spite of a prevalent anti-Semitism. Indeed, the interstitial area of Transylvania pioneered communal pluralism, with a similar mutual acceptance in Western Europe in the interstitial area of Alsace.

Of course, mutual acceptance was always relative and variable, with understood disparities of power and status. Once the peoples of the imperial periphery sought autonomy there were bound to be accelerating spirals of conflict with sanguinary massacres from time to time, or 'ethnic cleansing', such as regularly occurred in Greece, Bulgaria, the Lebanon, Armenia and Chechnya. Borderlands, with their unstable power structures and variable mix of peoples, were particularly susceptible to turbulence, above all where a minority could be viewed as a potential fifth column for another rival power (as, for example, Turks in Bulgaria or Christians in Mesopotamia). Alternatively, minorities could constitute powerful enclaves right at the heart of an empire or nation, and be subjected to popular violence out of fear and envy such as seemed to lie behind some of the early attacks on Jews in Spain and England. Clearly this kind of communalism militated against voluntaristic pluralism, because conversion weakened the unity of the group against its neighbours.

In any case, it may be that even this tolerated coexistence of enclaves came under pressure with the rise of nations and nationalism and the use of criteria such as common language and/or religion as the basis of belonging. An early case might be the expulsion of Jews and Muslims from Spain after 1492, and there may be a much more recent twentieth-century echo in the expulsion of historic Jewish communities all over North Africa and the Middle East. Certainly the rise of nationalism during the last two centuries in the eastern Mediterranean has meant the extrusion of communities once tolerated on both sides of the frontiers of Islamia and sometime Christendom, from Crete to the Lebanon and the Caucasus.

At the same time in parts of Western Europe and Latin America a type of nationalism arose which defined itself over against religion *as such*, and certainly against the previous state religion. This was most evident in France during the Third Republic and in countries under French cultural influence, but an early version is discernible in England over the whole period from the Henrician Reformation to the Commonwealth.[1] Initially in England the definities of heresy and treachery overlapped, but in time the criterion of compulsory belonging shifted from faith and heresy to patriotism and treachery, and that development might include a reluctant acceptance of elements of voluntarism. With the French Revolution the key criterion became treachery towards the Republic *and* to its ideals, so that compulsion not only turned on patriotism but political rectitude. Thus religion as such might be frowned upon as a basis for communal belonging, while minority identities, such as the Jewish identity, could be granted full citizenship, provided it took the form of individual subjection to the state at the expense of primary loyalty to the ethno-religious grouping. That meant a weakening of internal cohesion and with that the increased danger of secularization and assimilation, and the recognition of such a danger would generate strong prohibitions against defections from Judaism to voluntaristic faiths. Indeed, such prohibitions are also manifest today in Israel, where Jews are in a majority, because the mixed ethnic, religious and patriotic criteria of belonging to the nation would be corroded by conversion.

In Western Europe as a whole some such mix has been normal, with varying weights assigned to the national as compared with the religious criterion, according to the historical context. In Poland oppression ensured they were identical, so that to be Polish and Catholic gradually became synonymous, with unhappy consequences for Jewish communities. Voluntarism was virtually unthinkable, though it had actually existed in Poland centuries earlier. In less extreme cases the national myth would be positively associated with the majority faith, and the retrospective intellectual construction of historic national identity would play on the interlocking genealogies of faith, nation, native land and language. There were, however, partial exceptions, for example in the Czech Lands and Hungary, where the national myth could be associated with the Protestant minority.

The long-term drift is towards a criterion based on language, common culture and (maybe) political rectitude. Once again the key example is found in the evolution of radical liberal nationalism in France, but it has been present in many countries in Latin America, such as Uruguay, Guatemala and Mexico, and it is part of a reaction to the association of religion with political opponents, and with the traditional power structure. It happened with even greater violence and ideological rigour with regard to radical socialist nationalism in Russia and China, Ethiopia, Congo and North Korea. Radical socialist nationalism pre-empted the hegemonic space of religion, while at the same time deploying the faith of the heartland against the faiths of the periphery, as well as persecuting voluntary faiths as potentially treacherous and allies of foreign powers, in particular the USA.

There are parallel examples on the right, such as Nazism, which promoted a racial ideology based on pseudo-science which was to supplant Christianity or remake it in a racial image. Under fascist regimes the state colluded with the conservative authoritarianism of the Catholic Church and defined minority religions as defections from the nation. In Argentina, for example, there was a collusion of quasi-fascist organicism with Catholic 'intégrisme' under military auspices in opposition to liberal democracy, capitalism, individualism and Anglo-American Protestantism. One can say in general that throughout most of Latin Europe and Latin America up to the mid-century and beyond, Catholicism sought preferred status in the public realm, so that *de jure* pluralism is recent and *de facto* pluralism even more so. Yet, by a remarkable reversal in Latin America in the 1970s and 1980s, the 'national security' state pursued policies which aroused sufficient Catholic opposition for the military to court expanding evangelical minorities as alternative sources of legitimation. At the same time, such interludes, whether in Brazil or Chile or Mexico, have so far always ended with renegotiation and recognition of the special position of Catholicism.[2] What has altered, however, is the readiness of the state to incorporate Catholic norms into public law. Even in Italy recourse to divorce has been possible since the referendum of 1975. Both in Chile and in Poland the Church tried to capitalize on political credit built up during the period of dictatorship to secure the incorporation of religious concepts into secular law, and it failed. In that sense pluralism gains as the specifically religious becomes a matter of personal choice, not public regulation.[3]

Where the tide of nationalism recedes, as it has done in some countries of the West, such as the Netherlands or post-Franco Spain, it is almost a truism to say that pluralism has increased. Much depends on the historic relations in any given country between treachery and religious dissidence, and between identity and religious identity. These relations vary a great deal and are much affected by other factors, but if one takes the examples of the USA and Britain it looks as if the high tide of national pride and power is related to an invocation of broad religious identifications, in these cases the virtues of Protestant Christianity. It is understandable that nations in the course either of expansion or of resistance to foreign oppression look to their religious origins and traditions for mythic support, although as the case of Germany suggests these mythic elements can transmute religious figures into cultural heroes and appeal to non-Christian as well as Christian founders. Whatever the precise nature of the mythic construction of the nation, it is likely to include some genealogies and peoples at the conspicuous expense of others. However, given that in post-war Europe expansion and oppression are both less likely and cooperation encouraged, the ferocity of national attachments and enmities decreases and internal pluralism increases.

In the contemporary world, the USA provides a model and indeed an icon of the expansive pluralism which so widely influences global society, and it is a model allowing a vigorous nationalism to coexist with almost infinite religious variety. This is because the idea of 'America', so constantly invoked alongside the invocation of God, is attached to very broad values, such as enlightened optimism, which were long ago detached from roots in specific Protestant institutions. Different faiths and varied cultures bypass each other, more or less happily coexisting at a level well below the overarching sacred canopy. Change can occur almost invisibly by the switching of preferences, by the invention of new groups, by migration – and by the incorporation of fresh motifs in existing bodies as, for example, the incorporation of New Age motifs, whether or not recognized as such.[4] The USA includes sufficient cultural and geographical space even to incorporate the fundamentally different modes of integration and identity which underlie this analysis. There is, on the one hand, a primordial mode based on territory, similarity and a specific religious system, and on the other a looser mode accepting and even exploiting difference. In the USA this looser mode firmly separates ethnicity from citizenship.

At the same time, the broad values embraced are compelling to the point where those socialized in 'The American Way' have great difficulty in imagining alternatives or conceding that a country organized in the manner of Saudi Arabia can be truly in the modern world. American pluralism prevents its beneficiaries from recognizing just how problematic is its successful export, something that is well reflected in Francis Fukuyama's notion of an 'end to history'.[5]

One of the paradoxes of a plural and multicultural society is the nostalgia it breeds for modes of integration quite alien to it, which if they were actually experienced in the everyday life-world would be resisted as intolerable. In this way multiculturalism breeds is opposite not just in the form of the militant mobilization of distant cultures and civilizations rooted in territory and similarity, but in the form of yearnings for the simpler life of the communal or the communitarian. Ireland in particular has been the happy focus of yearnings for a place where times and schedules do not matter, in spite of a domination until recently of law and of personal morals by religion that would not be countenanced elsewhere for a minute. In the USA and in Britain the Irish theme and sentiment has also become a consumer item within a broader idealized current of Celticism, including an idealized vision of the Celtic Church, but it extends to theme pubs, riverdance and Celtic rock. Meanwhile, in the peripheries themselves there is conflict between those who object to the constrictions embodied in older modes of integration and those for whom the signs and symbols of that past, including language, provide the bedrock of threatened identity.

This same paradoxical nostalgia among metropolitan populations for communitarian forms and chthonic deities extends to indigenous cultures all over the world, and the advent of pluralism among indigenes is regarded as a major trespass on their authenticity. In this respect the intelligentsias of the West make common cause with nationalist intelligentsia against pluralism. As those who live in such cultures seek to inhabit the modern world and enjoy its options, even by adopting Christianity in some cases, those at a safe distance cherish and defend their cultural authenticity. By a further paradox any promotion of 'traditional values' in the metropolis is unacceptable, particularly if it takes a religious rather than an ethnic or cultural form. An authentic ethnicity is cherished but not its religious correlate, particularly if the religion happens to be the historic religion of the majority. Pluralism in the religious sense is not protected in the same way as ethnic and cultural pluralism, and what makes Muslim minorities difficult to assimilate and welcome is their refusal to distinguish properly between their good ethnicity and their objectionable religion.

Yet even the metropolitan centres of pluralistic societies conserve some signs and symbols of historic legitimacy and continuity and ideological rectitude. What is at stake here is the custody and central placement of the master-symbols of identity, such as the flag and buildings with iconic status. A great metropolis reserves spaces and protects architectural profiles, such as are recognized the world over as conveying the idea of Westminster or Washington, and in these quasi-sacred spaces alien symbols would not be tolerated. In less sensitive areas such as a Birmingham (UK) or Los Angeles suburb it is not so much the presence of Muslims that disturbs as the visibility of the minaret or the audibility of the call to prayer. Plural space is never unlimited.

What characterizes the pluralistic West today is the limitation of conflict within understood rules of engagement, so that the conflict of secular with religious nationalism, like the related conflict of left and right, is contained, even in France and Mexico, while the role of religion as a carrier of suppressed identity is less prominent, even in Poland and Ireland. The balance of forces, secular and religious, left and right, varies according to a country's historical experience, in particular the degree to which religion has been implicated in the resistance of traditonal to modernizing sectors or has supported national oppression rather than resisted it. The result is a continuum of outcomes, with Uruguay at one extreme forbidding the intrusion of religious symbols and liturgical seasons into public space, and Greece at the other, insisting that religion be acknowledged even on the national identity card, and greeting Easter Sunday with gun salutes.

In the West the previously dominant church takes its place in an expanding open space alongside other faith communities, and voluntary associations generally. There it generates social capital and the possibility of a critique. In particular the Roman Catholic Church, led by a resurgent and globally influential papacy, appears as the major transnational institution, and in an era of declining nationalism this lends it an edge over the established national churches. The possibility of a critique derives from a combination of available open space and a real though quite limited distance from power enabling the Catholic Church to exploit its traditional status and visibility, nationally and internationally. The effectiveness of moving between open critique and informal pressure has been evident in Korea, the Philippines, El Salvador, Brazil, Chile, francophone Africa and the USA.

Whatever the exploitation of a critical role, the established churches and the Roman Catholic Church alike have somehow to achieve a managed decline. This is inevitable because in Western Europe, which in this respect includes Britain, all churches represent a reservoir of motifs from older modes of integration where ecclesiastical and social hierarchies and the borders of the faith community and of the nation closely overlapped. From this follows an equally inevitable misalignment of discourses between churches and their social environment, given the contrast between older communal or organic motifs and current neo-liberal motivations. It is precisely this contrast which is attenuated in the USA, except in the clerical directorates. The pluralism of the USA was founded in the context of Protestant voluntarism on precisely the separation of the social and ecclesiastical hierarchies, and of religious and national borders, and thus the reservoir of communal motifs cannot be drawn on in the same way.

What remains from the past in Western Europe is the long shadow of earlier patterns. Though dormant for most of the time, they can spring to life when triggered by symbolic stimuli, as French *laïcité* was triggered by the issues of religious education and the wearing of Muslim headscarves at school. The state-sponsored *laïcity* of France has even promulgated a law designed to restrict new religious movements, while in Germany memories of the Nazi period affected the response to scientology.

Pluralism in the West today must lie close to its inherent limits since these are rooted in the criteria governing the very definition of what it is to be a society: some boundaries and some core values linked to a hierarchy of priority and power. It is clear that whatever the rhetoric of liberalism, no society, whether we think of the USA, Britain, Holland or Australia, will take large numbers of migrants with different loyalties and socialized in incompatible cultures. The West is under pressure to deliver in accordance with its rhetoric, but the very prospect of extending pluralism to include large populations socialized according to an antithetical communal principle brings out a 'reactionary' response from liberals and a firming up of borders.

These reactions merely echo in mild form the situation elsewhere, where boundaries are patrolled and aliens extruded because the core religious identity is so closely linked to social belonging as such. Even in places like Egypt, India, Indonesia, Nigeria and Bosnia, where there is some degree of mix and communal pluralism, clashes become cumulatively violent, the master-symbols of legitimate power are disputed – and the first building to be destroyed once conflict breaks out is church, mosque or temple.

With respect to the broad issues, Eastern Europe is part-way between the West and the rest of the world. Ethno-religion was stimulated by Ottoman overlordship and then stimulated further by state-sponsored secularism under the aegis of the Soviet Union. With the collapse of the Soviet Union, and so of the communist nationalism it promoted, ethno-religion moved into the vacated space, most dramatically so in the crisis years 1989–90. Since then some remnants of communist nationalism (operating most effectively in the Russian Federation) have linked up with ethno-religion in attempts to restrict religious pluralism, particularly when the new faiths come from outside.

The militant mobilization of territories in the rest of the world briefly colonized by the West or Russia leads to a reinforcement of the older modes of integration and to a subsumption of nationalism within religious militancy. The phenomenon is visible in Burmese Buddhism and the communal militancy of the Indian nationalist party, the BJP, and one can also point to minor manifestations, such as the reaction of Fiji Christians against the large migrant Indian minority. Islam is the most prominent case, however, because its mode of social insertion so closely links religious law and secular regulation as well as religious and social belonging. Wherever it recurs, social mobilization reduces toleration towards minorities, as is evident from the tensions present wherever Muslim, Christian and Hindu populations abut one another. The chances of opening up a competitive religious market are reduced and the equation of apostasy with death is reinforced.

Though such a competitive market may be quite recent in the West, it is irreversible and now expands to confront and indeed stimulate these militant mobilizations elsewhere. The expansion is rendered more problematic by such associations as may exist between 'MacWorld', competitive religion and the confident cultural and economic radiation of the American superpower. What remains of Catholic communalism in the West is also affected, to the dismay of the Vatican, which on particular issues like contraception even contemplates alliances with Islam, but the really dramatic confrontations are with the 'rest' of the world, where the rising tide of nationalism and ethno-religion can be regarded as the West's most successful export. What is receding in the West and belongs to an earlier phase is picked up elsewhere, but its nature changes because anti-religious nationalism enjoys a much shallower purchase in Islamia even where most successful, as in Turkey and Egypt.

In a situation where modern communication ensures almost every people becomes aware of contending global options, there is a search for the foundations, which are historically located in religion. This is what lends further colour to Samuel Huntingdon's controversial *Clash of Civilizations* (1996). The polarities written into our construction of 'the other' identify global rivals with deadly certainty. 'Occidentalism' as a construction confronts 'Orientalism' as a construction. This is yet another reason why all minorities on the wrong side of borders from Abkhazia to Ambon and from southern Sudan to Mindanao in the Philippines fear for their future. Inevitably the emissary of a rival faith is identified as the advance guard of political penetration.

So far the emphasis has been on the two main kinds of pluralism, communal and voluntaristic. However, one also needs to look at the main kinds of mission, which also lie along a continuum from the political–communal to the individual within the voluntary community. One means by this that mission may be mainly carried out by rulers bringing their peoples into a wider imperial entity or by (say) Methodist missionaries seeking individual conversions to a voluntary religious society. Clearly in practice the two kinds overlap, and there is also an intermediate kind involving dissemination along trade routes, but the political–communal form has been historically dominant, for example in the initial conversion of Northern Europe, whereas the voluntaristic form has been rapidly expanding only over the last half–millennium. It is, moreover, the consequence of a highly specific historical conjunction, which has briefly to be explored.

As that conjunction is very complex it can only be indicated by the crudest sketch, but it requires the coming together of the social process of differentiation whereby social spheres are separated off from overarching religio-political aegis (i.e. Church in collusion with State) and a religious repertoire that harbours a potential for 'faith' in the Protestant sense and the internalization of norms or conscience. These two preconditions, process and repertoire, actually assist each other's emergence, and that was further given historical momentum and global resonance by the shift of power from Rome and the Mediterranean to the North-west Atlantic littoral of Holland and England coming to fruition in the late seventeenth and early eighteenth centuries.[6]

If we seek for the origins of the religious repertoire, they lie in the Hebrew Scriptures with the idea of an inner law written on the heart and the amplification of that in the Pauline circumcision of the heart as carried forward by monasticism and the Reformation. The religious repertoire was incubated for world export in the protected island of Britain before being amplified yet again in the protected continent of North America, and the long-term consequence has been the triumph of the inner and the voluntary in the USA.

That this triumph is not unproblematic has been indicated by intellectual critiques as well as by the massive global reactions of other world civilizations. When we trace diminutions in the scope for voluntarism we are discussing the response of those world civilizations in the context of a relation between the expansion of pluralism and the cultural radiation of the American superpower. When we indicate the intellectual reactions as well, they run along a continuum from unease among classical Protestants to deep concern among thinkers in the Jewish community, to increasing degrees of rejection among Catholics, Orthodox and

Muslims, in that order. For a Jewish-American critique one could hardly do better than Adam Seligman's *Modernity's Wager*, which stresses the role of heteronomy in the creation of autonomy, while a striking Protestant critique is found in James Kurth's recent article (1998) 'The Protestant Deformation'.[7]

The focus here, however, is on the transitions from the political 'mission' historically associated with the staggered expansion of the two global forms of monotheism to the contemporary expansion of voluntarism through personal networks and worldwide communication. That requires some comparative sociology as risky as the historical sketch just offered. The most impressive exponent today of comparative sociology on this scale is S.N. Eisenstadt, but he emphasizes the link between a Christian millennial and sectarian tradition and European political Jacobinism whereas I want to emphasize the link between internalization and the emergence in Dutch and Anglo-American culture of competitive voluntarism.[8] Indeed, much of my recent work has been tracing a specific form of 'inward' Christian revivalism, parallel to a more outward Islamic revivalism, which is currently sweeping parts of the developing world in evangelical, Pentecostal and charismatic forms. This latter is a cultural mobilization, mostly outside the political sphere, and therefore non-violent (not to say predominantly female), which seeks an audible voice or a 'tongue' and unites the 'Expressive Revolution' of the mid-twentieth century with resources of inner conscience and discipline drawn from German Pietism and from Methodism. It is inherently modern in its competitive pluralism and peaceably seeks access to every kind of good, and to personal empowerment rather than to political power.[9]

Here, perhaps, I might interpose a personal recollection bearing on the tension between this vital and expansive voluntarism, as a 'movement' in the strict sense, achieved through a changed and portable identity, and Catholicism as a culture of continuous time and emplacement. The former appeals to the uprooted looking for inner reference points supported by a disciplined fraternity (or sorority) – fictive brothers and sisters – whereas the latter includes the whole society by a pre-emptive conversion via baptism. The fictive brothers and sisters in Catholicism are confined to the globally active religious orders. My personal recollection involved acting as a consultant to a meeting between Catholics and evangelicals in the USA to determine 'rules of engagement', and the point of maximum difficulty was precisely the Catholic claim to pre-empt whole populations through infant baptism, whereas for evangelicals and Pentecostals everything turned not on efficacious sacramental incorporation but on inwardly appropriated personal transformation.

The transition is, then, from periods when the two main monotheistic faiths spread by a combination of political incorporation and commercial radiation to a period of cultural dissemination along personal networks of transnational and global scope. Two or three periods have to be distinguished, beginning with what Jaspers called the Axial period from about 1000 BC to AD 600. Increasing unification and coherence in the sphere of the gods ran very roughly parallel to increasing unification and coherence in the political realm. Expansive empires became related to expansive faiths, as priesthoods and religious virtuosi worked over and integrated relgious formulas. In the cases of Christianity and Islam, both emerged from the periphery to take over the political centre, one very slowly and by conversion, one very quickly and by force, but once installed at the centre, Christianity, in common with Islam spread, as often as not, by force or at any rate by political choices, as in Northern Europe or when Kiev adhered to Byzantism or 'stout Cortez' forcibly incorporated the Aztecs. The other mode of adhesion in both cases was via trade routes, as in the Islamic advance into West Africa and Indonesia. In other words the main mode of adhesion was by metropolitan contagion or, if you like, political–commercial 'mission creep'. And that will always be the case to some extent because power in political terms is power in all other terms, so that one test of the efficacy of faith is political success, which is why many Christians in Byzantium converted to Islam once the icon of the Virgin failed to save their city.

Today the political power of the USA includes a powerful cultural radiation, except that we have to notice a major change in imperial modes since the great periods of Spanish and Islamic imperialism. The short-lived British empire worked mainly through native rulers and was more often based on sovereignty rather than on incorporation. Much conversion, especially in Africa, occurred as people sought to acquire the various kinds of power enjoyed by the British, for example in medicine, knowledge and science, but there was only a partial alliance between the Bible, the sword and trade. There was, from time to time, a reluctance on the part of administrators, traders or missionaries to endorse each other. This was the great age of the missionary, which is to say that it was an age of voluntary initiative, and the conversions were also, for the most part, voluntary, however much motivated by desire for advancement and empowerment.

In the contemporary world the USA, as the current superpower, and successor-state to the British imperium, has separated out religion and the state right from its foundation, and so its cultural radiation works quasi-independently of the political arm. Indeed, though the intelligentsias and political élites of many countries vehemently reject that cultural radiation (while ensuring access to its benefits for themselves), the masses in Latin America, sub-Saharan Africa, India and China are often attracted by it. The USA is an icon in itself. Moreover, the ideals of the USA can be used to criticize it, as was also the case with imperial Britain's professed democracy. For that matter, it is even the case that Spanish imperialism in South and Central America was also fought against by the native peoples appealing to the symbols of Christianity against their conquerors. If the peoples of the Ottoman empire appealed to the Koran or to the principles of the Ottomans to relieve their subordination, I am unaware of it. What, however, has plainly come about in the course of historical development is an increasing capacity on the part of the empire and the ex-empire to strike back, using the weapons put in their hands by superior political or cultural power. The Mexican 'La Luz del Mundo' has, as its name implies, a global outreach, which is expressed in spiritual conquistadors evangelizing the USA and Australia.

But, in any case, this is no longer the age of the missionary, no matter how numerous the American sending agencies, but of people travelling the globe in every direction taking their messages with them. So, though you have all kinds of missionary flow in every direction, such as the Brazilian Universal Church of the Kingdom of God in Portugal, lusophone Africa and South Africa, or evangelical Koreans in the Philippines, the main source of messages is through networks of people on the move. The transition to voluntarism is achieved as faiths are transmitted by personal contact, and that also implies the rapid indigenization of faiths, whatever the point of origin of the religious message. That is particularly the case with Pentecostalism, as a faith incubated in the swirling matrix of northern voluntarism and now taking advantage of such pluralism as is available in the contemporary world, above all in Latin America and sub-Saharan Africa.[10] Indeed, as already suggested, Pentecostalism is a peaceful harbinger of pluralism and its advance almost provides a global map of opportunity for competition from Benin and Congo to Costa Rica and Haiti. Naturally the same is true of non-Christian missionaries and their personal networks around the globe, such as have promoted Japanese New Religions in Latin America and the Pacific, or Baha'ism in the Caribbean.[11]

It is worth emphasizing just how much of the resistance to pluralism is cultural even though it may also be backed by law or other sanctions. If one takes Taiwan as an example, there was, until recently, some legal restriction (not including Christianity), but the core of resistance has lain in the negative response of the indigenous Taiwanese majority to external cultural radiation. As a result, initial Christian advances in the mid-century were stalled and forestalled by a reoriented and modernized Buddhism known as the Compassion Relief Foundation, with characteristics remarkably similar to Pentecostalism.[12] Like Pentecostalism, it gave form, purpose and meaning to the great trek to the mega-city, while lightening the weight of the ancestors and the extended family, as well as the weight of inevitable fate (*karma*) and the luck of poverty or riches. People on the move now related to a mobile fictive sisterhood and brotherhood, marked out by dress code and personal appearance. They became disciplined, altruistic, activist and aspiring in an atmosphere combining emotional release with meditation. Male irresponsibility was curbed, the corruptions of political activity rejected, and all this came about through an essentially lay movement displacing mediations and rituals by the charismatic authority of a matriarch, vigorous authority being a necessary feature of such movements if they are to offer a stable environment. Neo-Buddhism and parallel forms of Christianity often utilize modern rather than traditional style buildings, deploy modern media – and create their own welfare systems.

The key to the emergence of this 'functional equivalent' of Christianity lies in history and cultural context, which happens to be negative for Christianity in Taiwan (and Japan also) whereas it is positive in Korea. Cultural resistance is, of course, inherent in culture as such, and the variation in degree is explicable in terms of sociological principles. It varies even within the USA, so that the nation of Islam has a specific black constituency, to which it offers a renewed if modified version of primordial social integration – as the word 'nation' suggests. Overall a key factor in the spread of global pluralism is the cultural radiation of Anglo-America and English, but there are also regional sources of radiation such as Nigeria or Japan. Whether it is Christianity that is exported or a Japanese New Religion or Islam is a matter of context.

The main barriers to cultural pluralism are precisely the ethno-religious and communal consolidations mobilizing against it, in the Islamic world above all, but also in India, in some Buddhist countries and Japan, and in the remaining monopolies of radical secular ideology, such as North Korea and China. However, China is being hollowed out from the inside and there is a lively subterranean pluralism, both Christian and non-Christian. Perhaps the long-term mixture of traditions in China will in combination with the vacuum left by communist ideology open out into genuine pluralism. There is a pluralism inherent in shopping around among the gods according to their efficacy, and religious changes in the Chinese diaspora suggest how that may turn out.

In summary, the advent of pluralism is conventionally viewed as highly disadvantageous for Christianity, because it turns countries with crumbling establishments, like England and France, into 'Pays de Mission', and countries moreover highly resistant to all faiths because the psychological impact of decline is difficult to reverse, and the concept of the Church as a public service station inhibits self-service voluntarism.[13] However, those conditions do not obtain in the United States, where the corrosions come rather from a mutation of the idea of self-service in the direction of serving the self.

Elsewhere in the world, however, the modality of Christianity as shaped by its first voluntaristic and fraternal incarnation makes it the beneficiary and harbinger of pluralism. The internalization of faith, realized by the combination of universalism and voluntarism in primitive Christianity, has little enough to do directly with either democracy or pluralism. Indeed, it is cohesive and communitarian in a way which is today reinforced by the long history of Christianity as a communal faith of whole populations in a way providing Christian thinkers, particularly Catholics, with a critical edge *vis-à-vis* American individualism and voluntarism. Nevertheless, the foundation documents of Christianity are built around a contrast with ethno-religions, meaning by that territorial faiths with sacred lands, and holy temples in sacred cities, requiring ritual and outward adhesion to tables of public law and prescribed moral 'works'. St Paul has admittedly been described as a Roman jurisconsult, but the mature circumcision of the heart rather than the ritual circumcision of the new-born child profoundly amplifies the gospel injunction to avoid what pollutes within rather than what pollutes ritually without. Moreover, the Sermon on the Mount may and does have political implications of a very broad kind, but it is no kind of viable law or social blueprint.

There is, therefore, an open space in Christianity deriving from its sectarian rather than tribal origins, where a scheme of social regulation and ritual requirement might otherwise be. Indeed, it is dangerously open-ended to a degree which threatens its own viability and ability to reproduce, but it is nevertheless well adapted to a plural global society on the move.

As for the divine law and order of 'the Kingdom', it cannot be imposed by the actions of God's chosen Christian servants, although that was routinely attempted throughout the millennium and more of Constantinian establishment. Rather it comes about by the reserve powers of God in the eschatological future. Beyond that one has to recognize that whatever the ecumenical ideal may be, Christian practice in pluralistic conditions has been riotously fissiparous. Christianity is bound together today more by family resemblance than institutional unity. A better recipe for a pluralistic world where religion operates at the cultural level through voluntary forms is difficult to imagine. Each faith fastens on a sector of human existence, paying costs in its coverage elsewhere, and there are costs to be paid for Christianity's focus on redemptive love and its frustration, particularly in terms of its understanding of violence, conflict and the political realm, and that gap has to be supplied from elsewhere. It is equipped with an understanding of tragedy and personal and cosmic transformation but cannot simultaneously offer prescriptions for law and mass political action in the Islamic manner. Nor, as an exoteric faith, does it normally enter into the depths of the psyche as classical Buddhism does, which means that among élites, including those in the West, Buddhism is its real rival.

Notes

1   For accounts of this at the local and national level see Eamon Duffy, *The Stripping of the Altars*, New Haven: Yale University Press, 1992 and *The Voices of Morebath*, New Haven: Yale University Press, 2001; Diarmaid MacCulloch, *Tudor Church Militant*, Harmondsworth: Penguin, 1999; Brad S. Gregory, *Salvation at Stake*, Cambridge, MA: Harvard University Press, 2000.

2   The kind of renegotiation I have in mind is illustrated in the secret talks between the Brazilian Church and representatives of the military after Church–State clashes in the 1970s. See Kenneth Surbin, *Secret Dialogues*, Pittsburgh: University of Pittsburgh Press, 2000; and Anthony Gill, *Rendering Unto Caesar*, Chicago: University of Chicago Press, 1998.

3   See Michael Fleet and Brian Smith, *The Catholic Church and Democracy in Chile and Peru*, Notre Dame, IN: University of Notre Dame Press, 1997 and articles by Zdzislaw Mach and Katarzyna Gilarek in Tom Inglis, Zdzislaw Mach and Rafal Mazanek (eds), *Religion and Politics*, Dublin: University College Dublin Press, 2000.

4   See Linda Woodhead (ed.), *Reinventing Christianity*, Aldershot: Ashgate, 2001, particularly Introduction (pp. 1–26 and ch. 4, pp. 81–96).

5   Francis Fukuyama, *The End of History and the Last Man*, New York: The Free Press, 1992.

6   Jonathan Scott, *England's Troubles. Seventeenth Century English Political Instability in European Context*, Cambridge: Cambridge University Press, 2000.

7   Adam Seligman, *Modernity's Wager*, Princeton: Princeton University Press, 2000; James Kurth, 'The Protestant Deformation and American Foreign Policy', *Orbis*, Vol. 42, No. 2, Spring 1998, pp. 221–40.

8   Schmuel N. Eisenstadt, *Fundamentalism, Sectarianism and Revolution*, Cambridge: Cambridge University Press, 1999.

9   Paul Freston, *Evangelicals and Politics in Asia, Africa and Latin America*, Cambridge: Cambridge University Press, 2000 and Paul Gifford, *Ghana's New Christianity: Pentecostals in a Globalising African Economy*, London: Hurst, 2002.

10   David Martin, *Pentecostalism – The World Their Parish*, Oxford: Blackwell, 2001. For detailed material on Central America, the Carribean and Africa see André Corten and Ruth Marshall-Fratani (eds), *Between Babel and Pentecost*, London: Hurst, 2001.

11   See Peter Clarke, 'Japanese New Religious Movements in Brazil', in Bryan Wilson (ed.), *New Religious Movements: Challenge and Response*, London: Routledge, 1999.

12   Material largely drawn from Yu-shuang Yao, 'The Development and Appeal of the Tzu Chi Movement in Taiwan', Ph.D., London University, 2001.

13   Contrasting views of pluralism are available in Steve Bruce, *Choice and Religion*, Oxford: Oxford University Press, 1999 and in Rodney Stark and Roger Finke, *Acts of Faith*, Berkeley: University of California Press, 2000.

CHAPTER 12

What is Christian Language?

Prologomena

I want to think about the nature of religious language against the background of secularization. If secularization is understood as bound up in the evolution of modernity, and Christianity viewed as bound up in traditional society, then the language of faith falls into disuse, not for contingent reasons to do with restricted access or state repression and principled neglect, but because it is an archaic residue. That being the case, my attempt to characterize Christian language bears directly on the issue of secularization, because it attempts to exhibit religious speech as an irreducible mode, a manner of speaking which is *sui generis*, not a failed and inadequate version of realistic language.

I suggest that Christian language is a genre based on an alternative logic to that governing science, or indeed to that governing politics and academic debate, though the particular contrasts with politics and academic debate are reserved for treatment in Chapter 13. Religion is a mode of activity deploying its own grammar, and one which ought to be characterized without appealing to the validation of Christian theology, or even to such philosophical foundations as may be available, for example, in Heidegger or the later Wittgenstein. Philosophical implications are not entirely avoidable, but they can be kept to a minimum.

The position taken here rejects the Enlightenment myth of supersession whereby, in Ernest Gellner's terms, a great ditch is dug between the way people spoke in those days and the way they speak now.[1] Perhaps post-modernity, which in my view has disadvantages both as an account of our current condition and as a theoretical approach, at least helps undermine master narratives of supersession. Past modes are no longer forbidden to cross the abyss between the traditional and the modern. Clearly, that has implications for hard versions of secularization theory based on a master narrative of supersession. Such versions postulate a dominant mode of speech representing a single terminus rather than multiple modes leading to what S.N. Eisenstadt has called 'multiple modernities'.

What then is the broad understanding of religious language informing this initial exploration before I try to show how it actually works? First, let me say that I am restricting myself to *Christian* language because I believe it to be a quite particular and distinctive variant of the broader religious category. Clearly, I also include the language of the Hebrew Scriptures, but only as reviewed and integrated in a Christian Bible as the Old Testament. The affinities between 'Old' and 'New' are extraordinarily wide-ranging, and they work both backwards and forwards but, as Jonathan Sacks has recently argued, one must respect and honour difference, as well as candidly acknowledging it for purposes of analysis.

When it comes to differences between the world religions I accept as fundamental to my own thinking the argument of Max Weber as set out in his 'Religious Rejections of the World and their Directions'.[2] According to Weber, the positions embodied in the world religions represent a strictly limited spectrum or set based on their approach to 'the world', that is, the *saeculum*. Clearly, by taking variable attitudes to 'the world' as the key criterion governing the spectrum of difference, I am already hinting at the paradoxes of secularization, since these will arise quite differently in the different world religions. In Christianity, for example, the chief paradox of secularization emerges when faith conquers the world of the Roman Empire at the price of partial conformity to the imperatives of the secular, above all its glory, dominion and power. By using the religious language of glory, dominion and power in the context of the Constantinian establishment, I am suggesting how the original and vital Christian distinction between the dominion of Caesar and the dominion of God and of 'his Christ' has been radically reduced to a thin (though essential) demarcation: the City of God and the City of Man. I am also illustrating a quite distinctively Christian problem arising from the way its fundamental repertoire is rooted in the kingship of the lowly king, and in the eschatogical anticipation of a time when 'the kingdoms of this world shall become the kingdoms of our God and of his Christ'. In that particular text from Revelation all the attributes of majesty have been transferred to the 'sacred diadem' which on Calvary's hill was nothing but a crown of thorns. Such a paradox lies at the heart of Christian civilization and its discontents, above all the built-in oscillations between the power and the glory of the Church established on earth as the bearer of the keys of the Kingdom, and the power and the glory that belongs to a man expelled from the city as a blasphemer and a criminal.

That example allows one to see how the mutation of images works out in Christian history within the dominant tradition itself, and between dominant and subordinate traditions. As I argued in my *The Breaking of the Image* (1980), the radical elements in the original deposit of faith (for example the way all believers become kings and priests through the kingship and priesthood of Christ, or the way the lord of all becomes the servant of all) are expressed directly in subordinate traditions, while in dominant traditions the collusion between divine and human authority has to be placed in symbolic juxtaposition to the difference between them.[3] In the subordinate traditions the sign language of Christianity may be secularized in the sense of being earthed, as when all the faithful share equally at the fraternal meal or all have the right to speak in the assembly. In the dominant traditions it is secularized by having to conform to the hierarchy of worldly power – and yet the radical potential is all the same projected on to the iconographic screen as part of the original charter of faith. Establishments proclaim their own subversion. Every priest in the Church as established still has to pronounce the words 'Call no man father', which is why vernacular translation is so dangerous. Even in the iconography of established Christianity, death levels all and the Last Judgement brings all to the bar of justice.

If secularization carries different emphases and meanings in the dominant and subordinate traditions of Christianity, it carries strikingly different meanings when one compares Christianity and Islam. Christianity originates in a 'Son of God' and a 'Son of Man', who is defeated, and who is born and lives again outside the continuing cycle of the generations, while Islam originates in a prophet who succeeds as a conqueror and is part of a lineage. Thus the 'secular' understood in terms of power and lineage is not problematic for Islam, and because Islam is located quite differently on the spectrum of possibilities, it does not generate radical peace movements or monastic fraternities and sororities. Buddhism, by a further contrast, is very much the religion of the monk.

These are all examples of the operation of a religious logic, even though clearly looser than ordinary logic and expressed more in branching affinities than by strict implication. It follows that the 'world religions' are not haphazard assemblies of assorted empirical mistakes, or even useful wisdom hidden away in mythic form, but the strictly limited set of alternative logics delineated by Max Weber. That is why I am concerned here solely with the alternative logic embodied in Christianity.

Of course, it is also true that what one might call the standard deviation of a world religion on a spectrum of attitudes to the world includes a wider range which will intermittently reflect the 'shadow' of its rivals, in particular those with whom it is in close territorial rivalry. Yet this reflection of 'the other' will be inflected by the dominant tendency in an entirely characteristic manner. The shared theme will be orchestrated according to the logic of the original repertoire. For example, the shadow of Marian devotion in the 'Shekinah' of medieval Kabbalistic Judaism will still be controlled by the governing repertoire of the Hebrew Scriptures. Similarly, the Christian idea of martyrdom will be controlled and inflected within Islam by the governing repertoire of the Islamic revelation. It will *not* be the same, any more than the Virgin Birth in Christianity in just another instance in a general category of parthenogenesis. The particular paradoxes of Christianity, such as its oxymoron of dying to live, derives from its alternative logic exactly as delineated by Max Weber.

The logic of Christianity as I try to work it out below is *sui generis*, and it is based on transformation and deformation, acceptance and alienation, presence and absence, an image broken and an image restored, a fractured creation and a creation re-created and made new. Its primary virtues are faith, hope and love, and its supporting ancillary virtues patience, prudence, wisdom, humility, sincerity, judgement, mercy and care for the brethren.

Christianity is exclamatory, not explanatory, and it responds to the world as emblem to be 'beheld', and not as object to be known about and manipulated. It is vocative, not descriptive, and its patterns, above all the pattern of descent and ascent, are realized and recognized simultaneously rather than noted, anatomized and connected in causal sequence. Whereas science as a mode of knowing seeks generalization and abstraction according to the governing logic of the covering law, along the lines formulated by Carl Hempel, faith lies close to the modes of artistic creation, because it finds profound surplus and infinite overflow in dense and concentrated particularity. So, although broad and generalized translations of faith are possible, and indeed persistent, such as the brotherhood of man and the fatherhood of God, or our solidarity simply in being human, the modalities of faith resist any final conversion into a secular currency. Secularization encounters a limit. One may offer a partial translation by saying, for example, that we all sit and eat around one table, but that is not to be equated with the plenary embodiment of Christ in the body of the people of God realized in the eucharistic feast.

The analogy with art, and with the particularity written into the creation of the image, is best realized in the way the representations of faith participate in what they disclose and uncover. They are neither pure fabrication in being the expression of fancy or fantasy, nor are they reproductions conforming to the given, the datum. They are, instead, transformations of experience and the world, received as pure gift and absorbed without fragmentation or reduction. Where religious representation differs from artistic representation is best realized in the way the latter includes fantasy. Moreover, works of art are diffusely controlled by formal requirements and stylistic convention, not by the affinities governing the sign language of faith.

Spiritual landscapes are received, taken in and absorbed in the same way as other landscapes because not dissolved into more basic elements. The ensemble is itself basic. The sonic landscape of music, for example, is received as a whole 'fitly framed and joined together', and you do *need* to know either the structural elements analysed by musicology or the scientific and material basis of sound production. What you require is simply some preliminary acquaintance with what kind of music is being played. That sheep's guts can 'hail men's souls out of their bodies' is irrelevant, because the phenomenon as given in experience is as 'real' as the musicological analysis or the scientific reduction.

Perhaps this can be put in another way. The experience of the transforming spirit, whether with small 's' or capital 'S', is apodictic, irrespective of belief, but it is also inflected and shaped by the governing repertoire of the original deposit of faith. Our response will normally be affected by that inflection, which is what makes other civilizations initially opaque. A Western atheist is still a Christian atheist, and the modes of 'secular' society such as attitudes to the outsider and the victim or the solitary witness tried and tested or the vulnerable innocent child under threat of political violence are recognizable mutations of Christian themes.

The primal givens, as inflected by the initial repertoire, are mapped by names and locations. In time, as they acquire a necessary stability, they can also become fossilized. As a result the elements of contemporary scientific knowledge that philosophically minded Christians try to integrate with the deposit of faith, such as understandings of nature and the 'natural', tend to acquire extended coverage and legitimation on account of being built into revelation. Of course, as Charles Taylor has shown, the reverse also happens, in that religious concepts provide platforms from which scientific explorations may take off.[4]

Whatever the commerce in either direction between Christianity and secular scientific or philosophical understandings, the specific projections on which the map of faith is based are necessary. They are not arbitrary, certainly, though they are not the only possible projections either. They are necessary because they derive from the root position of the faith and because without them and their sign language, travellers cannot travel in company or recognize where they are in terms of where others have already been. When people en route see the sign of the cross and the shared meal, or the passage through water, they know where they are and recognize they are in some sense in the presence of 'church'. In other words, mapping and stabilization, with their associated signs, are required to express the fundamental orientation, to recognize continuity and the 'notes' of the church, and for tracking the trackless.

To be oriented, that is to be set towards the East and to know where you are in relation to the horizon of hope, does not require any specific attitude to the data of science. You do not have to decide on religious grounds how the world was created or even estimate the viability of (say) the anthropic principle, in order to receive and give back the language of faith. Maybe one can even be agnostic as to philosophic arguments about a realist or a non-realist account of God or, at any rate, find the whole presentation of the issue strange, given that the spiritual landscape is apodictically present to us all, 'believers' or not. As Goethe said, 'We *know* it, we feel it.'

The Spirit testifies with our spirit, and there are no other terms in which the testimony can be recast or demythologized other than its own. You do not ask what music means in terms of poetry or science, and you recognize the folly of the very suggestion. Demythologization is a modern myth born of not understanding the nature of religious language or the way it is ever ancient and ever new, *tam antiqua, tam nova*. It can be constantly recuperated, even if it is important that the recuperation is sensitive to context and the enveloping protective fabric of meaning. The New Testament is not a remote period piece (as Dennis Nineham has suggested) but a document or scroll that can be repeatedly unrolled, reopened and reread provided you respect and use the appropriate keys to its kingdom.

That is why 'children' can open up what has become opaque to the wise as, for example, Pentecostals all over the developing world are open to leadings of the Spirit 'into all truth', within the governing criteria of the original Gospel. I am not suggesting any developmental scheme here, such as the conventional enlightened division into the stage of the child and the stage of the adult. I am rather indicating a kind of direct vision, able to locate new resources, however culturally framed, which differs from the fragmented and fragmenting analytic purposes of enlightened scholarship.

The same is true of the contemporary revival of the ancient methods of typological and symbolic interpretation practised by the Early Church and the Fathers which are, of course, the methods of those who composed the Scriptures in the first place – as well as consonant with modern structuralist approaches. There is a recovery under way here, both of the signs rooted in the core repertoire and the decodings of their complex elaborations, for example, in Sarah Beckwith's *Christ's Body*, Leo Steinberg's *The Sexuality of Christ in Renaissance Art and Modern Oblivion* and Richard Taylor's *How to Read a Church*.[5] As one reviewer of Taylor put it, 'When we enter such places in our awkward, agnostic way, we are surrounded by such symbols', and discover this is a lost language which can be recouped as part of the appeal of Christianity to the contemporary imagination. When people attended the exhibition 'Seeing Salvation' at the National Gallery they saw what was already faintly familiar in broad outline brought to life as a coherent and encompassing universe of meanings. Moreover, they were guided to understand the universal in the particular rather than to abstract the universal from its concrete realization.

Typological and symbolic interpretation of the types and signs God has distributed in nature and scripture arises out of worship, as Pentecostalism does, and so out of the religious impulse, not out of intellectual distance adopted for particular analytic purposes. The types are, as Sidney Griffith has commented, commonplace rather than esoteric because Christ and the Gospel provide the exegetical focal point.[6] They are not commentary or attempts at extracting the kernel from the surrounds, but sacramental iconology. Religious language is not so much theology but rather the exclamations, dialogues, greetings and sequences of liturgy. We enter into the frames that govern a universe of meanings about kings and servants, wells, rocks and wildernesses, lions and lambs, gardens, cities and garden cities, vines and winepresses. The signs are not just helpful metaphors, but carriers and vessels bearing the full burden of meaning within themselves, and integrated within an iconographic scheme. The image of the king who became a servant, and was rich yet for our sake became poor, is irreducible beyond noting that its logic is one of reversal, incarnation, and the taking up of earth into heaven and humanity into God. We have here the underlying pattern of descent and ascent: 'he that descended is also he that ascended'. The reversals are understood as juxtapositions that were once enacted in a narrative but are now simultaneously and concurrently present in the semi-collapsed time-frames of liturgy and worship.

None of this has much to do with old myths having much to teach us moderns, as the enlightened myth of supersession would have it, but with transforming visions incarnated and enacted in particular narratives. Narratives, like poems, do not occur in abstracted, generalized never-never lands, but in a particular time and place, and in the here and now of liturgy. Specificity and particularity are no more a scandal in faith than they are in art, and just as they cannot be reduced downward, they cannot be assimilated upward in the manner of John Hick to some higher-order synthesis which claims to have extracted the relativities of time and place in favour of its own eternal and absolute revelation.

Christian faith is about an 'express image' and the story of the loving purposes of God in Christ. The text is woven into the action, Word into words, both now and in the circumstances of its original production within the lived experiences of the first communities of faith. That is true of most revolutions: the extended production of the Koran occurred in relation to the events it narrates, the storming of the Winter Palace is simultaneously Eisenstein and the original event.[7] We see and hear events as refracted in the *continuing* experience of those who undergo them and who seek to appropriate and understand them. These examples show how fundamental revolutions are a kind of journey or progress from here to there, historically and biographically. They go forward in their own re-enactments: *Vexilla regis prodeunt.*

One of the problems of the last five centuries, and of the literalism that came to dominate within it, arises from a 'Protestant' Bible seen as available and perspicuous to the common man through common sense. In practice it was always mediated through imagery, and the symbolic interpretations of the Bible were inscribed on the heart by psalm-singing and hymnody, but the received theory exercised a persistent pressure towards a crass literalism eked out by 'scientific', or common-sense, explanations, for example, of turning water into wine, or turning the sea into blood.

The impulse to disbelief often occurs when the Presbyterian and evangelical insistence on the literal word cannot be maintained in the face of enlightened criticism. In turn that has been mightily reinforced by the scriptural prohibition of idolatry, as revived by the Reformers and also by the thinkers of the Renaissance. Every image of divinity is viewed as a human invention falsely mediating between man and the living God. Such a perspective easily leads on to philosophical abstractions remote from the tangible imagery of religious poetry and narrative, and so without anchorage for mind or heart. In the Reformation itself the iconoclastic attitude fuelled an orgy of destruction and expropriation which inhibited the religious impulse for centuries and is present now in the dismissal of religious ritual and language as mumbo-jumbo.[8] In his *Hamlet in Purgatory*, Stephen Greenblatt has shown how the Reformation could result in the dismissal of poetry itself as merely fabulous, rather than in need of control by the initial deposit of faith.[9]

In common parlance religion is all too easily associated with the generic sacred. In fact, the Christian sacred embodied in the holiness of Christ and in the history of salvation may sometimes be drawn in toward the generic sacred, for example, the aura of monarchy or holy nation, and at other times be sharply distinguished from it. The 'glory' of God is not to be confused with *la gloire* in the sacred French republic, though they can move towards each other, for example, in the *Te Deum* and *Requiem* of Hector Berlioz, or the poetry of Charles Péguy. Notoriously the characteristics of religious language are apt to recur in relation to sacred monarchy, sacred nation, sacred leader and sacred party, but the criteria embedded in the initial deposit of faith as to the difference between God and Caesar, the emperor and the majesty of the crucified, persistently re-establish themselves. The rood screen is replaced by the royal arms and then the royal arms are themselves displaced.

Religious language is dense and intensive, based on a constant monitoring and scrutiny of the text. That is another respect in which it differs from discursive prose and from what Weber calls 'the romanticism of new ideas' dominating the academy and the media. There is a significant linguistic link here between the novel and novelty which is alien to the intensive scrutiny and contemplation required by faith. Faith is based on close reading. This is not to deny the importance of the novel or the new in general, but simply to draw out the religious mode. Faith requires sustained and intensive reading and redeploys the resources of the whole with reference to each particular moment and event. Thus the erotic imagery of the Song of Songs is brought to bear over and over again in the contemplation of the Passion and love of Christ, fusing *eros* and *agape*.

Finally, religious language includes creative contradiction and the coincidence of opposites. For every truth there is an equal and opposite truth. 'No man has seen God at any time', yet 'The Son of Man hath both seen him and known him.' Whereof we do not know we cannot speak, yet the Word obliges us to speak of what we know, even if we only stammer. The unimaginable must be embodied and made manifest.

How Christian Language Works

At the heart of faithful and inspired speech lies the fullness of the sign and the plenitude of the word. All the signs we make and all the words we use overflow in penumbras of meaning, but those animated by the indwelling of the spirit have a special density and range of implication, and they participate in what they denote. They are at the opposite end of the spectrum (as Peter Sellars has comented) from an advertisement briefly animated by the single idea of persuading you to consume a product, since their meanings are inexhaustible and emanate renewable energies.[10] A religious sign is analogous to the locked-up power of the atom awaiting release, or to light as it radiates out from a single point.

In ordinary discursive prose one thing follows from another either in terms of physical causation or in terms of the circumstances and motives giving rise to action, but in religious language all the elements are present at every point. The redemption is already prefigured in the Incarnation, and the child in his mother's arms is already the broken body of the crucified Christ awaiting burial. The medieval *Pietà* is, of course, an imaginative extension of the gospel narrative, but it faithfully represents the simultaneity of birth and death. Indeed, all human births and deaths are gathered together at key moments in the gospel narratives and we read our joys and sorrows into the story in a manner most recently illustrated by John Adams's *El Niño* and Harrison Birtwistle's *The Last Supper*.

Acts of repeated naming sum up and summon up the depths and heights of being; they invoke and evoke, call up, call out and call upon. To name over and over again is to acknowledge what lies hidden and overlain by mundane surfaces, and to bring full attention to bear on a constant grace and perpetual giveness: a donation. The manifold is evoked by iteration of the word: 'Sanctus, Sanctus, Sanctus, Dominus Deus Sabaoth.' Bach in his commentary on these words in the B minor Mass precisely renders the manifold by sets of threes circling above a ground bass which traverses the scale from end to end, alpha to omega. Indeed, in the classical and baroque periods musical translations of height, depth and finality use cumulative sequences and motifs of ascent and descent in a way which suggests musicians know what it is whereof the liturgy speaks.

Naming is complemented by enumeration and by loving inventory, as in Psalm 104: 'O Lord, how manifold are thy works' or the Benedicite *omnia opera*, 'O all ye works of the Lord, bless ye the Lord', or the Hymn to the Sun by St Francis. Both repeated naming and loving inventory resemble the language of love. As Elizabeth Barret Browning puts it in one of her 'Sonnets from the Portuguese': 'How do I love thee? Let me count the ways'. Through constant benediction and blessing the worshipper bestows a good word on what is 'most worthy to be praised'. Worshippers repeatedly pronounce and announce: 'Bless the Lord O my soul, and all that is within me, bless his holy name.' Such acclamations and appraisals are neither functional nor informative. We do not so much understand our words as stand under them; we do not possess them but are possessed by them.

The regularity of faithful speech approaches the condition of music in the way rhythmic utterance is linked to the stillness of complete absorption. We are taken over by 'the beauty of incantation': 'Lift up your voice with strength', 'Singet, singet, singet dem Herrn ein neues Lied'. Rhythm and measure are not adventitious aids to liturgical invocation and incantation, any more than they are mere ornaments in music. Measure is the regularity of heart and breath – hence inspiration – and a kind of mathematics serving to settle, confirm and establish. I quote here from one of my previous treatments of this theme:

> A powerful regularity not only establishes itself by a kind of intrinsic authority, but also establishes us within it. All the regularities of the body, its rhythm of limbs and blood, are objectified in the beat of words and sounds. There is a dance which links arteries and stars in a common circulation: outgoings and returns, openings up and stillings, rising curves which turn back on themselves and sink again into their originating ground. This bodying forth in measure is fundamental to expression and response. We do not receive these things but become them: in T.S. Eliot's phrase 'we are the music while the music lasts'.[11]

There are two key moments: embodiment and participation. We participate in what is embodied. Embodiment is intimately related to gestation and self-emptying, and so attracts comparisons with childbirth and coming-to-be. Both Jesus and Paul use the analogy of childbirth, as creative pain, delivery and release. Once again religious language about delivery and artistic language about conception and realization run in parallel. The artist and the prophet alike have foresight about what still lies locked in the unshaped material or the unformed time, and no one can say precisely what will be the hour or the day when delivery comes about.

The body is the document in which we read the glory and wholeness of the human as well as the darkness and the fracture. In the body of Christ, Christians read transfiguration and glorification as well as brokenness and vulnerability. The wounds of humanity are, through the body of Christ, taken up into God. Christ's body represents the gift of divine love offered to humankind, and the human response to that gift is to contemplate every aspect of what is offered, the outstretched arms and the wounded side, with all the ardour of the lover in the Song of Songs.

'Body' is a word which radiates surplus meaning in all directions and is identified with the coming-to-be of the divine Word. The divine Word begins its descent into the material world before taking flesh up into the Godhead. There is an entering into and a taking up, so that God participates in our humanity and gathers us into Himself. Human beings participate in the body of Christ both as sacramentally realized and as the body of all faithful people. The language of incorporation and mutuality is pervasive: Christians are 'in' Christ; the Son is 'in' the Father and the Father is 'in' the Son. The little words 'in' 'by' and 'through' convey participation and mutual union. 'We share *in* the body of Christ', since Christ is our portion, and we share his body with all other faithful people. In religious language persons are not discrete entities, but either incorporated so as to find themselves in the other, or lost and alien in a *massa damnata*.

This incorporation, vertically in relation to God, and horizontally in relation to 'neighbours in Christ', includes alteration by grace. Alter and alteration are bound together. Words like incorporation, alter and alteration, re-present and representation, do theology through a network of linguistic roots, reminding us that religious language is intimately related to language itself. Yet, as was suggested earlier, the way we articulate inclusion, mutuality and alteration does not provide information. *The informative yields place to the performative.* The sentences we use contain internal reinforcements, not external references: 'If any man be *in* Christ he is a new creature.'

As well as internal reinforcement, images and signs are reproduced at different levels. The Father sends forth the Son and the Spirit, and those in the Son and in the Spirit are sent out into all the world. The sequence of descent and ascent occurs at the highest level of incarnation and glorification, but is also echoed in going lower to go higher, and losing one's life to gain it. The double nature of Christ, human and divine, is reproduced in all the names and titles accorded him: the King of Glory who is also the Suffering Servant, the Cornerstone who is also the Stumbling-block, the Shepherd who is also the Slaughtered Lamb, the True Vine who is crushed in the Winepress.[12] These paradoxes derive directly from Christianity's simultaneous rejection and an acceptance of 'the world'.

As duality is constantly echoed, so the sequence of descent and ascent is understood as a transition and a journey from here to there, a coming and a going. In our own spiritual journey we follow the sequence undergone by Christ, who from being abased became highly exalted. The master's journey is the disciple's journey.

The spiritual journey may be, and most often is, a physical journey, and comings and goings are ubiquitous in both Testaments. Adam and Eve were ejected from Eden; Abraham set out not knowing whither he went; Moses led his people from Egypt into the wilderness in search of liberty and the Promised Land; the exiles in Babylon eventually set out to go to Jerusalem and rebuild it; wise men from the East followed the star to Bethlehem; Jesus 'set his face' to go up to Jerusalem; the disciples were sent out into the whole world, and all believers journey toward the City whose builder and maker is God. History is the long march of humanity, and biography is the long search of the individual soul to move from the status of an 'alien to the commonwealth' to citizen of the Celestial City. The story of the Prodigal Son coming to himself in a far country and going home in search of grace and acceptance is the same journey in miniature.

The paradigmatic stories are, of course, the Exodus and the Passion, each cross-referenced against the other. Together they provide the central narrative of sacred history and are enacted in the condensed drama of the sacred meal. This is the journey from slavery to liberation, trial to victory. Those who recite the narrative and re-enact the drama renew the journey and make the transition; they 'feel the blood applied' and the angel of death, spiritual and physical, passes over.

Once again, this fundamental pattern or sequence is repeated in different variations until inscribed on the 'fleshly tablets of the heart'. The sacrament of baptism, for example, reinforces the sequence by calling upon all the meanings of a passage through water. As the Children of Israel passed through the Red Sea, so Jesus has brought us through the waters of death to the further shore of resurrection. As Moses and Miriam the prophetess sang a song of triumph, so Christians raise the hymn of victory. Or again, the transitions of Easter can be superimposed on the story of Noah and the deluge: both are instances of re-creation. The ark is the Church enabling all creatures to pass over the flood to safety. Like the Children of Israel, Christians cross over Jordan, and like Jesus in his baptism in the Jordan, the dove of the Spirit alights on every head confirming their acceptance and sonship. People undergo the great transition to the baptism of the Spirit.

These are cycles of recapitulation with a difference, repetitions which also move forward, as the Mount of the Beatitudes recapitulates and moves forward from the law given on Mount Sinai; and they inform both the Bible's self-understanding and the Church's understanding of the Bible. Once the principles of recapitulation in a new form, and of cumulative cross-reference, are understood, then the poetry of Christianity, whether it is St Ephraem of Edessa or the seventeenth-century English metaphysical poets, or the eighteenth-century hymn writers, becomes an open book.

The Bible, then, contains both the cross-references of poetry and the condensed drama of narrative superimposed on narrative to yield an account of regress and progress. Progress and regress turn around the mighty oppositions of good and evil, light and darkness, order and chaos. The casting of good and evil in dramatic opposition makes any intermediate position or negotiated compromise difficult, because that would throw the essential difference into doubt. 'Woe to them that call good evil and evil good.' The unforgivable sin is to declare 'Evil be thou my good.' This is precisely why Christianity is politically dangerous: the moral field has to be so clarified by the oppositions of light and darkness that grey areas and negotiated deals reconciling conflicting interests rather than reconciling people with each other and with God cannot be countenanced.

Here I trespass by anticipation on the difference between religious language and political language, but clearly once the warfare of good and evil is superimposed onto the warfare of political interests, as is bound to happen, conflict is magnified and exacerbated. Moreover, Christians themselves lack a language in which to negotiate deals within the Church, which they certainly have to make but do not know how to talk about. This is where Wisdom literature has to be called upon as the necessary mediation between extremes.[13]

The opposition of good and evil is, then, constantly and necessarily simplified as part of the drama, and it comes to a climax in apocalytic expectation where time is fast-forwarded and the options starkly presented. We are to awake from sleep and choose. Once again, this sense of crisis is both psychological and historical: individuals and peoples are invited to decide now whom they will serve in view of the imminent day of the Lord. The apocalyptic books, above all as recapitulated in the Apocalypse of St John the Divine, summon up vast images of terror and destruction, and picture the perverted energies which bedevil human history. The message is that whatever may appear to be the case in terms of reigns of terror, death, pestilence and destruction, the reign of God is not ultimately impugned. In the tale of two cities, Babylon and Jerusalem, it is the peace of the heavenly city which in the end descends on the earth. The destroyer is destroyed. The Apocalypse is the prototype of all subsequent faith-fiction.

Not only is the story historical; it is also cosmic. In Paul's account of the drama the universe itself groans in expectation of deliverance. The redemption of man is also to be a redemption of nature, so that the triumph of love and humanity in the Resurrection of Christ presages the triumph of peace and love when lion and lamb lie down together in the kingdom set up on the mountain of the Lord. The imagery of light and dark in the moral world and the world of nature are placed in apposition. In the narrative of the Passion, Judas goes out into the night, the disciples file out into the shades of the Garden of Gethsemane, the light of the world goes out in the preternatural darkness of Golgotha, and on the third day before the advent of dawn the Sun of Righteouness has already risen with healing in his wings. In a similar way the lesser light of the star comes to rest over the greater light of the child in his mother's arms, and the impersonal fate written in the heavens concedes primacy to divine providence. Christ walking on the water and stilling the storm is simultaneously an analogue of the Christian safe in the barque of Christ and a recapitulation of the way the Word brought order out of the original chaos. So the Second Adam and the re-creation of the New Covenant recapitulate the original Genesis. 'In my end is my beginning.'

Summary, Assumptions

What then in summary, and what assumptions lie beneath my account of Christian language? As to summary, I have suggested that Christian language is a distinctive genre and an alternative logic based on affinities, not on rigorous implication. It is located at a crucial point on a spectrum of attitudes to the world that render the term secularization paradoxical, such as conformity to worldly power in the dominant traditions, and earthly translation in the subordinate traditions. *The paradoxes of Christianity derive directly from its attitude to the world*: we reject and accept the world, we die to the world and 'live to God'.

The logic of Christianity centres around brokenness and transfiguration, descent and ascent. Breakage is fundamental, but set against the horizon of reconciliation. It is invocatory in relation to 'givenness', not manipulative in relation to empirical data. You *can* offer translations of it, but attempts at reduction only turn it into something else. Like art, Christian language is particular and specific; moreover, it is an ensemble where the whole is implicit at every point. Liturgical simultaneity complements narrative sequence.

Christian signs carry and participate in what they denote; and they are set in a spiritual landscape to provide the orientation necessary for historical and biographical journeys from darkness to light. They are echoed at different levels, from cosmic to psychological, and they constantly recapitulate each other with a difference, as in the Passover and the Eucharist. We invoke and we enumerate the manifold of the divine to make it manifest. We do not dissect the divine Word, but handle it, absorb it and flesh it out. As in poetry and music the Word constantly overflows with divine surplus: it cannot be contained or captured. Every attempt at containment breaks down; every formula encounters an element that resists incorporation.

Christian language is *performative* in that it actively frames the breaking of the divine image and anticipates in the here and now, a reconciliation that lies in wait, always 'not yet'.

Naturally, characterizing Christian language is itself a translation, that is, a theology, because it involves an attempt to draw out elements normally implicit and taken for granted. At the same time, it is a translation that stays close to the particularity of sign and the narrative, affirming their primacy, not turning them into abstract universals like human dignity or solidarity or reverence for life.

I am engaged in reconstruction, not deconstruction. My attempt at characterization is not a quest for the core in the manner of Harnack or for the existential underlay as in Bultmann. Rather the kernel is the Gestalt. The universal is manifest in the specific, and that is found in the concrete journey from slavery to liberty through trial and judgement; from a proclamation of a world to come against the powers that are, to crisis, death and resurrection; from the requirements of law to the gifts of grace. These are generic social experiences set and framed in a narrative, a landscape with signs, and dramatized in the concentrated time-frame of liturgy.

These social experiences, undergone in company, are built into the structure of language itself as a kind of proto-theology, above all in words like re-presentation, in-corporation, alter-ation and participation. We re-present, in-corporate, alter and participate in order to bring the past into the present simultaneously re-presenting the breakage of the body and the fellowship, and anticipating and prefiguring reconciliation and unity.

Notes

1 Ernest Gellner, *Thought and Change,* London: Weidenfeld and Nicolson, 1964.

2 Max Weber, 'Religious Rejections of the World and Their Direction', in Hans Gerth and C. Wright Mills (eds), *From Max Weber*, London: Routledge, 1948.

3 David Martin, *The Breaking of the Image*, Oxford: Blackwell, 1980.

4 Charles Taylor, *Sources of the Self,* Cambridge: Cambridge University Press, 1989.

5 Sarah Beckwith, *Christ's Body*, London: Routledge, 1993, and *Signifying God*, London and Chicago: University of Chicago Press, 2001; Leo Steinberg, *The Sexuality of Christ in Renaissance Art and in Modern Oblivion,* Chicago: University of Chicago Press, 1993; Richard Taylor, *How to Read in Church: A Guide to Images, Symbols and Meanings in Churches and Cathedrals*, London: Rider, 2003.

6 Sidney Griffith, 'The Eucharist as "Living Medicine"', in Sarah Beckwith (ed.), *Catholicism and Catholicity*, Oxford: Blackwell, 1999, pp. 115–16.

7 W. Bruce Lincoln, *Sunlight at Midnight*, Oxford: Perseus Press, 2001, ch. 8.

8 Carter Lindberg, *The European Reformations*, Oxford: Blackwell, 1996, pp. 375–7.

9 Stephen Greenblatt, *Hamlet in Purgatory*, Princeton and Oxford: Princeton University Press, 2001.

10 Peter Sellars, introductory comments to John Adams's *El Niño* at the Barbican, 25 June, 2003.

11 David Martin, 'The Beautiful, the Holy and our God-forsaken liturgies', *Epworth Review*, Vol. 10, No. 3 (1983), p. 52.

12 Neil MacGregor, *The Image of Christ*, London: National Gallery, 2000.

13 Stephen C. Barton (ed.), *Where Shall Wisdom be Found?*, Edinburgh: T. and T. Clark, 1999.

CHAPTER 13

The Christian, the Political and the Academic

If for the sake of argument we agree there has been a return in sociology to culture and cultural analysis, then we are once again given full permission to visit the classical sites excavated by Max Weber concerning the great issues of Christian civilization. The issue I raise here could hardly be more fundamental: the language of Christianity about power, politics and violence in the context of secularization. One of my founding texts is Max Weber's 'Politics as a Vocation' because in that great essay he analyses the characteristics and constraints of the political role as contrasted with the religious and the academic roles.[1] The religious, the political and the academic form the triangle in which I conduct my enquiry.

Politics is about many things, such as the negotiation of rival interests, but minimally it is about power and potential violence. Politicians are of many kinds, including place-men, fixers, conscientious representatives and dictators, but the exigencies of responsible power mean politics can be a vocation. It can engender its own kind of moral heroism. For many people that is a surprising thought, almost a contradiction in terms. We resist the idea of the political vocation and its potential heroism, because we live in moral environments saturated in the combined effects of enlightened universalism and versions of Christian universalism. By that I mean that we assume the imperatives of reason and love are laid upon us all in the same way and that we all walk in a uniform moral space rather than in different walks of life, including politics. Consequently we fail properly to distinguish the political walk or vocation from the religious or the academic. All three vocations are circumscribed in their different ways, but the practice of politics is the one most hedged about by limits while having to operate in a moral atmosphere created by the critical universalisms of love and reason. This constitutes the triangle in which I am interested, with its three cultures in dialectic tension. Clearly any cultural analysis that deals in different vocations and kinds of heroism is bound also to be a moral analysis. The sociology of culture is necessarily a sociology of morals.

My triangle depends on Weberian typifications: the Christian, the political and the academic, and includes some extension of the academic to cover media commentary. If the political provides the hypotenuse of the triangle, because so highly constrained, the academic side of the triangle provides a background contrast because most completely given over to the idea that we are autonomous actors, just persons as persons, ideally safeguarding our integrity and authenticity in uniform moral space. The Christian commentator, who in practice figures most largely in what follows, lies in between, neither so constrained as the politician nor so autonomous as the academic. By concentrating on Christian commentary about the political I relegate the academic to the status of occasional foil and one characterized by what Max Weber called 'the irresponsible romanticism of new ideas'. Perhaps I should add that events following 11 September 2001, in Europe as well as the USA, are clandestine presences throughout.

Of Christian Language

I have to begin with a brief initial account of Christian language before turning to the context of secularization. Of all world religions, apart from Buddhism, Christianity is the most ambivalent about power and control. It virtually prohibits violence, insists on a reconciliation far beyond the mere negotiation of rival interests, and invokes a heavenly kingdom where power is understood as strength perfected in weakness. All basic social institutions and arrangements, such as borders and territory, family and lineage, authority, violence and possessions, have a question mark put against them.

That characterization of Christianity and its language is partly dependent on my second foundation text from Max Weber's other great essay 'Religious Rejections of the World and Their Direction'.[2] It is the distinctive Christian tension derived from simultaneous acceptance and rejection of the world, the goodness of creation and the demanding presence of an alternative kingdom, which gives rise to the paradoxes of Christianity and Christian civilization, above all dying to live and the power of the Cross to salvation.

But politics is defined by power, so faith in an alternative kingdom, once it is socially influential or established, is bound to end up colluding with the kingdoms of this world, that is, secularized. The power of the Cross will be converted into the violence of the crusade. When that happens any witness to the pacific and fraternal ideal will have to be made by subordinate and dissident groups or individuals. Moreover, once Christianity has been so suborned by 'the world', the contrast with the pristine Gospel becomes so striking that Christian civilization is exposed to critical irony from within and without, though most persistently over the past few centuries by the partisans of universal reason. If one wanted an example of criticism from the partisans of love, it would be Leo Tolstoy, especially in his essay on 'The Kingdom of God'.

Enlightened Myth

What is not, perhaps, sufficiently noticed is the way the Enlightenment itself is just as much suborned by the permanent exigencies of power as Christianity, so that pure reason is converted into *raison d'état*. The record of Enlightenment attracts less notice only because not embodied in a continuing, identifiable institutional presence, like the Church, capable of being held to account, and indeed even going so far recently as to apologize. Somehow Stalin and the Security Police can be elided from the account as not genuinely enlightened, whereas Torquemada cannot be dismissed as not genuinely Christian. Yet the collusions with power are identical in both cases.[3]

More than that, and in spite of the enlightened commitment to social science, the reconciliations proposed by reason are as much mythic and visionary as the reconciliations proposed by love. But just as the heirs of Enlightenment evade historical responsibility, so they evade the mythic status of their governing concepts. Even Voltaire, as archpriest of Enlightenment, could do no more than satirize the chronic gap between the idea and the reality in *Candide*. Without some consciousness of the deterioration and fracture written into human projects, the chronic gap stays unaccountable, and so, in enlightened theory as in practice, empirical reality is bent to conform to the requirements of myth through hidden hands and harmonies, and the *telos* of progress. What refuses to conform is censored as too 'sensitive' to mention. That has become the current meaning of 'sensitivity'.

An example of the pressure exerted by myth can be found in contemporary Europe, pacified for over half a century by living in the ambit of American power. People suggest the continent enjoys Kant's vision of 'perpetual peace'. Intellectuals, and even Christians, hail a new age as if it had really dawned universally. Yet in reality this 'distracted globe' remains obstinately Hobbesian, with only modest intimations of perpetual peace, let alone the *koinonia* of Christian peace and love.

Secularization, Secular Language, Pemanent Secularity

What of secularization? I have already complicated matters by characterizing the conversion of the cross into the sword as secularization and conformity to the world. Though this usage is paradoxical, it derives directly from the Christian pattern of world acceptance and rejection. By overcoming the world Christianity succumbs to it, and the pristine language of the primitive faith is driven down to the bedrock of liturgy and iconography. Socially it is carried in muted form by monasticism or by clandestine and subordinate traditions. Clearly secularization is something more profound than declines or changes in belief and practice.

All the same, paradox apart, there is a standard usage of secularization, meaning, in particular, social differentiation, or the freeing of successive sectors of social life and thought from ecclesiastical oversight and religious concepts. Social differentiation erodes the links between Christian language and emerging secular languages, for example, those of science and politics, and breaks down the comprehensive institutional coverage once provided by the Church. The theological mode ceases to provide the overarching frame.

Yet, in an important sense, social practice is always secular, even when religion provides the dominant mode of understanding. One example might be the perennial pursuit of pleasure and survival which has broken out now in mass consumerism and widespread satiation; but most relevant for the present purpose are the perennial dynamics and exigencies of power. Christian rulers have always behaved much as other rulers do, and the secularization of power by Machiavelli in *The Prince*, though for centuries regarded as a diabolical incursion, was only a change in understanding, not in behaviour. No renaissance duke altered his ways for the worse because Machiavelli had articulated the theory of his practice. For that matter nothing much changed when power became legitimated in secular rather than Christian terms.

There is a genealogy of secularization here, running from William of Ockham, Marsilius and Machiavelli to Hobbes and Cardinal Richelieu, and from Rousseau to Clausewitz and Nietzsche. In explicit theory or practice this secularization brings out the tension between Christian virtues and the virtues of the citizen, between Christian martyrdom and republican heroism. That is one reason why established Christianity has always needed supplementing from other sources, in particular from stoicism and also from concepts of nature which, however malleable and selective, are still points of reference today in bioethics or issues of sexual behaviour like paedophilia. The just price, and in our particular context, the just war, have provided the criteria for Christian political thought, though it is once again malleable in practice and always subject to prudential considerations of survival. For example, the criterion which requires an excess of good outcomes over bad can, in the kind of situation that arose in 1936, make the pre-emptive strike a moral imperative. The alternative turned out to be a policy of waiting until Hitler had a good chance of winning a war in which fifty million died.

Secularization: Throwing Christian Language into Relief

Politics has always been a rough trade, even though Machiavelli traumatized Christians as much as Darwin did. However, the gain from these successive secularizations is the way they throw into high relief the intrinsic character of the original Christian language, particularly as embodied in liturgical drama and poetic imagery. In this respect, as in others, like patriarchy, the Reformation was loss as well as gain, because it stressed the perspicuity of the literal word to the common people at the expense of imagery, whether sculptural or poetic. In due course that loss in devotional tangibility condemned Protestant evangelicals to a much greater trauma than Catholics on account of the enlightened fragmentation of the biblical text.

I realize this is controversial, but I am suggesting that successive secularizations, including what used to be called 'scientific' history, but also other critical approaches, have made possible a recovery of Christian language as a distinctive mode of speech, and as an alternative logic, unencumbered by partial fusions with earlier scientific and philosophical conceptions or by a literalism treating the Bible as science or history as now understood.

That has further implications. First it implies the danger of today attempting forced intellectual unions which ignore differences in kind, of logic and genre. I am, of course, deeply impressed by the work of Christians who are scientists, such as Arthur Peacocke and John Polkinghorne, in throwing bridges across the gaps, but I am, in principle, uneasy about synthesis. Perhaps the physical and biological sciences are different from the social sciences, but one only has to imagine the monstrous progeny that might have resulted had a religious liberalism tried to marry Christianity to *The Prince* or to Herbert Spencer's *Principles of Sociology*. Indeed, something like that has happened rather frequently, for example, in Paley's *Evidences of Christianity* and in the partial conflation at one point of Liberation Theology with Marx.

The other implication is that Christian language is not some mish-mash of assorted empirical mistakes and historical myths, somehow malingering through the rigours of modernity into the kindlier, gentler climate of post-modernity. Rather it is a mode of understanding based on transformation and deformation analogous to art, and like art resistant to reduction. To reduce it is to denature it, and that implies a limit to secularization similar to the limit proposed by Rodney Stark with respect to the permanent anxieties of the human condition, or the limit proposed by Thomas Luckmann with regard to self-transcendence, or Pascal Boyer's genetic programme for the production of socially useful delusions.[4]

So, in order to make sense of the dialectic triangle between the Christian, the political and the academic, and to understand in particular the nature of Christian political commentary and action, we have to restate more fully what is involved in this Christian language. I have already suggested that, as a direct consequence of the pattern of combined world rejection and world acceptance delineated by Max Weber, Christianity puts a question mark against all established institutions in the name of the coming kingdom. That in turn creates a continuing potential for turbulence in Christian societies which is released on the cue of social circumstance, and is as much propagated by seeds blown over the borders of the Church as by seeds nurtured in the cultivated plot of the official institution. I am not saying that the fissionable material lodged in the foundations of the Christian city make the idea of a 'normal' Christian civilization impossible, but it does lead to a continual questioning of Christianity on grounds both Christian and non-Christian, and to a pervasive irony springing out of the contrast between the Gospel and Christian practice. More than that, as Adam Seligman has argued in *Modernity's Wager*, there is a potential inwardness and subjectivity secreted in the foundation texts from Jeremiah to Jesus, and from Paul and Augustine to Anselm and Luther.[5] This is always liable to crack open the organic frames of Christian society. The inner forum, our self-awareness *in foro interno*, disturbs the outer forum of the republic, the *res publica*.

Christian language is exclamatory not explanatory, intensive not discursive, particular not abstracted. It has a logic of responding to the world as emblem rather than treating it as object. It has a narrative sequence of injustice, sin and judgement rather than a sequence of historical cause and effect. It has a logic of symbolic affinity rather than rigorous implication, which is one major source of its malleability when it comes to political inferences or moral casuistry. Crucially, its mode of address is personal and direct, not analytic.

Christian language, more especially as embedded in liturgy, carries forward close organic kinds of human relationship rooted in the idea of incorporation, all being one in the body of Christ and in receiving that body. The idea of incorporation brings organic relationship into the present and the future by aspiring to a more perfect union, human and divine. Christianity pursues the reconciliation of differences through Holy Communion, by remembrance and anticipation, anamnesis and prolepsis. All this has implications for Christian political recommendations because there is a vigorous tension between incorporation 'I in you and you in me' and the individualism or inwardness that has its roots, though *not* its full contemporary realization, in Christianity and, indeed, in Judaism. Holy Communion as the symbolic enactment of the ideal of holy community, or the ecstatic dialogue of Pentecostal tongues, has scant relation to price or exchange value or negotiated compromises. Its basis remains reconciliation, atonement and new creation. At the heart of liturgy is obedience to the heavenly vision and sustained commitment rather than open-ended negotiation and renegotiation as circumstances require. A key text such as 'He is our peace who has made both one' is not in any way a realistic social model but an enactment of hope and the realization of a presence through gesture and sign. It brings together identity and difference.

How, then, does Christianity construe identity and difference, concepts at the heart of religion and politics alike? Christians share identity in being one in Christ and also because they find in Him an exemplar for imitation: 'having the mind in you that was in Christ Jesus'. However, Christianity also expresses difference, not only on account of unique subjective awareness, but because each person inhabits a distinctive social character or role. The two conceptions of difference, one based on inwardness, the other on the character of the role, are a further source of tension, particularly in the modern situation where inwardness and uniform moral space occlude our appreciation of particular roles, above all for our purposes, the political role as distinct from the religious and the academic.

The figure of Christ Himself illustrates the difference because while He provides the common universal pattern for Christian emulation, He also bears the unique character of the Lamb of God, offered by, to and for Christians. It is out of this difference that we derive vital differences in Christian political commentary and action. Those who adopt the role of witness combine the role of Christ the exemplar who inaugurates the alternative kingdom of peace with the role of Christ the anointed one and saviour who in His reconciling sacrifice refuses the way of violence and points the path to peace. Effectively such a witness amounts to the end of ordinary politics and represents eschatology brought forward into the present. What remains is only the politics of gesture, placard and procession practised by the little flock, by the few who have found the kingdom. Since they are necessarily 'the few' they often paradoxically recognize that to be a witness is itself to adopt a specific role complementing others in differentiated moral space. That is not, of course, to impugn its value, since moral enlargement in part depends on distinctive moral roles.

Christianity and Normal Politics

However, those who accept ordinary politics and remain in what George Fox called 'the mixture' not only recognize the problem of imitating Christ the exemplar but, above all, recognize that they cannot reproduce the action of the Passion in the world of politics. Rather, they appropriate its benefits as grace and grace alone. There is an irreducible gap between us as citizens and Christ as saviour. To contrast 'the witness' with those 'in the mixture' is simply to restate the difference between Anabaptist and Lutheran. Once Luther tried to take monasticism out of the monastery into the world he found the whole enterprise vitiated by a gap, by the break, between the language of the heavenly city and the inherent character of the City of Man. That was hardly a new discovery, because the limit reasserts itself in every generation, as when Augustine and Gregory the Great much earlier tried to convert the anamnesis and prolepsis of the Gospel and of the liturgy into a working fraternity. The malignant worm constantly revisits.

Yet, if Christ as saviour cannot be realized in full, nevertheless aspects of His role and fragments of religious consciousness continue to float freely in contemporary society in the form of sacrifice for others, victimhood, concepts of the massing of evil in the system and of collective solidarity in social guilt as well as secularized conceptions of a war to end war, of an end to war and the oppression of the poor. Academics, otherwise given over to notions of autonomy and unique potential, pick up these fragments of religious consciousness, and sometimes joyfully immolate their subjective conscience and consciousness on the altar of the party and its revolutionary vision. The seeds of Christianity, blown over the wall, can, as Eisenstadt suggests, generate Jacobinism, or utopias of love complemented by utopias of rational harmony, and all oblivious that Utopia, like Erewhon, means Nowhere. This utopian sentiment, patently present in the banausic sentimentality of lyrics in popular music, combines with the notion of uniform moral space to render the specificity of religious and political roles opaque. We are all supposed to be in pursuit of our own authenticity at all costs, rather than fulfilling what Bradley called 'My Station and Its Duties'. The idea of character as taking up or bearing a specific role in the sense of Chaucer's Knight or Priest, or Castiliogne's Courtier or the characters delineated in Earle's *Microcosmographie*, requires an educated leap of the imagination. The role of the Prince, transmogrified in contemporary terms as the politician, offends the universality of both love and reason.

The result is a cynicism about politics, and a culture of complaint and affronted righteousness well documented by sociologists such as Inglehart. It holds that those in power always break their promises, which is true because public aspirations are such that the promises which politicians have to make cannot be fulfilled. People are let down. The rise to power always turns out to be a fall, a disobedience to the original vision, a treachery to the faithful, and a heresy to the creed.

By a further extension, given the stress on inwardness and the assumption of uniform moral space, we have difficulty grasping the communal weight that in earlier times assembled behind the obligations attendant on specific roles, not noticing how many analogues of these remain in contemporary life. Jephtha, in the Bible story, makes a solemn vow in his role as leader of the Israelites that in return for the victory of his people he will sacrifice whatever greets him first on his return. When his daughter comes out to greet him the vow to God and the communal weight resting on his shoulders require he redeem his promise. We dismiss that particular story as barbaric, but variants of its structure are present whenever it is expedient that one or some 'die for the people'. When Prime Minister Blair said he would face his Maker over his decision to send soldiers to kill and be killed in Iraq, he showed something of the specific gravity resting on those bearing political responsibility. Every day we hear people saying they *had* to do what they did not *want* to do on account of the responsibilities of their role. The whole Western dramatic tradition from *Antigone* onwards should have inducted us into this understanding, otherwise we cannot follow what tragedy is about. Great modern operas such as *Peter Grimes* and *Billy Budd* still pivot on the weight of the communal falling on the outsider or the innocent, and on the obligations of responsibility. In *Billy Budd* the innocent boy is hanged by his reluctant captain in accordance with naval law. In *Peter Grimes* the fate of the outsider implicitly and distantly echoes the Passion of Christ, whereas in *Billy Budd* the echoes are close and explicit.

Christianity as Very Personal and Very General

So far I have concentrated on how Christian language rejects the world and sets a question mark against all established institutions in the name of the transforming vision. But there are other characteristics which define the difference between the Christian and the political. Christians say they do God's will and find God's anonymous presence whenever they give a cup of water to the thirsty or have compassion on the beggar at the gate. That is at once very general and intensely personal. It does not take us very far on public policy towards rough sleepers or even suggest whether we should offer money to feed somebody's self-destructive habit. Moral apothegms and parables require a great deal of prudence in their application and the trail of inference to politics is long and loose, as Mrs Thatcher showed when she pointed out to the General Synod of the Church of Scotland that if you are to be a Good Samaritan you have first to engage in wealth creation to pay the money to the innkeeper.

Again, the religious time-scale is very different from the political time-scale. Faith is about today and eternity, politics about the next few weeks and the next five years. You cannot break into the political time-scale regarding pensions and insurance by taking no thought for the morrow, or throw cold water on wealth creation on the grounds that some people gain the world at the expense of their soul. You cannot publicly forgive your political opponents sitting on the bench opposite by excusing their venality on the ground that we are all miserable sinners. Not even the most devout politicians turn the other cheek in political debate but, as in outright war, they fight to win. In almost every respect the political resists the Christian, because Christianity rejects the categories of power and violence apart from the power of a final judgement, affirming the ultimate supremacy of the good.

How, then, does the Christian respond to the imperatives of such a faith in the meantime, which seems to be as much time as we are likely to have? It is not that there are few resources. Where there is gross injustice and inhumanity, Christianity, including its incorporation of the Hebrew Scriptures as an Old Testament, has recourse to many concepts and images opposed to 'the principalities and the powers'. It may, as Liberation Theology and Minjung Theology have done, appeal to the shared humanity of our common genesis, the reversal of the condition of the poor and the release of the prisoners in the alternative kingdom, to the exodus from slavery in Egypt and the ending of exile in Babylon, and to the prophetic condemnation of laying field to field and oppressing the widow and the fatherless. It can point to the sharing and caring community of the Eucharist and to the priesthood and kingship of all believers. It can set out a dramatic scenario of good embattled against evil where all is not lost even when 'good is on the scaffold' and evil on the throne. In times of crisis it may ask for fundamental choices, not grey compromises, and it can look forward to a peaceable kingdom where each and all live under their own vine and their own fig tree.

But if faith is endlessly resourceful where injustice and inhumanity are rampant, which in human history is normal enough, it is still the case that every resource has the disadvantages of its advantages. Every concept is capable of misuse as circumstances change. You can cry 'peace, peace', where there is no peace, and you can divide the world into good and evil, with your own nation wholly on the side of good in opposition to the evil empire. You can appropriate the elect status of God's Israel or God's Messiah as historical privilege and domination rather than as historical responsibility and redemption. 'God with us' may mean the presence of the Prince of Peace, but it can just as easily turn into the idea that 'The Lord is a man of war'. All the categories, like peace or, indeed, the poor and the stranger, are general and prone to sentimental invocation. The presuppositions are often those of an organic society, for which there is nostalgia on right and left, as corporatism or as socialism, but the costs of which are neither fully faced nor really desired. Above all, the lack of causal analysis inherent in a personal mode of address necessitates supplementation by social science with all the hazards of unforeseen consequences that social science knows about but does not know how to circumvent. So, as the history of Liberation Theology and the base communities suggests, the time of crisis is the time for the deployment of all faith's radical resources, but with the desired return of what we have to call 'normal' politics the Church ceases to be a principal channel of political action, and those who have used it as a temporary shelter shift to more secular models and modes of political action.

Christian Political Options

The Christian, face to face with the political, has several options, of which I have already touched on two: the Anabaptist embrace of the heavenly kingdom come what may, and the Lutheran prudential separation of the heavenly kingdom from the earthly, with the earthly dominant in the meantime. So far as the Anabaptist option is concerned, as represented by such distinguished contemporary figures as Stanley Hauerwas and the late John Yoder, Christianity has to be a gesture made by those, presumably a small minority or saving remnant, who have opted out of the culture of power and control and rejected war outright.

However, there is another option, often adopted in the liberal mainstream, which is based on a meliorist view of progress, and in principle always leans in the pacific direction. It rejects all pre-emption but keeps the realist position in reserve should the situation become intolerable. As already pointed out, this has the disadvantage of giving potential enemies every opportunity to improve their chances and increases the likelihood of maximum loss of life on all sides. A chance is taken on the optimistic calculation that leaving well alone will probably turn out for the best, while pessimistically lamenting the way the political world is so evidently given over to imperial greed and will-to-power. But if that really characterizes even the actions of the democracies, what price optimistic bets on good outcomes as compared with preparation for the worst? Can you really leap from such adamant worst-case scenarios to hoping for the best?

A further option, alongside that of the witness and the pacific optimist, emerges where the Christian can identify with a particular cause such as the liberation of a people, where few concrete policy decisions need to be faced beyond the goal of liberation. In the case of Christian leaders, if they survive, the political project has a limited life-span, and so is another instance of the politics of crisis and the interim. Achievements of the goal may take a long time but eventually the project lapses. The prototype is Moses, and the obvious modern examples are Archbishop Romero, Martin Luther King, Nelson Mandela, Archbishop Tutu, Archbishop Luwum and Aung San Suu Kyi. This is where the politics of martyrdom, of the gesture, the placard and the procession, and the liturgies of the streets and the open air prove their power. The threat behind the non-violent gesture stays implicit and the promise of a future exodus to life and liberty is transmitted by sign language. As we have seen, Christianity and Judaism are replete with such signs.

This is where the events of 1989 in Eastern Germany offer almost a paradigm case of liturgy used in the politics of liberation. Because Christian sign language is focused in broad issues of creation and peace, it was able to find political expression with regard to the pollution of nature and the militarization of adolescents. On the question of pollution the communist government claimed it was confined to the Western world, which allowed Christian commentary to point out that this was not quite the case. With regard to the militarization of young people, it so happened that the Russians had presented a sculpture to the United Nations of swords turned into ploughshares. This allowed Christian protesters and others to adopt this sculpture as a badge on their sleeves. When this was duly banned they ripped the badge out and went about their business with a hole in the sleeve.

So the body, with its wounds and markings, is a sign, and a political communication. Even when the body is killed it still communicates, because it remains an incarnation of the righteousness of a cause and the cost of liberty or redemption. The gestures of unarmed bodies in procession made by those who lead and those walking in their company are a reserve language when all other kinds of speech have failed. A frail woman in Burma, Aung San Suu Kyi, remains a walking placard of her cause, at once invulnerable and in great danger. St Paul refers to Christ as 'placarded' for us, and Christianity seems born out of what happens when the unarmed procession into the city stirs up frightened authorities to act. It can only be brought fully into play in a particular kind of crisis, before the world carries on as before, but it remains the paradigm of all confrontation between naked truth and vested power.

A distinct variant on this, perhaps as much resembling the Zealot nationalists of Masada as the peaceful men of Galilee, comes about where church leaders are identified with the spirit of repressed nationhood. In varying degrees this identification can lead to serious moral ambiguity, as the examples of Archbishop Stepinać of Croatia, Archbishop Makarios of Cyprus and Father Tiso of clero-fascist Slovakia indicate. The religious character of Christian leaders, and their capacity for personal moral address, is too easily compromised by the kind of ethnic politics requiring suppression of the truth, covert collusion in indiscriminate violence, argument by slogan, the automatic assumption of one's own innocence in the face of the automatic guilt of the enemy, and the mutual litany of hate based on the principle that they never change. So the word of forgiveness and mercy, healing and reconciliation, remains unspoken.

The moral dilemmas vary between cooperation with an oppressor and outright terrorism. Laslo Tokes, sometime pastor, later bishop, spoke for the Hungarian minority in Romania, but his attempted arrest sparked off the Romanian revolution of December 1989. Cardinal Wyszynski was long the anchor of the Polish national spirit under communism, later followed by Karol Wojtyla, and by Lech Walesa as lay leader of Solidarity. In all of these cases, whether or not morally ambiguous, the religious role of national icon or leader tends to be for the interim. Once the goal is achieved the processions and the placards disperse, and the solidarity fragments. What was once so urgent with meaning turns into rites of commemoration.

Critical Solidarity and Its Constraints

A different role which can be taken up in democratic countries where the Church is a recognized presence, involves a version of critical solidarity. The Church stands for and upholds a different order of priorities than the State, a different sector of concerns. A church leader or commentator seeks to insert dialogue rather than set-piece confrontations, committed propaganda and self-promotion. Commentators can hardly appeal to the ideals of the kingdom in terms (say) of giving all you have to the poor, but they can deploy aspects of the prophetic tradition of peace and justice, sometimes in concert with secular intelligentsias.

One constraint bearing on the role of critical solidarity arises from the danger of compromising the authority of the preaching voice by vulnerable political judgements, and appearing too frequently to second-guess politicians. Christian interventions need, therefore, to be occasional, and there are understood rules governing just how specific and overtly technical or partisan they may be. Vatican pronouncements, for example, are cast in generalities which require close reading and may carry loadings pointing in several directions. The Christian commentator is by convention expected to take up broad moral aspects and not become involved in purely prudential political judgements about the utility of particular proposals. Once that happens Christian commentators confuse their publics, within and without the Church, by sounding like shadow ministers of state, and can end up being accorded the same degree of credibility. They have damaged their standing by talking in two kinds of voice. After all, a totem is not supposed to talk too much, and a ritual leader is bound by the rules of the role. Rites become invalid when ritual leaders break ranks and offer opinions like anyone else. To lead is to be constrained.

However, the constraints on ritual leadership are not quite those bearing on the politician, such as the need to retain power, respect and foster foreign compacts, identify the national interest, and respond to party and electorate. What the Christian commentator seeks to do is to recognize the constricted moral space of politics while trying marginally to enlarge the range of options and shift the order of priorities. Options are not foreclosed by political reality, even by *realpolitik*; another voice can be attended to and, after all, no law decrees that the marginal cannot also be crucial. In any case my own view of the fruitfulness of the specifically Christian tensions turns paradoxically on the faithful imagining the improbable.

When it comes to the internal politics of the Church, Christian commentators find themselves practitioners, constrained by precisely the pressures of power and control they note and regret in politics. Though these may not include matters of life and death or direct electoral accountability, there are plenty of analogues of political dilemmas. Rival lobbies have to be taken into account, unity maintained, ecumenical relations fostered, and the economics of survival attended to. Such modest degrees of freedom as faith enjoys when speaking truth to power sharply diminish when it comes to ecclesiastical politics, and the public persona of the

Church can easily be impaired if it appears little better in practice than the institutions it criticizes.

In practice the administration of churches is thoroughly bureaucratic, so that, whatever the misleading overlay of unction, the criteria deployed and the psychological tests administered would certainly have excluded the majority of the saints. People are persuaded by the loosest of inferences from biblical or liturgical texts, while love and sacrifice prove remarkably effective persuaders, especially when it comes to time and money. The rhetoric of stewardship offers a cornucopia of pious reasons for adopting prudential courses, as no doubt it needs to. As always, in the end, needs dictate the means.

Different Distances from Power

So far we have explored the consequences of a language evoking the imminence of a better kingdom characterized by unity, fraternity, Christian liberty, humility and love. On the one hand this introduces a long-term ferment affecting all the major institutions of law and power, as well as the family; on the other hand it is not attuned to the dynamics of power in the secular city. It also leaves large open spaces where other faiths might provide detailed ritual or moral prescription, such as would anchor Christian identity. Of course, detailed prescription does emerge in the course of Christian history, but the principle of putting man before the Sabbath and of setting the inner condition before outward conformity is always present as the final arbiter. In particular I mean the way the dialectic of Jesus concerning the inward and the outward plays into the Pauline dialectic of grace and the law. It is this inner liberty before the law which is momentous for Christian civilization, including its capacity in the long run to undermine the reproductive capacity of the formal moulds of Christian identity. Complete inwardness corrodes outer form, which is why Catholicism survives better than Protestantism.

In this respect Islam is very different because it works in the reverse direction, from outward conformity to the inner condition, and reinforces the identity and the social identifications secured by ritual law and its demarcations. Again, its view of the place of religion in society is maximal, whereas in Christianity the latent impact of the difference between inner and outer, and between God and Caesar, leads, under the pressure of Protestantism, Enlightenment and secularization, to a limited view of the place of religion. At the same time, this decrease in institutional scope terrifyingly increases the impact of Christianity on the structures of the self, and so creates, as Charles Taylor has taught us, a major paradox of secularization: the unacknowledged and unacknowledgeable Christian markings on the secular soul.

So far as our focus on the political is concerned, the maximal role of religion in Islam complements its easy attunement to the dynamics of power. The prophet, as celebrated by Carlyle in his lectures *On Heroes*, was a man of action, a military leader and a family man. He did what he had to do politically in a context where religious and political action were closely intertwined. Concepts like martyrdom, which might seem to be shared with Christianity, are quite differently inflected, because based on a much more ready acceptance of the way of the world than on world rejection. In all these respects there surely is a clash of civilizations, which what Jonathan Sacks calls the dignity of difference requires us to acknowledge and respect. It is Islam as it is programmed for global success which throws into sharp relief the Christian problem with power.

The Special Licence of Academic and Media Commentary

So far we have explored the extent to which Christian commentary can exploit a degree of freedom not available to the politician. But what, finally, of that wider community of commentary represented by the academy and the media? Because they are not responsible persons whose actions and opinions are taken to be representative of a continuing institution, academics and media people do not need to answer for an institutional past or even reveal their full position. The media commentator and the academic no doubt face certain constraints on total freedom, but they can ask questions without needing themselves to answer them, just as they can demand apologies without ever having to give them.

The people of the academy and the media fire from hidden positions while requiring others to be transparent about where they stand. They can be righteous or antinomian according to taste or tactics, and have no standards to keep up before the public except the limited ones governing their specific role. They can cite previous comments, promises and failures, as though collectively incurred by the politician or public servant, without themselves being cited or meeting the demands of consistency over time. They are the prosecuting lawyers and the judges, and their style is forensic, making out the case and levelling the accusation. Above all, they are chronically prone to generalize from the degree of freedom they enjoy to characterize all incumbents of roles, though they are in fact quite differently placed. They can come up with an idea and let it run without ever having to follow it through, bear its costs, or take the blame. Once it has done enough damage they can bid it farewell as no further business of theirs.

This, then, is what Max Weber pilloried as the 'irresponsible romanticism of new ideas' and what Karl Mannheim labelled with ambivalent admiration 'the unattached intelligentsia'.[6] As celebrated in their own eyes, these are always the true, the fearless, and the incorruptible revealers of corruption. They are the real moral heroes, apart from artists, because they speak according to the dictates of their inner freedom and integrity. If that freedom includes the relativization of all morality or a totally indiscriminate respect for all moralities, which is the same thing, their moral heroism is intact and unimpugned. The privilege of the academic and the media commentator is pure judgement without responsibility. That is always the prerogative of the unattached intelligence, and it is why lack of attachment is embraced with such enthusiasm. It is also the closest approximation possible to uniform moral space bereft of appropriate differentiation. And one must, of course, say that it is an absolutely necessary ingredient in democratic debate.

What can the occupants of responsible roles in Church or State possibly say in response to a moral heroism so effortlessly achieved at their expense? Their disadvantages are admittedly severe and, apart from the consolations and erotics of power, politicians can only defend themselves with talk of tough choices, tough love, the meaning of opportunity cost, and complaints about the culture of complaint. The question still remains, however, as to whether a political role, to which Max Weber granted the high title of vocation, might not have a heroism of its own, perhaps secretly enjoyed and motivated by reasons not easily advertised or revealed without inviting yet more righteous indignation if not expulsion from power for intolerable honesty. It is perhaps part of the sociological imagination to consider in just what qualities such a moral heroism might reside and in just what situations it might emerge.

Notes

1   Max Weber, 'Politics as a Vocation', in H. Gerth and C. Wright Mills (eds), *From Max Weber*, London: Routledge, 1948, pp. 77–128.

2   Max Weber, 'Religious Rejections of the World and Their Direction', in H. Gerth and C. Wright Mills (eds), *From Max Weber*, London: Routledge, 1948, pp. 323–62.

3   J.F. Talmon, *Political Messianism: the Romantic Phase*, London: Secker and Warburg, 1960.

4   Pascal Boyer, *Religion Explained*, London: Heinemann, 2001.

5   Adam Seligman, *Modernity's Wager*, Princeton: Princeton University Press, 2000.

6   Karl C. Mannheim, *Essays on the Sociology of Knowledge*, London: Routledge, 1952.

Index